Recollections of
a Picture Dealer

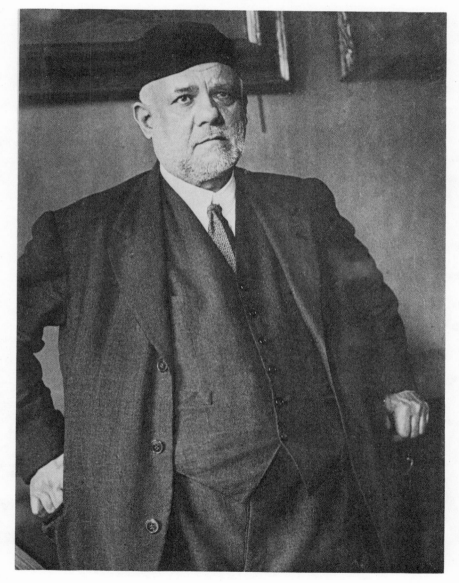

Recollections
of a
Picture
Dealer

AMBROISE

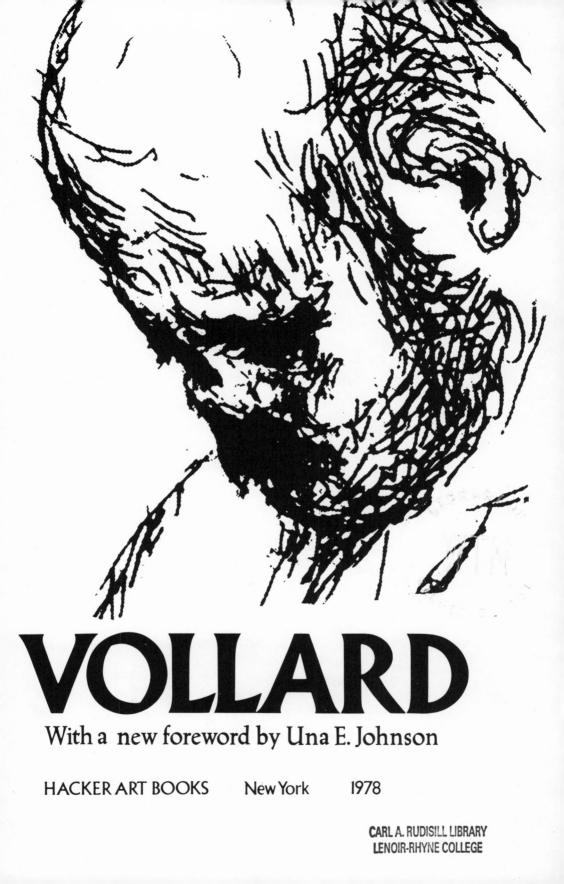

VOLLARD

With a new foreword by Una E. Johnson

HACKER ART BOOKS   New York   1978

Translated from the French by Violet M. MacDonald

N
8660
.V6
A 2
1978
Dec 1999

Frontispiece
AMBROISE VOLLARD 1934
(Photo Brassai)

First published 1936, Boston.
Reissued 1978 by
Hacker Art Books, New York.
Library of Congress Catalogue Card Number 77-76778
ISBN 0-87817-218-1
Printed in the United States of America.

CONTENTS

ILLUSTRATIONS

ILLUSTRATIONS FOLLOW PAGE 326

FOREWORD

This Foreword is based in part on the writer's recent book, "Ambroise Vollard, Editeur," published by the Museum of Modern Art, New York, 1977.

In the early 1890's, Ambroise Vollard, a young and unknown French colonial, opened a small art gallery on rue Laffitte in the Montmartre section of Paris. Locally called "the street of pictures", rue Laffitte was the address of many important art dealers in the city. Vollard's unobtrusive letterhead carried in small type, in its upper left corner, the notation: "Tableaux Modernes / Editions de livres / et d'Estampes moderne / 6 rue Laffitte 6". Among his modest holdings were five paintings by Paul Cézanne that Vollard had acquired, for something less than a thousand francs, from the auction sale of Père Tanguy, a color merchant and staunch befriender of many struggling artists. In his gallery, Vollard featured only paintings by artists who were generally unfashionable or unrecognized. He firmly believed in their ideas and the imaginative daring of their paintings. Willing to take the risks of buying and selling these works, Vollard brushed aside the disapproving opinions of the academicians and the ridicule of the critics and other dealers in Paris.

As it turned out, Vollard was a many-faceted genius. Not only was he amassing a collection of unusual paintings (and a growing fortune through their sale): he was also publishing albums of prints and editions de luxe by the same unfashionable artists whose paintings he so assiduously promoted. Furthermore, Vollard found time to record in his own writings his personal observations of, and many amusing anecdotes about, his artist-friends, especially Cézanne, Renoir and Degas, whose paintings he greatly admired. Vollard's writings culminated in his autobiography, "Recollections of a Picture Dealer", published in the United States in 1936.

It was as a dealer in avant-garde paintings that Vollard first achieved fame and, perhaps, a calculated degree of notoriety. In 1895, he gave Cézanne, who was then fifty-four

years old, his first one-man exhibition. At this exhibition,
a few prominent collectors decided to acquire their first
modern paintings. The Cézanne exhibition was followed
in 1901 by an exhibit of the early paintings of Picasso, who
had only recently arrived in Paris. In 1902, Vollard assembled and exhibited some terra cottas, bronzes and a tapestry
by an unknown sculptor, Artistide Maillol. Two years later,
he exhibited the pre-fauve paintings of Henri Matisse. It
was thus that Vollard assumed his exceptional position in
the art world of Paris. His little gallery seldom lacked
visitors. Aggressive, enterprising and, especially, shrewd,
Vollard carried forward his unswerving policy of buying
directly from the artist and often in quantity. The artists
complained about the low prices he offered, but he was one
of the few dealers who did buy and sell their paintings. In
his instinctive ability to foresee the probable acceptance
of these "new artists", in his willingness to take the risks
of acquiring their works, and, finally, in his ability to interest these same artists in working on his numerous publishing
ventures, lay his special genius. In their company he was
witty, charming, knowledgeable and, above all, persuasive.

For Vollard, no effort was too great so long as his projects
continued to materialize. He established Maillol in an
adequate studio at Villeneuve-Saint-Georges. For many
years, Georges Rouault occupied a studio on the third floor
of Vollard's residence on rue de Martignac. It was Vollard
who requested that a heavier press be designed and built
in order that the printer might achieve the rich blacks of
Rouault's images. It was also Vollard who prevailed upon
Renoir, then seventy-three and in precarious health, to
embark on a career in sculpture. Vollard suggested that
Renoir select a number of his figurative drawings to serve
as basic studies for the sculpture. Vollard knew an able
and talented young sculptor, Richard Guino, who would
carry out Renoir's directions. Guino had worked with
Maillol and was amenable to working in a style that was
not his own. Their method of working together was carefully developed, with Vollard supplying all materials as well

as paying Guino's salary. This proved to be a happy and productive arrangement, and a number of fine plaster models were made. Vollard, in turn, had them cast in bronze. A man of taste and obvious ingenuity, Vollard was always the astute businessman, and he managed to gain exclusive rights as sole agent for the Renoir sculptures. Vollard had previously issued bronzes by Maillol and five early pieces by Picasso.

As Vollard's reputation and fortune grew, he was soon able to withhold from the market a few of his favorite paintings for his own collection. Is is a recognized fact that most of the great paintings created during the last decades of the 19th century and the first decades of the 20th had passed through Vollard's hands. In 1933, some forty paintings from his collection were shipped to New York and shown at the Knoedler Galleries with considerable acclaim and fanfare. These works, never before seen in New York, were accompanied by the famous impresario himself.

Although Vollard gained a fortune through modern paintings, it is to be noted that he was in no sense avaricious. He proceeded to spend that fortune on his most cherished dream—that of being known as a great publisher of the most distinguished books and prints created in the 20th century. To discern how well he succeeded, one needs only to reflect on the quality and range of his publications. However, this immense venture proved unremunerative in his lifetime. The albums were mostly lithographs in color by various painters of his choosing. His first albums did not appeal to print collectors, who much preferred the stylized and less imaginative work of professional engravers. Vollard's first edition de luxe was *Parallèlement* by Paul Verlaine, with freely rendered lithographs by Pierre Bonnard. Vollard chose the French Government Printing Office to carry out the printing. However, the director of the Printing Office belatedly decided that the text was too controversial. After some changes in the title page, the book was completed. It was to be acknowledged many years later as one of Vollard's most magnificent publications.

In 1913, Vollard was persuaded to send a few of his paintings by Cézanne and others to the Armory Show. He also included a few of his publications. *Parallèlement* was among them. They were casually shown on an open display table; each volume was priced at about fifty dollars. They were not considered important enough to be listed in the official catalogue of the exhibition. Vollard always maintained that it was his publications that gave him the greatest satisfaction. Perhaps nowhere but in Paris were to be found more skilled printers, more inventive fabricators of fine handmade papers, and more dedicated engravers, who deftly and faithfully rendered the artists' designs. Vollard knew and greatly admired these capable artisans. He tirelessly sought them out and demanded of them their best efforts.

Over a period of forty-five years, Vollard published, mostly under commission, approximately twenty-five illustrated books and numerous albums of prints. There were handsome albums of lithographs by Bonnard, Vuillard and Denis, and black-and-white lithographs by Redon, Fantin Latour and Rouault. Vollard also published lectern-size books illuminated by Rouault, including *Les Réincarnations du Père Ubu, Cirque de l'etoile filante* and *Passion* with text by André Suarès. Rouault's "Miserere" remained unpublished until ten years after Vollard's death. Picasso's graphic work was well-represented in the Vollard publications, beginning with the Saltimbanques series issued in 1914, continuing with the illustrations for Balzac's "Le Chef-d'oeuvre inconnu" in 1931 and, finally, with the famous Suite Vollard. Another two dozen of the Vollard projects, including impressive works by Chagall, Derain, Picasso, Rouault and Dunoyer de Segonzac, remained unpublished. During the next several decades, Vollard's unpublished books continued to set a distinguished mark in 20th-century graphic art as they appeared under the imprint of other publishers in Paris.

Along with his extensive and remunerative activities as a dealer in modern art, and his not-so-successful publishing ventures, Vollard found time to write of his experiences with some of the artists whose work he especially admired. At the beginning of World War I, he was forced to close down his picture gallery and move its contents to his own private quarters. Under the auspices of the French Information Service, he was sent abroad to lecture on Cézanne and Renoir. He traveled to Switzerland and Spain, where he was happy to renew contacts with his foreign clients. His lectures formed the basis for his anecdotal biographies of Cézanne, Renoir and Degas. The work on Cézanne appeared in 1914 in an edition of a thousand copies. A few critics complained that it was "too little Cézanne and too much Vollard". Vollard never considered his writings to be critical or scholarly. He explained, "I tried to write simply, colloquially, so to speak, eschewing the slightest hint of criticism." Gertrude Stein, on reading his Cézanne, found it "extremely good". Roger Fry, in his review of the work, remarked: "M. Vollard has had the wit to write about Cézanne and not about his pictures. He has played Vasari to Cézanne and done so with the same directness, the same narrative ease, the insatiable delight in the oddities and idiosyncrasies of his subject." Vollard continued this refreshing style of writing in his biographical sketches of Renoir and Degas. They record Vollard's keen observations and insights and his amused enjoyment in his artist-friends, the masters of the School of Paris.

Early in his career, Vollard had been highly entertained by the adventures and brazen declarations of the outrageous reprobate Père Ubu, a surreal character originally created by Alfred Jarry and presented in a play in 1895 to a shocked Paris audience. From time to time, Vollard spun out further adventures of Ubu in ironic and sometimes disturbing stories. These were privately printed as small, inexpensive brochures and sent to Vollard's friends. In 1923, Vollard published a more ambitious work, entitled "Le Père Ubu á la Guerre", with illustrations by Jean Puy. Nearly a decade later, Vollard, still fascinated by Ubu, published the entire series in a single volume of lectern size. Carrying

the title "Les Réincarnations du Père Ubu", it was illustrated by Rouault and printed on elegant but sturdy handmade paper. Vollard's own conception and Rouault's
heroic-comic symbols have much in common. However,
Rouault lifted Vollard's Ubu to a plane of somber drama.
Where Vollard permitted Ubu the extravagance of mim-
icry, Rouault, with his customary fervor, gave to Ubu a new
and ominous meaning. He made Ubu the strange prophet
of fanatical and ruthless ideologies.

The adventures of Père Ubu are a far cry from Vollard's
somewhat romantic story, "La Vie de Sainte-Monique".
Undistinguished as the text may be, it is generously illustrated with etchings, lithographs and wood-engravings by
Bonnard. With special grace and charm, Bonnard impro-
vises on a slight but pleasant theme, one which brought to
Vollard nostalgic memories of his childhood on the faraway
French colonial island of La Réunion in the Indian Ocean.
Vollard's final book was his autobiography, "Recollections
of a Picture Dealer", published first in English, in 1936,
and in French the following year. Similar in style to his
books on Cézanne and Renoir, it was a simple and unpretentious testament of a singularly eventful life. It was his
answer to those associates who had urged him to write a
candid and revealing personal history. If they hoped for
answers to any sensational rumors concerning his lineage,
his personal "affaires" and his shrewd dealings, they were
doomed to disappointment. Vollard was content to let stand
those rumors and enigmas concerning his life. Written
when Vollard was nearing seventy years of age, it is full of
engaging anecdotes of artists and authors with whom he
had dealings. It also chronicles the amusing scenes and
small ironies of life that Vollard never failed to enjoy.

Vollard's death shortly before the beginning of World
War II was the result of an automobile accident. M. Henri
Petiet, well-known art dealer and a younger colleague of
Vollard, recalled the somewhat bizarre circumstances that
caused his death. It was Vollard's habit to spend week-ends
at his country house outside of Paris. His chauffeur of many

years drove him on these short trips. His cook always prepared an iron pot filled with a creole stew for these occasions. It was carried directly from the kitchen and placed
on the shelf behind the rear seat of the car. On this particular weekend, the chauffeur, in order to avoid an accident,
suddenly braked the car, causing the heavy lid of the pot to
slide off. It struck Vollard in the back of the neck, severing
the cervical vertebra. Vollard, in great pain, was finally
taken to a nearby hospital, where he died the following
day. The Gazette des Beaux Arts reported that obsequies
for Vollard were held at the church of Sainte-Clotilde,
across the square from his residence on rue de Martignac.
Many in the art world of Paris came to pay him homage. It
was the last time before the outbreak of World War II
that the most important artists in France came together.
Marc Chagall, the last living member of this splendid company of artists, recently reflected: "Ambroise Vollard was
not so much a dealer as a mystic, with a great enthusiasm
for an art, then unknown, that followed the Impressionist
era of Durand-Ruel. He was a great precursor."* Vollard
was as much of an innovator in his way as were the many
artists whose works he so consistently promoted during his
lifetime.

The present re-issue of Vollard's "Recollections of a
Picture Dealer", long out of print, is a welcome event in the
field of meaningful books on modern artists. It again makes
available the exceptional story of Ambroise Vollard, distinguished and unique impresario of the art of his time.

Una E. Johnson

*from Chagall's notes to the Museum of Modern Art, New
York, Spring, 1977.

I FROM THE ISLAND OF LA RÉUNION TO THE FACULTÉ DE DROIT IN PARIS

I was born on the Island of La Réunion. When I refer to my native country, people ask me: "How big is this island of yours? What is its population?" I once read somewhere that La Réunion is smaller than the smallest of the French Departments, that of the Seine excepted; but of the number of its inhabitants I have no idea.

What I do know, on the other hand, is that the first nucleus of the colony consisted for the most part of aristocratic French families, our kings having decreed, by successive Orders in Council, that it was not derogatory to "go colonising." French peasants came too, encouraged by Colbert to settle on the territories newly attached to the Crown. At the time of the Revolution many aristocrats—"ci-devants" whose lives were threatened—sought refuge in the Islands; and there were also Frenchmen of all classes whom the spirit of adventure led to expatriate themselves.

My maternal grandfather was one of these. A native of Northern France, he had dreamed in his early youth of becoming a painter; but having no patrimony, he ended by seeking his fortune in La Réunion, where he married a girl whose parents came from Provence. I remember that among the papers he left, I discovered the draft of a letter addressed to a friend in France, in which he spoke of " the divine Ingres." This epithet " divine," attributed to the painter, made the greater impression on me as I had never before heard it applied to a human being.

As for my father, whose family had never strayed

B

beyond the ancient province of the Île de France, he came to La Réunion to enter a notary's office, and ended by purchasing the business. A few years after his arrival in the Island, he married, and by this union he had ten children, of whom I was the eldest.

Surrounded as it was by foreign elements that had found their way little by little into the Island, the white population took the greatest care to maintain its racial integrity and traditions. The children were brought up with the strictest vigilance.

A friend of my aunt's went one day to the Vice-principal of the Lycée, to ask for leave of absence for her son, so that he might go with her into the country next day.

" All right," said the Vice-principal, " but you will have to give him a note for his master, to say he has been ill."

" What! Set my Edouard an example of false-hood! " she cried. " Never! If it comes to that, he must go to school as usual."

The education of the girls was bound by rules of decorum and propriety that would be laughed at to-day, though I have come across the same sort of upbringing among South American girls in Paris; for young Chilians, Uruguayans, Paraguayans have the same teachers that our girls had in the old days of La Réunion—venerable nuns who maintain in their *pensionnats* the customs and the courtesy of old-time France. I remember my astonishment at seeing a Brazilian girl with her magnificent black hair coiled upon her head.

" What! You haven't cut your hair? "

" You see, if I did, I should be pointed at in the street when I got back to Rio."

Two years later I met the charming foreigner again. This time she had fair hair, cut *à la Jeanne d'Arc*. And I wouldn't swear that nowadays the girls of La Réunion themselves . . .

As far back as my childish recollections go, I see a parrot mounted on its perch. I longed to possess one of its lovely feathers, but I had watched it crushing the hardest seeds in its beak, and knew better than to go near it. Young as I was, however, I had noticed that everything I did was imitated by a little nigger-boy who was allowed to play with us. So I pulled a feather out of the tail of a domestic hen, and then, pointing to the parrot, said to him: " You too take a pretty feather." But he drew back with a grimace: " *Ça pas bon.*" Round the perch, which was set up in the courtyard under a mango tree, a regular little garden had grown up, in which, among other plants, magnificent sunflowers bloomed. One day I was fighting one of my brothers for the possession of this garden, when my aunt, separating us, said: " We'll move the perch somewhere else, and as soon as there's another little garden, you can each have one." I asked my Nannie: " How does the parrot's little garden grow? I never see him digging or sowing seeds." " That creature, he cunning," she replied. But I soon discovered that in shelling his seeds, the parrot scattered some around him. This accounted for the profusion of plants springing up in so delightful a tangle.

At that time I had a veritable passion for flowers. As a reward for good behaviour I was allowed to pick a few from the beds. What joy to make a posy! My favourites were the roses; dahlias pleased me less because of something metallic about them that made them seem less alive. I had not then seen dahlias painted. When, many years later, Renoir gave me the choice of two of his paintings, one of roses, the other of dahlias, I found it difficult to decide.

In our drawing-room there was a cabinet in which, alongside of native curiosities—stuffed *bengalis*, butterflies in a glass case, shells—the eye was regaled with bouquets of flowers made of raffia dyed in various colours. My Aunt Noémie, who was considered by her friends to have a pretty talent for water-colours, took pride in copying these artificial flowers in her sketch-book.

" The flowers in the garden are much prettier," I ventured to point out to her one day.

" So they are. But raffia flowers never wither," retorted my aunt.

I learnt later that Cézanne's most sumptuous nosegays were painted from paper flowers, for the same reason.

I was for ever tormenting my parents to let me alter things to my own taste in our garden, but they invariably answered: " We'll see. . . . Some day, when you're bigger. . . ."

Meanwhile I made my Nannie move the parrot and his perch from one bed to the other, from the carnations to the balsams, and thence to the roses; and I was entranced with the variety of effects I obtained in this way. In the arrangement I liked best of all, the bird with his blue-and-yellow plumage made a splash of brilliance in the midst of a group of lilies. I had a little sandy cat, too, and one day I found him lying beside a border of forget-me-nots. I knew nothing in those days of what are termed complementaries, but my eye was delighted with this juxtaposition of colours.

Another day, having picked a bunch of little white flowers, I noticed they were not all of the same shade. Of course I was told that white on white was monotonous; but to me, on the contrary, the mixture appeared ravishing. I happened one day to be telling Renoir of the combinations of colour I had made as a child, and I mentioned the white posy.

" On the contrary," he said, " an effect of white on white looks extremely well. Nothing is more exciting to paint."

One of my childish ambitions had been to become

a slave! I had heard grown-up people say that in the old days there were slaves, and that they were for ever running off into the woods.

" So then," I said, " the slaves' Nannies let them run away? "

" The slaves hadn't any Nannies."

How lovely to go into the woods all alone, and not to have a Nanny! But one day, as I was looking at an old print representing a negro at the top of a coconut tree, surrounded by gunmen whose dogs were tearing furiously at the trunk of the tree:

" That's a runaway slave," explained my Nanny. " He's waiting for his master to fire at him."

" Why? "

" Because he hopes to get something broken, and then he won't be able to work any more. He was a lazy fellow, I guess."

This explanation cured me of all temptation to venture alone in the woods, where one ran a risk, it seemed, of meeting with nasty, chestnut-coloured negroes. From that time onwards, when on our walks we passed by a thicket, I used instinctively to squeeze my Nanny's hand a little tighter.

At the age of four I commenced collector. Not that I had any idea of what that meant. I simply had a lively sense of property. As I had been specifically forbidden to touch anything in the house, I fell back on things in the garden, such as no one would dream of disputing with me. I began building up a heap of big pebbles, and I had made a very fine " collection " of them, when one day they all disappeared. Materials had been needed to repair a wall, and my pebbles had been commandeered.

Undaunted, I turned my attention to the bits of broken crockery I found lying about. My favourites were the fragments of blue china. But my relations thinking it unwise to let a child play with sharp-edged objects, my lovely bits of china disappeared in their turn.

It seemed I was fated to have my " collections " taken from me. But nothing hindered me from contemplating the treasures in our native museum— stuffed lions, tigers and birds, shells and a variety of other objects. The live lions and tigers I was shown in France in later years were not more impressive than these.

And in the courtyard of the museum there was a real, live porcupine. For a halfpenny its keeper would let us touch its nose with a stick, and it was a marvel to see its quills rising up. Meanwhile its " showman," with watchful eye, stood ready to check our covetous hands: " Hi, you! Take care not pull out his *feathers*! "

" Now that you are a big boy," said my father when I was six years old, " you must begin to work seriously with Aunt Noémie."

This was my mother's elder sister. An old maid, she had dedicated herself wholly to the upbringing of her nephews and nieces. My mother, absorbed by the duties of housekeeping, found her an invaluable help. Tante Noémie brought to the care of the children confided to her the anxious solicitude of a hen with her little ones; even in the circular gesture of her arm beneath her cloak one saw the jealous movement of a broody hen gathering her chicks under her wing.

My Aunt Noémie lived in terror of the Evil One. I saw her constantly making the sign of the cross over her breast. " It is to keep a pure heart, my child, so as not to fall a prey to the Devil." And she would read me the *Life of the Curé of Ars*, in which the Devil, for ever at the Saint's side, was to be seen taking the most diverse forms.

I noticed my aunt, when we went to see my Uncle

Buroleau, making little signs of the cross before a picture of a lady in a low-cut dress: a copy of a *Virgin* by Raphael. This lady did not frighten me at all, and I thought innocently that if that was one of the shapes the Devil appeared in, he wasn't so dreadful as they made out. But one evening I woke up with a start. The candlestick on the night-table had fallen down, and I saw the candle go running across the room. . . . I screamed. A maidservant rushed in. Trembling, I pointed to the bewitched candle, which had stopped short against the wainscot. She picked it up, and said simply: " The rat, he fool, his hole too little for candle go in."

So it was only a rat running away with the candle, after all. From that moment my terror of the Devil grew less.

The time came for my father to take our education into his own hands.

Though tenderly attached to his family, my father was very hard on himself, and thought it natural to exact a great deal from others. And in his view his children's future could only be assured by their obtaining University degrees. I did not dislike study, but I had little disposition for certain subjects, such as mathematics, geography, drawing. Drawing was my *bête noire*. I could not so much as produce the little mannikins with which most children cover the margins of their exercise-books.

At meal-times we heard of nothing but the marks we had obtained for our tasks—the places we had got in competition. Even the end of the day did not see us set free. After dinner we had to repeat our lessons, and have our tasks checked, for the next day. My younger brother and I, who were near in age, were coupled together for study. Our father attached the greatest importance to Greek and Latin, and as our exercises were never good enough to please him, we were made to get up before daylight and go over them

again.   Candle in hand, we went down from the first
floor, where we slept, to the ground floor, where
my father had his room.   We were only moderately
appreciative of this solicitude, in fact we considered
ourselves much to be pitied.   But when Papa was our
age . . .

A simple notary's clerk, my father had educated
himself, devoting a part of the night to the completion
of his studies.   By the time he became a notary, he
cared for none but books whose titles alone give me
cold shivers to this day, such as the *Logic* of Port-
Royal, Descartes' *Discours de la Méthode*, Malebranche's
Recherche de la Vérité.   Thrown in upon himself in this
way, his mind had acquired a sort of dryness, a touch
of puritan asceticism which made itself felt all about
him.   I used to fancy protestants must be like that.
So that, brought up though we were in the Catholic
religion, we had not even the benefit of that cheerful-
ness which it permits to its most scrupulous adherents.
I remember my father's indignation when, for my
twelfth birthday, my mother, on the faith of a catalogue of books for the young, bought me a copy of
Andersen's Fairy-tales.

" Show me that book," said my father to me.
And chancing on the tale called " The Emperor's
New Clothes ": " What's this? " he cried.   " Here's
something about a naked man! "

But my father's greatest terror was *la femme*.   A
theatrical company on tour in the Island gave a
performance of *Marie ou la Grâce de Dieu* at St. Denis,
where we lived.   My uncle took me to see it, and
Papa could not conceal his anxiety at the thought of
my witnessing a spectacle where the mere sight of an
actress might fill my young head with " evil notions."
I was then about fifteen!   Our maids, I need hardly
add, were chosen for their ugliness.   And not only
the maids.   It had been settled that I was to learn
English, so I said one day to my father: " I'm told

there's a certain Madame Bocage who has a splendid method of teaching modern languages." This Madame Bocage was an amiable widow in the forties, whose opulent contours offered a lively interest to my young eyes. My father, without answering, shot a severe glance at me. Not long after, he said to me: " I've found a teacher of English whose pronunciation is even better than that of *your* Madame Bocage." However this may have been, I was soon to discover that Mademoiselle Génier, my destined teacher, had ill-looks and to spare.

Happily the severe discipline to which we were subjected was relaxed during the two months' holiday that we all spent at Le Brûlé. Le Brûlé, 1000 metres above sea-level, meant, to me, a tangle of ferns, hydrangeas, tree-camellias, a network of plants of every sort, such as one sees in the engravings of Bresdin. It meant a river with a thousand windings, forming pools and cascades everywhere. At sunset a blue mist descending from the heights, an impalpable down, which in a few moments spread darkness everywhere, a darkness made of those silvery greys that enchant one in Whistler's canvases.

From the summit of Le Brûlé, when the sky was exceptionally clear, one saw in the far distance another peak, entirely white, the Piton des Neiges. When I was sixteen I obtained my parents' permission to go there on an excursion.

" That's white, if you like! " I exclaimed as we drew near.

" That blue too, m'sieu'," said a negro behind me.

Looking more attentively, I saw he was right: the snow had blue reflections in it. How then, with so much blue in it, did it achieve such dazzling whiteness? Many years later, watching a laundress rinsing out fine linen, I asked her: " Why do you put blue in your rinsing water? "

" To make my linen nice and white," she replied.

One day I came across an album that had belonged to my grandfather, full of pictures of French officers' uniforms, and I was enraptured at the sight of so many magnificent soldiers. If only one day I could be dressed like one of these!

The naval doctors and apothecaries chiefly excited my admiration. They wore caps trimmed with so much gold that they were indistinguishable from the *képis* of the generals, and they had besides a marvellous golden sun on the back of their tunics. These two uniforms were so equal in beauty that I was unable to choose between them. Neither of these professions attracted me in the least, I must say, but merely the idea of one day donning their glorious clothes. In the end, after examining them in the minutest detail, I gave my preference to the naval doctor, because of the red velvet backing his gold braid. The apothecary's velvet was a beautiful green, but the gold did not show up on it with the same brilliance.

From now onwards my cry was: " I want to be a naval doctor! "

" In that case," observed my father, " you would do well to begin by obtaining better marks at the *lycée*."

So I resolved to give every satisfaction to my professors. For our next competitive exam. in French we were given as a subject: " Compare the grotesque in ancient and modern times." I remembered that the theme had been treated by Victor Hugo in the *Préface de Cromwell*. As luck would have it, I had the book in my desk. I coolly copied out the poet, and was classed . . . last of all! No doubt you imagine the professor had tumbled to the trick. But for all his pretended idolatry of Hugo, Père Jayot had swallowed the bait. He thought my transcription such ridiculous balderdash that he read my composition aloud, to show my schoolfellows to what lengths bathos could be carried, and the whole class was convulsed with

laughter.   In my vexation I was about to give myself
away, when I remembered that our Aristarchus was
not only a worshipper of Hugo, but one of the examiners
for the *baccalauréat*.

The *baccalauréat* carried as much weight among the
families of La Réunion as it inspired terror among the
scholars themselves. To crown all, the Examining
Board was recruited in part from among the magistrates
of the Tribunal, and it is easy to imagine the terror
of the boys brought suddenly face to face with the
Procureur de la République, or with the examining
magistrate: they were not scholars, but prisoners
awaiting sentence.

Now, there were some things at which I was hopeless,
notably history and geography, and to make things
worse, the examiner in these branches was the President
of the Board himself, *Monsieur le Procureur de la République*.   Only a miracle could save me—and the miracle
happened. Just as the *Procureur* was opening his
mouth to question me, a negro policeman, breaking
into the room, rushed up to him. He had come to
tell him that on the topmost branch of a tamarind tree
in the gardens of the Hôtel de Ville they had found an
Indian hanging, a " free labourer." This was the
name given to the Indians brought from their native
country to take the place of the negroes, who since
their emancipation had come to consider work of any
kind unworthy of politically conscious electors.   Our
" free labourer," seized with home-sickness, had hit
on this ingenious means of breaking his contract.
By his death he was making sure, moreover, of the
great advantage of coming to life again in his fatherland, according to the religious belief: " *Planté
ici, repoussé Madras.*"

The policeman wanted to know if he was to cut
the rope.

The magistrate went off in a hurry with him;
the coast was clear, therefore, so far as I was concerned.

And as good things never come singly, it was another member of the Board, an old friend of my family, who went on with the exam. And that was how I got my bachelor's degree.

Now I could set out for France to study medicine! Having noticed that doctors always wrote and signed their prescriptions in a totally illegible fashion, I began practising a spidery scrawl. But these preparations for a medical career were thrown away. My father had the shrewd notion of taking me to the hospital, and letting me see an operation performed. The mere sight of the surgeon, his hands red with blood, nearly made me faint, and I realised, though sick at heart, that I must give up all hopes of the military braid and the golden sun on my back, which I had so dearly coveted.

The medical profession being thus closed to me, it was decided that I should go to France to study law; and after a short stay at Montpellier I found myself in Paris.

II ARRIVAL IN PARIS: THE QUARTIER LATIN AND MONTMARTRE

Paris! The very magic of the name predisposed me to admire everything. My hotel was situated in the rue Toullier, near the Luxembourg, where I went first thing the next day. I was disappointed. It took me many years to realise the beauty of that incomparable garden and the magnificence of its planning. For the moment it merely seemed to me vaster, and at the same time less intimate, than the " Jardin du Roi " of my native isle. As for the monuments, their hugeness seemed to bear down on me and crush me. I went to see the museums, and all I got by dragging myself for an hour through their endless rooms was a very bad headache. I was a long while adapting myself.

How absurd it is for tourists who have rushed round the world to talk of the countries they have seen as though they really knew them! It was only during the War, by moonlight, with all other lights extinguished, that I suddenly became aware of the incomparable charm of St. Julien-le-pauvre. And it was not at first sight either that I discerned the beauty of the mass, at once so powerful and so ethereal, of Notre-Dame de Paris. And the Sacré-Cœur! How many times, going from the Boulevards to my shop in the rue Laffitte, had I not passed it without really seeing it at all, till one day, at twilight, I became aware all at once of a mysterious citadel rising up before me.

But if the big things made no impression on me at first, the little things—the shops with their goods displayed outside, the narrow streets of the Latin

Quarter—interested me enormously. Above all, I was fascinated by the quays and bridges of the Seine, where the second-hand booksellers had their boxes. As I have said, there was something of the collector about me from childhood; and hunting about in these boxes, I developed a passion for engravings and drawings. Those were the days when for three francs, or even two, you might pick up some such treasure as a fine, lively drawing by Guys.

I must confess I was actuated chiefly at first by the instinct of possession. I was beside myself with joy, for instance, when for eighteen francs I succeeded in purchasing a little china plaque of a girl with a broken pitcher, signed Laure-Lévy d. Bonnat. I had once read a story of a girl who was given three *louis* on her birthday, and exclaimed: " Now I can treat myself to that fine engraving of *Job on the Dunghill* by Bonnat! " I now concluded that Bonnat was a woman, and Laure-Lévy her maiden name. But I did not really care much for the painting, and was not particularly disappointed to discover that the " d." before Bonnat signified " d'après," that Bonnat was a man, and that the original of his " broken pitcher " hung at the Louvre for all the world to see. I went there for the purpose, and was so slenderly impressed that I decided for the future not to judge pictures solely by the fame of their authors, but to rely more on my own taste. One day, pottering about the Hôtel Drouot between two lectures on law, I fished out a little picture of peasants dancing in front of a fire, which I thought a marvel of *chiaroscuro*. I bought it for a small sum. It was signed Innocenti, so I was still a long way from Cézanne. All the same my bargain procured me a great deal of respect among my compatriots in the Latin Quarter. One of them, whose opinion carried weight—we were all impressed by the 350 francs a month he received from his parents —declared it was as good as a Rembrandt.

As a result of this purchase I became acquainted with the artist, who invited me to visit his studio at Neuilly, and it was through him that I came to know the future director of the *Union Artistique*, where, as will be seen, I was to make my first campaign as a picture dealer.

Innocenti, like many others at that time, was greatly smitten with the idea of a " Mediterranean Federation." To further it, he executed a painting of three figures, life-size, suggesting France, Italy and Spain. In the middle he placed General Boulanger, at that time the idol of the Parisians; on either side of him the Kings of Spain and Italy. The painter had the greatest hopes of this allegory, expecting to see it reproduced on brooches pinned to ladies' bodices. This dream was not realised, but he had the joy of seeing his picture included in the *Exposition Universelle* of 1889. His friends had prophesied the *médaille d'honneur*. But the political tendencies of the picture were no doubt disquieting to the jury, who awarded him a bronze medal only. Innocenti bore them no grudge, and generously bestowed his work on the French State, which rewarded him with the *Palmes Académiques*.[1] At official ceremonies, even at private dinner-parties with French people, he was always careful to wear his decoration: " One should show honour," he would say, " to the country that has paid one homage."

Montmartre, the artistic quarter *par excellence*, attracted me more than the École de Droit, and I decided to go and live there. This was about 1890.

How unlike the Montmartre of that day, the Montmartre of the first *Moulin Rouge*, of which Bonnard

---

[1] A civil decoration that is generously distributed, and may be awarded, among others, to foreigners, and Frenchmen residing abroad, who have " contributed to the intellectual, scientific or artistic expansion of France " (*Larousse*). The recipient, on all but ceremonial occasions, wears a small strip of purple ribbon in his buttonhole. See p. 97.

painted a famous picture for me, is the post-war Montmartre with its lugubrious night-clubs!

At the time when I lived in the rue des Apennins, the only amusement I could afford was to go of a Sunday to watch the procession of smart carriages from under the trees lining the Avenue des Champs Élysées. But one day, waiving the principles of economy which had enabled me so far to hold out, I went and drank a *bock* at the cabaret *Le Chat Noir*. There was a big picture there by Willette, his *Parce Domine*, which I had been told rivalled the most celebrated compositions of the eighteenth century. A further attraction of the *Chat Noir* was its waiters, who served their customers dressed as Academicians.

Willette was known to me through the *Courrier Français*. That splendid publication had brought together most of the best-known draughtsmen of the day, beginning with Forain. The best-known, which was not to say the best-paid. Willette had fervent admirers, but praise is a meagre diet. And the painter Louis Legrand, in his tiny lodging in the Avenue de Clichy, had already engraved some of his finest plates, but he did not succeed in selling them till the day when, to their mutual advantage, he met with the publisher Pellet. Rivière too had acquired a greater reputation by showing his shadow-play *La Marche à l'Étoile* on gala nights at the *Chat Noir*, than by the admirable woodcuts that were piling up in his portfolios.

Of all the artists of Montmartre, one's thoughts turned inevitably first to Forain—and above all to his drawings—although his corrosive and satirical vein was the exact opposite of the Montmartre spirit. (What a far cry from that shuddering woman of his, slipping her key into her door, the *Inconnu* she has brought back with her close at her heels, to Willette's little Pierrots singing hymns to the moon, or fighting Harlequin for a Pierrette!)

There was another establishment of Montmartre, kept by Aristide Bruant, where the customer on entering was bombarded with the most ill-sounding epithets. This cabaret achieved a vogue at least as great as that of the *Chat Noir*, and ended by disappearing in the same way. But of Aristide Bruant's day there remain to us not only his work as a *chansonnier*, but the magnificent posters that Lautrec executed for him. As a poster artist Lautrec, though little appreciated at that time as a painter, rivalled Jules Chéret, whom the exquisite acclaimed as another Watteau.

Given the least encouragement, Lautrec might even have developed into a great painter of frescoes, judging by the panel he executed for the booth of La Goulue, another of Montmartre's celebrities. This woman, after dancing the *cancan* at the *Moulin Rouge*, set up as an exhibitor of lions and other wild beasts; but the exhibition soon proved a failure, and the collection was dispersed. La Goulue died in neglect and the direst poverty, and the adventures of Lautrec's panel began. After passing from hand to hand, it was cut in pieces by its latest purchaser, this practically-minded individual judging it to be more saleable in sections. These fragments, reassembled as the result of protests by the artist's admirers, were bought for a respectable sum by the Administration of the Beaux-Arts, the same Beaux-Arts which, twenty years earlier, would have laughed Lautrec to scorn if he had begged for a wall to decorate for nothing.

The whimsicality that characterises Lautrec's work showed in his behaviour as well.

One evening I came home to find my maidservant rather worried.

" A funny little gentleman has been here," she said. " I told him M. Vollard was not at home, and when I asked him his name, instead of answering, he picked up a piece of charcoal that was lying about, drew a

c

little *bonhomme* on the back of that canvas of M. Bonnard's, and went away."

Bonnard just then was at work on a decoration for my dining-room, and on the back of one of his sketches Lautrec had left me a silhouette of himself by way of visiting-card.

As I said, the Beaux-Arts would have been highly diverted if they had been asked to give Lautrec a commission for a fresco: after La Goulue, the next person to put the walls of her *salon* at the great artist's disposal was the proprietress of a celebrated *maison*.

The *Café de la Nouvelle Athènes*, in Montmartre, was a meeting-place for Degas, Cézanne, Renoir, Manet, Desboutin, and art critics such as Duranty. The latter had constituted himself champion of the " New Painting," though his praise was not without reservations. He complained of Cézanne, for instance, that he painted with a bricklayer's trowel. In his opinion, Cézanne's reason for putting so much paint on his canvas must be that he thought a kilogramme of green would look greener than a gramme.

Nor did Manet, for his part, set much store by the painter from Aix. To Manet, the refined and elegant Parisian, the artist in Cézanne was but the counterpart of the " foul-mouthed " man. But to tell the truth, the vulgarity of speech that he was reproached with was actually a pose adopted by Cézanne for Manet's benefit, irritated as he was by his standoffish airs. Once, for instance, when the painter of *Le Bon Bock* asked his colleague if he was preparing anything for the *Salon*, he drew upon himself the retort:

" Yes, some nice dung! "

It has sometimes been said that " Degas and Renoir, with their dissimilar natures, were not made to understand one another." As a matter of fact, although Degas disliked the fluffy texture of some of Renoir's paintings—" He paints with balls of wool," he would say when confronted with them—at other times, on the contrary, I have heard him exclaim, as he passed his hand amorously over one of his pictures: "Lord, what a lovely texture!"

On the other hand, there was no greater admirer of Degas than Renoir, although secretly he deplored Degas' desertion of the art of the pastellist, in which he was so entirely himself, for that of the painter in oils.

Notwithstanding their esteem for one another as artists, Renoir and Degas did, however, manage to quarrel. It happened in this way.

The painter Caillebotte, being about to die, wished to indemnify Renoir for purchases he had made from him at prices he was now ashamed of. In his will, therefore, he bequeathed to Renoir any one of the pictures in his collection, at the artist's choice.

Renoir was just beginning to " sell," though his prices were not yet very high. Having heard that an admirer was prepared to pay 50,000 francs for the *Moulin de la Galette*, Renoir, very naturally, would have liked to select this picture. But Caillebotte's executor pointed out that as the collection was to go to the Luxembourg, it would be a pity if he were to beggar it of one of his most characteristic works. The same objection was made with regard to the *Swing*, on which his choice fell next, and finally, as the bequest included several pictures by Degas, Caillebotte's brother suggested to Renoir that he should take one of the *Leçons de Danse*; and Renoir agreed.

But Renoir soon tired of seeing the musician for ever bending over his violin, while the dancer, one leg in the air, awaited the chord that should give the signal for her pirouette. One day, when Durand-Ruel said to him: " I have a customer for a really finished Degas," Renoir did not wait to be told twice, but taking down the picture, handed it to him on the spot.

When Degas heard of it he was beside himself with

fury, and sent Renoir back a magnificent painting
that the latter had once allowed him to carry off
from his studio—a woman in a blue dress cut low in
front, almost life-size. This work belongs to the same
period as the famous picture *La Dame au Sourire*. I was
with Renoir when the painting was thus brutally
returned to him. In his anger, seizing a palette-
knife, he began slashing at the canvas. Having reduced
the dress to shreds, he was aiming the knife at the
face:

" But, Monsieur Renoir ! " I cried.

He interrupted his gesture:

" Well, what's the matter? "

" Monsieur Renoir, you were saying in this very
room only the other day that a picture is like a child
one has begotten. And now you are going to destroy
that face ! "

" You're a nuisance with your wise tales ! "

But his hand dropped, and he said suddenly:

" That head gave me such a lot of trouble to paint !
Ma foi ! I shall keep it."

He cut out the upper part of the picture. That
fragment, I believe, is now in Russia.

Renoir threw the hacked strips furiously into the
fire. Then taking a slip of paper, he wrote on it the
single word " Enfin ! " put the paper in an envelope
addressed to Degas, and gave the letter to his servant
to post. Happening to meet Degas some time after,
I had the whole story from him; and after a silence:

" What on earth can he have meant by that
' Enfin ! '? "

" Probably that at last he had quarrelled with
you."

" Well, I never ! " exclaimed Degas. Obviously he
could not get over his astonishment.

La Nouvelle Athènes was at the height of its fame at
the period of *La Loge*, for which Renoir had so much
difficulty in obtaining the 425 francs he needed to pay

his rent; the period of Manet's painting of a woman
in a white satin jerkin, lying on a sofa, and two
kittens playing with balls of wool, for which at Nadar's
sale in 1895 I watched the bidding: it failed to reach
1500 francs. About the same time, at Hoschide's
sale, Claude Monet's famous *Dindons blancs* sold for
less than 100 francs. And in 1900 or thereabouts, a
big dealer on the Boulevards, wishing to get rid of a
lot of Impressionist paintings which he fancied were
injuring the sale of his more " finished " pictures,
could think of nothing better than to deposit them in
a little shop on the outer Boulevard. The proprietress
used to lure admirers of Impressionism inside, saying :
" I have a bargain for you."

One day, as I was walking along the Boulevard de
Clichy, curiosity drew me into a little restaurant whose
signboard bore the device " *Au Tambourin*." Inside
were to be seen a large number of tambourines on
which artists had painted all sorts of subjects. And the
tambourines were not all: there were canvases too,
in colour-schemes that might be termed startling.
Someone who came in at the same time as myself
inquired of the landlady :

" Has Vincent come? "

" He's this minute gone out. He came in to hang
up those *Sunflowers*, and went off again at once."

And that was how I just missed meeting Van Gogh.

As may be imagined, the owner of this shop, a
certain Madame Segatori, did not grow rich by her
clientèle of artists. She ended by seeing the whole of
her stock, her tambourines and her Van Goghs
scattered haphazard at auction—for Van Gogh's
success so far was but a *succès de rire*.

III A GOLDEN AGE FOR THE COLLECTORS

We were passing through a fortunate period for collectors. Masterpieces everywhere, and going, so to speak, for a song. Not only was Manet's *Woman on a Sofa*, which had belonged to Baudelaire, knocked down at the Hôtel Drouot for 1500 francs; but his portrait of Zacharie Astruc, for which less than 2000 was asked, found no bidder. A canvas by Renoir, the *Femme Nue*, now at the Musée Rodin, was for sale in my little shop in the rue Laffitte for 400 francs, and I remember a " great " admirer saying to me: " If I had 400 francs to spare, I should buy that painting to destroy it, it grieves me so to see my friend Renoir so badly represented. What woman ever had hands like that? " A reproach, it may be said in passing, that the painter incurred all his life with regard to the hands of his sitters.

The most admirable lithographs by Redon, limited to 25 or 30 copies, were sold at seven francs fifty, and for ten years to come did not exceed that price.

And Gauguin, who by then had proved himself a master all along the line—as painter, as ceramist, as sculptor—Gauguin on his return from Tahiti was to see his finest paintings refused by the Musée du Luxembourg, which, it must be added, was at the same time, owing to indignant protests from the *Institut*, rejecting seventeen of the canvases of Caillebotte's bequest.

Caillebotte's brother, meeting me one day after this repulse, said, " Vollard, you know Bénédite " (at that time custodian of the Musée du Luxembourg); "couldn't you get him to store the outcasts of the lot in the attic" (the outcasts were Renoir, Sisley, Cézanne and Manet), "so that if the wind should change, he could hang them later on the walls of the museum?"

I ran off to Bénédite. I think I can still hear him: "I, in whom the State has put its trust, am *I* to make myself a 'fence' for paintings that the Commission has excluded?"

A few years later Renoir said to me: "It seems that the 'Friends of the Luxembourg' would like to have something of mine. But I don't want to appear to be forcing the doors of the Museum. Look here, you take this pastel" (it was his *Madame Morisot and her Daughter*) "and go and tell the President of the 'Friends of the Luxembourg'—you know, M. Chéramy—that I'll sell them this picture for 100 francs. The worst of it is, they'll imagine themselves obliged to come and thank me."

I took the pastel to Chéramy, who drew back in alarm before the "responsibility" of introducing a Renoir into the Luxembourg without further ceremony.

"Please assure M. Renoir that we have all of us the greatest esteem for him, but explain that in order to avoid criticism we have decided to submit all our purchases to the judgment of M. Bonnat."

I ventured to say to M. Chéramy: "And something of Cézanne's? Would the 'Friends of the Luxembourg' . . .?"

M. Chéramy, looking severe:

"You surely wouldn't suggest . . .?"

The man in the street thought no otherwise. Having arranged an exhibition of Cézanne's work, I heard an outcry one day outside my window. A man was holding a woman by the wrists before one of the pictures. She was struggling, and shouting: "Fancy forcing me to look at that horror, me that got a prize for drawing!" And the man who had thought out this excellent form of marital punishment was retorting: "That'll teach you to be nicer to me another time!" It is true that this objector did not belong to the ranks of art criticism. But one of the writers most noted among these for his modern tendencies deplored, on the occasion of this same exhibition, that "Cézanne's scanty knowledge betrayed him," declaring that he failed "in the art of separating his planes, of giving the illusion of distance."

It was the same with Van Gogh: the boldest were unable to stomach his painting. Even when, in 1897, I held an exhibition of this artist—the first big exhibition of his work ever given—and the finest of his paintings were offered at about 500 francs, the connoisseurs could not make up their mind to "plunge." After all, this reluctance on the part of the public was not to be wondered at, when the most emancipated of the artists themselves, such as Renoir and Cézanne, were to be heard, the one reproaching Van Gogh with his "exoticism," and the other saying: "Honestly, yours is the painting of a madman."

If the older artists had so much difficulty in making their way, it was still harder for the younger ones such as Bonnard, Vuillard, Roussel, Denis, Aristide Maillol. I do wrong, though, to name Maurice Denis among the "*jeunes*" who found it difficult to sell their work, for he made his mark at once. It was M. Arsène Alexandre, I think, who wrote: "The great event of the week is not the fall of the Ministry, but Maurice Denis's show at the *Indépendants*."

And yet as early as 1892 it had looked as though the work of the *jeunes* were going to win the day. A dealer who went in for "furbishing up" old pictures, Le Barc de Bouteville, influenced, I fancy, by Vogler, a pupil of Sisley's, tried, as he said, to get " a little fresh air " into his shop, and organised exhibitions of the *jeunes*. But after a short fit of curiosity on the part of the public, everything fell flat again.

Le Barc de Bouteville was not the only one to go ahead. Earlier than he an old artists' colourman, " Père " Tanguy, had become interested in the new painting, to the extent of allowing credit to the artists who painted " light."

This worthy man, who had been arrested by mistake as an insurgent during the last days of the Commune, and had barely escaped being shot, had ended, in all good faith, by convincing himself that he was a genuine *réfractaire*. Having been spared he knew not why, and established himself later on as a colour-merchant, he patronised the new painters, in whom it pleased him to see rebels like himself. I may add that he gave credit likewise to those who painted " dark," but on condition that they distinguished themselves by the regularity of their lives— in refraining, for instance, from going to cafés and betting at races. For this *communard* by suggestion was the most bourgeois of men, and nothing could have rid him of the conviction that with good conduct a painter must infallibly " arrive." If Tanguy did not grow rich by his trade, he gained the esteem of the artists. Émile Bernard led him to appreciate Cézanne. Van Gogh did several portraits of him; one of which, a life-size painting with the model seated, is now in the Musée Rodin. When people tried to buy it from him, Tanguy would coolly demand 5000 francs, and if they exclaimed at the " outrageousness " of the price, he would add: " You see, I'm not anxious to sell my portrait." It was not till after his death that Rodin was able to purchase it.

At Tanguy's sale I bought five of Cézanne's paintings for about 900 francs. I remember that after the sale, when we were paying for our purchases, the auctioneer, M. Paul Chevallier, said to me: "You've got some pluck! I admired the doggedness with which you held out against the other bidders." The compliment made it all the more embarrassing to have to confess that I possessed only 300 francs. I suggested handing this over to him by way of deposit till I should be in a position to take delivery of my purchases. He looked at me for a moment. "No! Take your pictures. You can pay me for the lot as soon as you're able to." A real good sort, M. Chevallier! And what a good turn he did me that day! This reminiscence may account for the many outstanding accounts that were found in his safe at his death.

One day, turning over some of the books exposed for sale in the Galeries de l'Odéon, I came upon Huysmans's *Certains*. What he had to say of the Satanism of Félicien Rops made me anxious to know that artist. I had discovered among the boxes on the quays an unsigned engraving which looked to me like a Rops. They wanted five francs for it, but I got it for three francs fifty. Taking my courage in both hands, I knocked at the door of the artist's studio. From my reading of Huysmans I was prepared when the door opened to penetrate into the den of a sorcerer. I found myself confronted by a jovial young man with a little box of rouge in his hand. Only one side of his face was made up so far. For all costume—it was summer—he wore a green shade to protect his eyes, and at his waist, hanging by a string, something that resembled an infant's bib. He received me none the less without the least embarrassment. He told me that the etching I had brought to show him was a very rare work, of which he himself possessed no proof. He proposed an exchange, and gave me instead a water-colour drawing of a naked woman wearing gloves and a hat. Her perverse eyes appeared to be lighting up at the sight of a monkey prancing about behind the bars of its cage. I returned from my visit proud in the possession of a work so characteristic of the artist's manner. I was later to hear Rops referred to as the " Belgian Cabanel." I happened to repeat this to Renoir, who said : " The funniest thing about that is that they probably intended it as a compliment to him."

Rops liked to be thought a great lady-killer. He did not even conceal his discomfitures in that respect. He got a letter one day which read : " Monsieur Rops, when I was a little girl you used to say, ' I'd like to paint your portrait, you little rogue.' Well, now I'll come to your studio." Rops could not remember anything about her, and his impatience to see what would turn up was great. A heavily-built woman, with greying hair and a moustache, presented herself. " How stout you've grown, M. Rops! You remember, you were always trying to kiss me; but now I'm married, so you must behave."

Again, when two or three years before his death I went to see Rops in his studio, he said to me : " I'm expecting a woman." I suggested retiring. " No, stay," he said. " When the bell rings three times, you can leave by the other end of the studio." After a little while the bell rang three times and I took my leave. Without thinking, I looked over my shoulder. It was an old *bonne*. " Come now," she said, " it's time for your *tisane*."

Rops had an old friend, Doctor Filleau, to whom he introduced me : he had got together an admirable collection of the great Impressionists. The hours I spent at his house were among the pleasantest of my life. Every Tuesday there was a *dîner du pot au feu*, to which the *habitués* of the house had a standing

invitation; and after dinner we listened at times—
what a treat it was!—to Mme Filleau, the future
interpreter of Vincent d'Indy. Among the intimates
of the house was M. Dumay, senior clerk at the
Ministry of Public Worship, a circumstance which
provided Dr. Filleau with an ardent following of
ecclesiastics; for the latter, not daring to approach
M. Dumay directly, hoped to secure their host's
mediation. One prelate sent the Doctor a superb
lobster, adding, on the card which accompanied the
gift, these words, which at that date seemed to me
the height of wit: " *Sur votre table il deviendra* CAR-
DINAL." Another time an aspirant to the episcopate
brought two pretty nieces for the Doctor to examine—
or at any rate two young persons who made themselves out to be such, and needless to say were not
sparing in their praise of their excellent uncle. These
shallow little tricks were of course all given away to
the senior clerk of Public Worship. He took careful
note of them, that no adventurer might creep into
the flock under his care; for, anti-clerical though he
was, M. Dumay would have no trifling with the
prestige of the ecclesiastical hierarchy.

It was on one of those Tuesdays that I dropped a
brick, the memory of which still haunts me after
more than forty years. A very loquacious lady,
whom I had never seen before, appeared to be talking through her nose. " Don't you think," I said to
one of my neighbours, by way of starting conversation, " that lady would be well advised to sound
her trumpet less often? "

" You bet I do! I've not been able to get used
to it these thirty years."

And as I stared at him, horror-struck:

" Yes. I'm her husband."

One day when I was leaving the Doctor's house
with Rops, my eyes still dazzled by the pictures that
adorned the walls:

" Well, now," he said to me, " all that stuff's mad, don't you agree? "

" I'm not so sure. I think it's jolly nice to look at, anyhow."

" Then I'm sorry for you. It's all up with you. Once one has got that sort of painting into one's eye . . ."

Nevertheless it was seeing pictures of that kind that enabled me to find my line.

Not long after this, having profitably disposed of the *Femme au Singe* given me by Rops, I devoted the proceeds of the sale to the purchase of a water-colour by a painter who has not yet obtained the recognition he deserves : John Lewis-Brown. Delighted with my acquisition, I ventured to call on him.

On entering his ground-floor flat in the rue Ballu, I was flabbergasted to find myself confronted by a General on horseback in the midst of a little garden. It was one of the painter's models.

" By the by," I said to Brown, " I've seen an astounding drawing of horses on the Boulevard Montmartre."

" At Boussod's, you mean? Why, man, it's by Degas, the greatest of living painters! "

" I see that it's only by painting from nature . . ."

Brown interrupted me :

" *He!* He does his painting on the third floor, with little wooden horses for models."

And seeing my astonishment :

" Of course Degas goes to the race-courses, at Auteuil and Longchamp, but it's in his studio, twiddling his little wooden horses about in the light, that he succeeds in reconstituting nature. Ah! when one has a painter's eye! It's like Daumier. His friend Boulard told me that one day, at Valmondois, Daumier said to him : ' I'd like to do a study of ducks.' Boulard took him into the poultry-yard :

the birds were all let out, and the whole time they were disporting themselves on the pond, Daumier was smoking his pipe and talking of something else. Said Boulard to himself: 'He's forgotten all about the ducks.' A few days later, going to see his friend at his studio, what was his amazement to come upon a study of ducks. Said Daumier: 'You remember, it was at your place I saw them.'"

"I haven't got that gift of memory," Lewis-Brown went on, "I'm obliged to have a model. Fortunately I live on the ground floor."

The advantage of living on the ground floor, to a painter of horses working from the life, was still further impressed on me not long after, when in another block of studios I came upon a man on horseback waiting outside a door on the second floor. My astonishment was all the greater as the painter who lived there specialised in little birds.

It turned out that this painter had exhibited at the *Salon* a picture of a lark, executed with such an astounding degree of finish that it had brought him a great many commissions. Among his customers was an Argentine, who asked if he could do a portrait of a horse with the same perfection.

"Why not?" replied the artist.

"And me upon it," the Argentine added, suggesting at the same time an appointment for a sitting in the studio.

"At my place?" cried the artist in dismay. "What are you thinking of? I live on the second floor!"

"Bueno!" said the Argentine. "In our country, horses go upstairs."

I told this story to Lewis-Brown at another of my visits to his studio. I found him fulminating: "I've just seen the *Angélus* again, and it's brand-new! To think that when I saw that picture last, it was all over cracks!"

The painting, it must be explained, had since passed into the hands of M. Chauchard, the director of the Magasins du Louvre. Now, M. Chauchard never bought anything but masterpieces, and his esteem for the Old Masters was such that he could not dream of letting their works appear in his house showing the slightest defect.

IV MY APPRENTICESHIP AT THE *UNION ARTISTIQUE*

I had told Rops I should like to be a picture dealer, and asked him if he could not give me an introduction to some important Art gallery, where I could be initiated into the business.

" I deal directly with my purchasers," he replied, " and have no relations with any of the dealers."

Then after a moment's reflection:

" All the same I may be able to help you."

And taking from a drawer the photograph of a very youthful Rops, he wrote on it: " To the Georges Petit of to-morrow, Ambroise Vollard," signed it *F. Rops*, and gave it me.

More embarrassed than pleased by this testimonial, and resolved not to make any use of it, I went nevertheless to Georges Petit's Gallery, having by chance a letter of recommendation to the firm, given me by a rich banker. Even so I dared not ask for the owner himself, but went up to a member of the staff and showed him my letter.

" How many foreign languages can you speak? " he asked.

" None. But I don't expect much. I won't ask for anything to begin with."

" We can get as many assistants as we want, who are prepared to come for nothing, and can speak foreign languages into the bargain."

And after casting a glance at me, he went off.

It was M. Georges Petit himself.

About this time I made the acquaintance of M. Alphonse Dumas, a gentleman of means who went in for painting in a dilettantish way, and with whom I eventually obtained a " paid job." Dumas was a pupil of Debat-Ponsan, an artist whose speciality was cows in meadows, and portraits of Ministers, particularly those who were natives of Toulouse.

M. Alphonse Dumas had opened a picture-gallery, which he called the *Union Artistique*. It was not with a view to making money: he merely wanted to balance the expenses of his own painting by the profits to be made out of selling other people's. Perhaps in his secret heart he looked forward to seeing passers-by stop to look at *Torses de Femme* and *Nymphes au Bain* signed Alphonse Dumas.

But he was particularly anxious not to be taken for a dealer.

" You see," he said, " I come of a family of artists. It's not a shop I've opened, it's a *salon*. I am a gentleman serving as intermediary between the artist and the customer. Debat-Ponsan will let me have his work; my friend Gillou has promised to bring the members of his club, and there are all the other people I know in other ways."

It may be said at once that the members of Gillou's club were not the slightest use to the *Union Artistique*. They came and gossiped sometimes from six to seven, but that was all. One evening when Dumas had had to delay shutting up the shop for a quarter of an hour, he said:

" The fact is, I'm simply burning gas for nothing. But what are all those people doing over there? " And he pointed to the terrace of a *café* which was crowded with customers.

" They are drinking their *apéritif*."

" Instead of buying pictures for their homes! I tell you what it is, Vollard, nowadays people live too much in public."

Our customers certainly were remarkably few. Once, though, we did have hopes of getting rid at

D

one go of a lot of Debat-Ponsans. An American came in. I was alone in the shop. In a great hurry, because he was on the point of sailing, he asked if we could furnish him with a dozen pictures of animals. Debat-Ponsan, as I said, painted cows to perfection, but he had told us that to suit the taste of customers, he would be equally pleased to paint horses, donkeys, sheep, or even poultry.

"You see," the visitor explained, "I'm at my office from morning to night, and when I come home, I want something to look at that will be a change from all the people I've had to see. I'm off to-morrow night. Show me some samples, and I'll give you an order."

When M. Dumas came in, I told him what had happened.

"Quick! Run and tell Debat-Ponsan the good news! America's a big country! When they see the pictures over there . . ."

He had visions of boat-loads of Debat-Ponsans sailing to both the Americas. But that day, unfortunately, Debat-Ponsan hadn't a single picture of cows ready to show.

"Well," cried Dumas, catching sight of a canvas against the wall, "what about that magnificent bull?"

"Ah, no! Only the under-coats of that picture are done."

"Isn't that enough to give an idea of the style?"

"I have sworn"—M. Debat-Ponsan raised his hand—"that I will never let a painting go out of my studio with only the under-coats painted. When a picture is finished, I defy anyone to discover how I've painted it; but in that state a painter would tumble to my process at once, and bag it. And who's to say your American isn't an artist in disguise?"

We shuddered at the thought, and were obliged to

let the American catch his boat without having
bought anything from us.

We were to some extent compensated by a customer
who commissioned two pictures next day. He wanted
two paintings, each of a soldier.

" I don't know the names of any military painters,"
he told us, " but I want my commission executed by
someone *hors concours*. And I want one of the soldiers
to be a Zouave. The other doesn't matter, so long
as he doesn't belong to a crack regiment. You see,
I was a Zouave myself. . . . If I had the time to
sit . . ."

His greater difficulty would have been to suggest,
even remotely, the hypothetical Zouave of long ago,
with the belly that had grown on him, and his
enormous chops. When he hinted that lack of time
alone prevented him from sitting, the woman accom-
panying him—a very pretty woman—was unable to
conceal a smile; and it struck me that whether or
no he had once been a Zouave, there was every
likelihood that he was now a cuckold.

But Alphonse Dumas' concern was to satisfy his
customer.

" How about a cavalryman taking a toss, as a
companion picture to the Zouave? "

" I've no wish to hurt anybody," said the fat
man, " I merely want the regiment to be inferior."

" Well," said M. Dumas, " shall we say a soldier
of the line? "

" That's it. A mud-thumper."

I must admit that M. Debat-Ponsan, so supple
was his talent, made an extraordinarily good job of
the " novelty " demanded of him. The Zouave was
magnificent: as for the infantryman, he looked as
though he had just done it in his pants.

Meanwhile the painter had finished his bull. The
picture, which we at once put in the window, attracted
a passer-by whom I suspected of being an ironmonger.

I had heard that people end by assimilating the character of their surroundings; and this man, with his pointed elbows and knees! . . . His whole person suggested a vendor of files and nails. He gazed at the Debat-Ponsan with increasing admiration.

" That powerful bull and those delicate flowers—what a charming antithesis! "

" This is an ironmonger-poet," thought I.

" And what is the title of the picture? "

" Virility," I began. And I was about to add: " That is the title the Master gives it himself," but I stopped short, so great was the disappointment I read in my customer's face. Debat-Ponsan had authorised me to alter the titles of his paintings according to circumstance, so I went on: " That at least is the title which a coarse mind, insensitive to the poetry with which the painting is saturated, might hit on."

" So then, really, it's called . . . ? "

" April," I declared stoutly, " April, the month of flowers, in which nature, under the fragrant breath of spring . . ."

The ironmonger's eyes lit up at this decent title, that would allow him to take the picture home without laying himself open to ridicule from a possibly unsatisfied spouse, or scandalising his daughters.

" April! What an admirable symbol! . . . Monsieur, I am professor of æsthetics at the Faculty of Letters at X. I shall acquaint my students with the name of Debat-Ponsan. April! What images may be called up by the magic of a single word! I will buy the picture. But . . ." The professor's face grew suddenly pensive. " What is that patch of blue among the branches at the top of the tree? It suggests forget-me-nots. But how can there be forget-me-nots on a tree? Myosotis turned parasite? "

As it happened I had asked the very same question of the painter:

"Doesn't it look as though there were forget-me-nots growing among the branches of your oak?"

"To hell with you!" the artist had replied. "What does it matter if it does? That's a tone-echo." And he added condescendingly: "That's a matter for painters, my lad."

Aping the Master's assurance, I repeated my lesson to my customer:

"That patch? Why, it's a tone-echo! That's a matter for painters, you know."

"There is no end to the mysteries of art!" exclaimed the professor. "The profane, looking at this picture, would say, 'How can an oak produce forget-me-nots?' And *we* say, 'Tone-echo'!"

His face lighted up with a mischievous smile:

"I'll stump my botanical colleague with *that* myosotis."

Things were very quiet at the *Union Artistique*. There was a momentary slump in Debat-Ponsans. One day, actually, a some-time enthusiast who had bought a *Heifer and Calf*, one of the most successful of the Master's pictures, came to ask Dumas to take it back.

Then came better days. Three Debat-Ponsans sold one after another. And a gentleman came in to buy a painting by the Bordeaux artist Quinsac: a girl warming a turtle-dove on her very dainty little breasts.

"Is it all right to give a picture like that to one's *fiancée*?" our new customer asked timidly.

We assured him it was.

"Every day, on my way to the office," he confessed to us, "I've been going out of my way to have a squint at that juicy little bit. It's nice, isn't it, giving presents that one can enjoy oneself?"

After he had left the shop:

"If that's his idea of a present," I said to Dumas,

" he'll be giving his wife a sporting rifle for her birthday one of these days."

A friend of the Dumas' who happened to be present, appeared rather embarrassed by my remark. I discovered later that he was also in the habit of giving his wife " useful " presents. One day, for instance, on the anniversary of their wedding, he brought her, to her astonishment, a magnificent meerschaum pipe. " Don't you see? " he explained, showing her the old man's head that formed the bowl of it; " it's the very image of your father."

In honour of the tenth Debat-Ponsan that we sold, Dumas gave a garden-party at his house at Neuilly, to which I was invited. In the park, towards the end of the day, the guests were admiring the effect of the sun breaking through the clouds:

" Oh, look! " cried somebody, " a regular Monet sky! "

" What says the Master? " asked Dumas of Debat-Ponsan, who was studiously contemplating the sky.

" Of course! . . . Of course. . . . There's a lot in a sunset. But in nature, as in everything else, one must pick and choose."

At that moment there was a peal of thunder.

" You see! " cried one of the guests, " a sky like that isn't natural."

" As for me," added another, " when the sky takes upon itself to play the Monet, this is all I have to say for it."

And he went back indoors.

" But," said another guest, " shouldn't art imitate nature? "

" All I know is this," retorted M. Debat-Ponsan, " I'm a gold-medallist. When your Monet can say as much, we'll discuss the matter if he likes. If nature is going over to the painters who paint without knowing how to draw, so much the worse for nature! Corot—you wouldn't call him a fool, I suppose?—Well, Corot said that the artist must be able to correct nature. It's the formula of the ancients: *Ars addit Naturæ.*"

"*I* nearly let myself in for one of those bloody Impressionists," another visitor remarked. "One day, without looking at the signature, I bought a picture of the very bit of the Oise where my wife and I are fond of going for a walk. It was the very image of the place. When we saw it in the window, we couldn't help it: we went off with it at once. Then one day someone said to us: 'What! You've got a Pissaro in your house?' I wasn't long getting rid of it, I can tell you! To begin with, Impressionist painting is against my principles; and besides, my wife says that when one has daughters, one must be careful to give a good tone to the home."

This gave M. Dumas to think; for he had four daughters to marry off.

The next day he brought a large portfolio to the *Union Artistique.*

"I have a youthful sin to confess to you," he said. "I knew Père Noisy at the beginning of his career, when he was dealing chiefly in books—certain romantics that I was very keen on. He came to me one day and said: 'I want to take you to see a painter who is beginning to be talked about.' 'Noisy knows what I like,' I said to myself; 'I may be in for a good thing.' And then he took me to a studio where everything was of a modernism! . . .

"I was standing there gaping, when Noisy, who was talking to the painter, called me over. 'M. Dumas,' he said, introducing me, 'is afraid to ask you for anything, but perhaps he might take away one or two little studies at your choice?' I was caught. The painter took some drawings from a portfolio and a framed water-colour from the wall, made a little parcel of the lot, and handed it me. That little joke cost me ten good louis. I didn't think it funny at the time, I can assure you. To-day, it appears, the stuff is beginning to go up in value. All the more reason to get rid of it. My ten louis have been lying idle at least ten years in there!"

Dumas opened the portfolio, and took out Manet's gorgeous water-colour, *Olympia*—the framed sketch the artist had taken from the wall—then a roll containing the original drawings for *Le Chat Noir et le Chat Blanc*; a " state " of the coloured lithograph *Polichinelle*; several admirable drawings in red chalk and a dozen sketches of cats.

" I think that's all," he said.

But on his shaking the portfolio there fell out a delightful study of a woman, painted on parchment.

" How my friends would have ragged me if they had seen that! . . . Now make it your business to get rid of the lot for me, at the best price you can. But of course, nothing in the window! You understand, if Debat-Ponsan were to drop in unexpectedly and see himself exhibited alongside a Manet! . . ."

Good things must have some mysterious force of attraction in them. Although, following the instructions of my chief, I only showed the Manets with the greatest discretion, in a day or two they were all sold. Only one thing vexed Dumas: the customer who bought *Le Chat Noir et le Chat Blanc* had insisted on our relieving him of a Sisley.

" And I had sworn," said Dumas to me, " never to buy an Impressionist! We must hope you'll find an opportunity of passing this Sisley on to some chance customer. Anyway, do your best! And more than ever, sale on the strict q.t., you understand. This is not a time to do anything foolish, when we're just beginning to make a little headway."

It was true, the shop was beginning to attract custom. Only the day before we had got rid of two flower pieces by Jeannin, and if only we had had

some paintings of fruit, we could have sold one of
those too. Besides all this, one of our good customers
was talking of commissioning a portrait by Quinsac
and a study of sheep by Debat-Ponsan.

One afternoon when he was about to go out,
Dumas said to me: " I'll be back in an hour. I've
got an engagement at the Club." Sure of my freedom of action in the interval, I resolved to pull off
a bold stroke. I removed the Debat-Ponsan that
was in the window and put the Sisley in its place.
Five minutes later it was sold. This was not because
the Impressionists were in favour (the year was 1892)
but it just happened like that.

Dumas' first words when he came back were:
" That Sisley, you know, really . . . Look here,
Vollard, you'll have to go to the collector who foisted
it on us, and ask him to take his picture back at a
low price."

" But I've sold it."

" Never! To someone we know? "

" No, to a stranger. He talks of coming back some
day to see if we've got anything else of the same
kind."

" Of course you told him the firm doesn't deal in
that sort of stuff, and it was only by chance . . ."

Life in these surroundings was beginning to be
more than irksome.

Now, one day, having nothing to do, I was leaning
against the hand-rail of the window in the *entresol*,
watching the passing show of the street. Suddenly
the rail gave way, and I was about to be precipitated
into space, when I felt myself held back as though
by a hand. It was a bit of metal fixed into the
wall. A moment or so later a locksmith's workman
appeared on the scene: " I've come to unscrew the
iron bracket by the window of the *entresol*. I was to
have come yesterday, but my little boy broke his

leg." "Well," I said, "it's a jolly good thing for me that your little boy *did* break his leg," and I told him my adventure. The man looked furious. He evidently considered me a hard-hearted brute.

No harm, on the other hand, came to the girl who, unwittingly also, preserved me from death. It is true that a stranger came off very badly in my stead; but that was actually a punishment for his curiosity.

I had climbed to the top of an omnibus that was waiting at the terminus, when I caught sight of a ravishingly pretty girl walking along the pavement. I said to myself: "That girl probably has no idea how delicious she is. She ought to be told." And getting up, I prepared to leave the omnibus.

"Excuse me, sir," said a passenger whom I brushed against in passing, "I often see you take this omnibus. May I ask what advantage you find in the seat you always try to secure on the right of the driver?"

"A very great advantage," I said. "But excuse me, I'm in a great hurry this morning. I'll tell you all about it another time, since we often take the same bus."

I had not indeed time to tell him that once I was seated, I liked to lean on one arm; that being left-handed, it was my left arm that supported me best, and in that particular seat I was able to rest it on the driver's box. My interlocutor took my reply for the bluff of a person with a secret he refuses to give away; and hoping no doubt to discover for himself what the place I had just quitted had to offer, he got up there and then and went over to it. And the omnibus started, bearing him away to his destiny.

Meanwhile I had approached the girl. I discovered at once, with pleasure, that I had to do with a very respectable person, for she did not attempt to tell me she was *sérieuse*, as most girls do who allow themselves to be spoken to in the street. I also saw she was a foreigner. But when she was at a loss for some expression in our language, she made up for it in very effective and amusing dumb-show. Seeing a tram approaching, she told me she must take it, and when I pressed for a *rendez-vous*:

" It's too late now," she said, " my *fiancé* is coming back to-morrow. He will be delighted to see how I have got on with my French in his absence, thanks to all the kind gentlemen I have met."

So much for the girl who was never to know she had just saved my life, a fact which came to light the next day. I took my usual bus at the head of the line, with the same driver, and he told me with considerable emotion that not long after I had got off, just as the bus was passing a house that was being pulled down, a brick had fallen on the head of the only passenger on the upper deck—the identical one who had taken my place.

As I told Dumas the story, I noticed he had a preoccupied air.

" I can't make up my mind," he told me at last. " I've got three hundred thousand francs to invest. I've been offered two equally interesting concerns, and I'm torn between them like the donkey that . . . well, you know the story of the two bundles of hay."

" If I were you, I should spend my three hundred thousand francs buying Renoirs, Cézannes and Degas —all the great Impressionists, in fact."

Dumas would listen to no more.

V I COMMENCE PICTURE DEALER

I have often been asked about my beginnings in the trade. They go back to the time when I was reduced to living on ship's biscuits because they were cheaper than bread. Even so, my last resources were pretty well exhausted, and I was obliged to try to turn to account the few drawings and engravings I had collected out of my savings as a student.

I heard one day that a certain wine-merchant went in for buying modern drawings when his business happened to be doing well. I lived at the lower end of the Avenue de Clichy; the potential purchaser at Bercy. But I was not afraid of the distance; for economy's sake I did the journey on foot. I took with me a drawing by Forain, as I had been told that artist's work was likely to please the wine-merchant.

"What do you want for your drawing?" asked my collector.

"A hundred and twenty francs."

"I'll give you a hundred for it."

And he took a note out of his wallet. A hundred francs! It was very tempting. All the same, I wouldn't give in. I had been very much struck, a little while before, by the tactics of a colleague when a customer was trying to beat him down over a drawing by Rops:

"What do you want for your Rops?"

"Forty francs."

"Too much. Thirty if you like."

44

" You want to beat me down, do you? All right then, I'll take fifty."

And the collector had paid the fifty francs.

I tried the same dodge.

" You want to beat down my Forain? " I said to my client. " Very well, it's no longer a hundred and twenty; I want a hundred and fifty for it."

" I'll take it," said the collector. " But you have some cheek, I must say."

When the hundred and fifty francs were in my pocket, I thought I would celebrate this success by treating myself to the theatre and a little supper at one of the big restaurants. I decided to see *Michel Strogoff* at the Châtelet. What an evening that was! I had an excellent seat, right at the top, for one franc fifty. Beside me sat a family—father, mother and a boy of about ten. The latter appeared to take a passionate interest in all the vicissitudes of the play. When it came to the entertainment given by the Emir, in the course of which the executioner passes a white-hot sword in front of Michel Strogoff's eyes to blind him, the boy could not contain himself: " That wouldn't have happened to him if he'd killed the other one properly with his pistol, when he was fighting with him in the beginning."

" Well, but, you silly," retorted his father, " if the other had been killed straight away, nothing more would have happened. You would never have seen the Emir's gorgeous entertainment."

" Oh! well then . . ." said the child.

Obviously the brat would not have minded a few more eyes being burnt out for the sake of still further marvellous adventures.

After the theatre I went to the Restaurant Weber, where in those happy days one could get a plate of York ham, a pint of dark beer and a generous slice of cheese, all for two francs fifty, including the tip. Sitting there at my table, among all the lights, the women in evening dress, the elegant men, the attentive waiters, I felt I was taking part in fashionable life. As I ate my supper I made up my mind that whenever I brought off a good deal, I would treat myself to the theatre and Weber. But once I was home again I thought: " All the same, that makes four francs less in my pocket."

So much for my first customer.

So now I was in business. The whole of my stock-in-trade had hardly cost me more than five hundred francs. The fact that I was able to pull through was due to a " banker " who believed in me. He was a very decent sort. He lent me money at 150 per cent. in sureties worth at least double the loan. As he reminded me every time I borrowed from him, it was to my interest that his business should prosper, since otherwise he would not be able to advance me anything more. He did business on anything and everything; and to encumber his premises as little as possible, he had done away with all his own furniture, even to domestic utensils, using for his needs only the objects that had been left him in pawn.

This arrangement was not without its inconveniences. For instance, one of his customers borrowed on a parrot; but the creature could not open its beak without saying " s . . . t," and our good man, who had nice feelings, could not bear foul language. When his daughter married, the wedding feast was to have been given at his house; but as fate would have it, the very day before, the whole of the crockery, chairs and so forth, that he held in pledge, were taken out of pawn.

These mishaps induced him to give up a business in which one was sure of nothing; and losing my sleeping partner in this way, I came near to going out of business myself. However, I would not let myself be discouraged, and carried on with the precarious means at my disposal. My stock consisted almost exclusively of drawings and prints, the most expensive of which had not cost me above thirty francs.

At that time, for a surprisingly modest sum, one could still pick up real works of art. I paid ten francs for a monotype by Degas that I fished out of a box on the quays. A fine Guys drawing might be had for the same sum, and I remember even to have seen some at two francs.

With these marvels going for so low a price, it was obviously not with the dealers that I could hope to do good business: it was indispensable that I should get into direct touch with the collectors.

One day a brother in the trade spoke to me of a client of his who was on the look-out for Forains, Guys, Rops, Steinlens, everything in fact that passed at that time for " advanced " art. " I know you have some of these," he said to me, " and if you care to get rid of the lot, I'll take them."

I replied evasively. I thought it would be more to my advantage to treat with the collector myself; but before I could do that, I must get hold of his name.

This same dealer, who made himself out to be very knowing, had once said to me: " When a man talks to me about a thing in ambiguous terms, I repeat to him, word for word, everything he's said, and it's very seldom he doesn't let fall something that puts me on the track."

I tried the same trick. Meeting him again a little later, I repeated everything he had said to me: " I have a client who buys Forains, Rops, Steinlens, all the modern school, in fact."

" I can guess who that is," he said.

" I know you're as sharp as they make them, but how on earth, with such a vague hint as I have given you . . .? "

" What would you say if I told you his name? "

" Unless you're a wizard . . ."

" Your client is M. Maurice Y. . . ."

" Well, really now, that's extraordinary! "

I had the name! It remained to get the collector's address.

Turning to my interlocutor, I said:

" I'm just writing to M. Maurice Y. Have you anything to say to him? "

" No, I don't think so."

On a bit of paper that he was so kind as to furnish me with, I informed the potential customer that I had some Forains, Rops, etc., etc. . . . When I had written the name on the envelope, I said:

" I shall have to go home. I have forgotten the address."

" Why, don't you keep all your addresses in your head? Here, without so much as looking in my book . . ." And taking the letter from me, he wrote in the street and the number.

Two days later someone knocked at the door of my room. It was M. Maurice Y.

I spread out my collection for him to see. M. Maurice Y. went away with a thousand francs' worth of merchandise, which he paid for on the nail. With this sum in my hands I felt like Rothschild.

The following week, happening to pass the shop of a colleague, what was my surprise to see one of the things I had sold to M. Maurice Y. exhibited in the window! I went in, and found the entire lot he had bought from me.

" That," said the salesman, " is not stuff that's been lying about in the junk shops. We had it from a gentleman traveller. People who have something to sell think they'll do a better deal with an *amateur* than with a dealer, and in the end it's they who get done in the eye."

VI AT MADAME MANET'S

In 1893 I forsook the heights of Montmartre, where two little garrets had served me as living-rooms and business quarters combined, and settled into the rue Laffitte. I took a tiny shop at No. 39, and later moved to No. 41.

I had had a hard struggle so far, and my setting up shop was not enough to improve my fortunes.

One evening, at closing time, one of my clients came in and said to me:

" I've just been talking to a little dealer. I'm not going to tell you his name. The fellow wants me to come back in a week's time. He says he's unearthed some ripping drawings."

" Didn't he give you any details? "

" He says there are a heap of them in a place where nobody would dream of looking. And he expects to sell them to some relation of the artist's, who will be tremendously interested in them."

" And that was all he told you? "

" Well, he did say, ' Won't (we'll say Dupont) sit up when he hears of it! After all the fuss he made about having discovered three or four pictures by the artist in question. . . . And as for the *jeunes*, who can talk of nothing but " synthetic drawing," this will take the wind out of their sails, I can tell you! ' "

" That's a bit of luck I could do with myself," I thought, when my customer had gone. " But who on earth can he have meant by his Dupont (who isn't Dupont)? Though even if I knew who Dupont was, I'd still have to discover the famous cache."

E   49

I knew the enterprise to be a mad one, but I could not keep my mind off it. I wandered along the street in a fit of abstraction. The moon was at the full. Suddenly, while I was looking up at it, it put me in mind of a pumpkin perpetually rotating; and at that same instant I ran into M. Marcel Sembat. I didn't notice him, I was so lost in thought, and it was he that spoke:

" You look very preoccupied ! "

" Can you tell me," I replied, " why, when I'm thinking of Dupont, the moon should suddenly suggest a pumpkin rotating upon itself? "

" Why, of course, it's a reminiscence of De Musset's *Dialogue of Dupont and Durand*:

> *Et le globe rasé, sans barbe ni cheveux,*
> *Comme un grand potiron roulera dans les cieux.*"

I gave a shout. Dupont? It was Durand! Durand, the great picture-dealer. He it was, precisely, who had just unearthed some pictures by Manet, several at one go. The place where no one would have thought of looking was probably the house of some member of the painter's family. And the relation who would be so much interested, mightn't that be Mme Berthe Morisot, Manet's sister-in-law? Everything fitted in admirably! But none of this told me where the drawings were to be found. I was about to give up trying to solve the puzzle, when, on passing by a rubbish bin, I heard a ragman exclaim, as he kicked a dog out of his way: " Get out, you dirty *cabot*! " The word *cabot* evoked the notion of synthesis, and at the same time the thought of Père Noisy. A strange concatenation of ideas which is to be explained in this way: Before the visit of the customer who had so much excited my curiosity with his mysterious discovery of drawings, a painter had come into my shop. He had shown me an album of lithographed portraits of actors, entitled " *Cabots!* "

" You'll admit that drawing like this is *synthesis*," he said. " Well, I've just been showing these to old Noisy, and he couldn't make anything of them."

But now *I* was tumbling to something. The little dealer my customer had referred to, who laughed at the word *synthesis* that the younger painters were so fond of, must of course be Père Noisy. In that case it was he who had discovered the hoard of drawings by Manet. It only remained for me to find the cache and make the haul myself.

I happened to have an old score to settle with Père Noisy. He had once bought from me, for a good price, a page from the sketch-book of an artist formerly the rage—the designer Renouard.

" You know," he said to me at the time, " he did a lot of studies of the people at the Vatican, and I'm after them." A few days later, by good luck, I saw the whole series at the Hôtel Drouot, where I ran into several of Noisy's customers. One of them, with more pluck than myself, had the lot knocked down to him.

" In return for this," he said to me, " I shall get that old fool Noisy to give me a Degas I've had my eye on for ages."

The next day I happened to be in Noisy's shop when the purchaser of the Renouards turned up.

Said he to Noisy:

" What would you say to twenty-seven of Renouard's best drawings? "

" I should say you'd better hurry up and get rid of them as soon as you can."

" You won't even look at them? "

" No need. I sent them to the Hôtel Drouot myself."

The other having gone away considerably crest-fallen, Père Noisy turned to me:

" They tell me you bid too. Just because I paid you fifty francs the other day for a little sketch !

You took me for an idiot that day. You didn't see that I was leading you on. Ah! You think yourselves very clever, you youngsters!"

I had resolved to "have" him one day in my turn. And the complicated affair I was trying to disentangle was perhaps going to give me my opportunity. Calling in at Noisy's place, I found him talking to the collector who had put me on the track of the mysterious drawings.

"A little patience," Père Noisy was saying; "I'm expecting to mop them up in a week's time. There's no danger. Nobody would dream of looking for them there. It's like everything else that stares you in the face: people go right past it. Only here I have to do with a woman. And with women it doesn't do to be in too much of a hurry."

My earlier deductions had led me to conjecture it was Manet's drawings that were in question: why shouldn't they be in the possession of the artist's widow? I went at once to Madame Manet's house, where I found a whole collection of drawings by the Master, which, as I discovered later, were known to quite a lot of people, only nobody had wanted them because they were merely sketches, and at that time things of that sort were not valued. I managed to buy up the despised collection; and I arranged a little show of them, which had a tremendous success with the artists and helped to give me a start.

After this visit to Mme Manet, I had occasion to see her again more than once. The first time I was there I met a very charming young man, in whom, however, I at first apprehended a competitor.

"My brother Leenhoff," said Mme Manet, introducing him.

When I left, he asked me when I should be coming again.

"Since you are interested even in the unimportant

things," put in Mme Manet, " I'll tidy the house up
a bit, and see if I can't find some of the stuff the
dealers declared was unsaleable. I've left it all
lying about; for since I put on weight it tires me to
move about much. Leenhoff can help me to look
for them. Only the other day he found quite a nice
water-colour of my husband's on the top of a cupboard.
I managed to get rid of it through Portier."

I have spoken elsewhere of this strange dealer in the
rue Lepic, whose dining-room did duty as show-room
for the canvases that accumulated pretty well everywhere in the modest *entresol* he inhabited with his
family. Many a time I saw, alongside a marvellous
" *Place Clichy* " of Renoir's that wouldn't " go off,"
that masterpiece of Manet's—a picture of a man and
woman standing beside a child's perambulator, in a
public garden. And I shall always remember Portier's
air of triumph when at last he was able to announce :
" Things are on the move ! I've found a purchaser
for my Manet. Two thousand francs ! "

Mme Manet told me that this picture had originally
been given by Manet to the painter de Nittis, in
exchange for one of his own. At Manet's death
Mme de Nittis came to see his widow :

" My dear friend," she said, " in memory of my
husband, I would like to have the picture back that
he exchanged in the old days."

Mme Manet, whose tenderness for the memory of
her husband was no less, was glad to accept, and the
paintings were exchanged once more.

There were not only sketches left with the widow of
the great painter. What a number of fine canvases
the collectors had refused ! I was reminded of this
when, at the triumphal exhibition of Manet's works in
1932, I was present at the unpacking of one of the
Master's pictures which had arrived by aeroplane,
under the care of a " nurse " whose duty it was, while
the exhibition lasted, to superintend the temperature

of the layer of air between the canvas and the glass that protected it.

A famous picture of Manet's which was not treated with such care was one of the variants of the *Exécution de Maximilien*, as important as that which is the pride of the Mannheim museum. Mme Manet's brother considered this variant inferior because Maximilian, and the generals executed with him, did not appear to him as " finished " as in the other painting. The family feared that if they put both pictures up for sale at the same time, it might injure the chances of the more finished one, for which, as it was, they were unable to obtain six thousand francs. So the replica, which was considered too cumbersome to be hung on the wall in Mme Manet's flat at Asnières, was taken off its stretcher, rolled up, and put away in the lumber-room, under a cupboard.

One day it occurred to Mme Manet's young brother that perhaps after all there was something to be done with this picture, considered unsaleable till then: the sergeant loading his rifle, for instance, shown by itself, might easily pass for a *sujet de genre*. The sergeant was immediately cut out and handed to Portier. What remained of the picture after this mutilation was all the less easy to market, that a line of cracks ran right across the bellies of the soldiers about to fire. Yet even reduced to these proportions, the *Exécution de Maximilien* was too voluminous to be thrown in the dustbin. Rolled up again, it was replaced under the cupboard, whence M. Leenhoff fished it out once more to offer it to me. I remember Mme Manet's wistful expression when these remains were spread out before us:

" What a pity Édouard took all that trouble with it! What a lot of nice things he could have painted in the time! "

I concluded the bargain. But how was I to get the fragment to the repairer? I could not think of taking the omnibus with this sort of stove-pipe in my arms. I went for a cab. Seated inside it, with my Manet on my knees, I had to be perpetually on the look-out to preserve it from the dangers of the journey, holding it upright like a church taper when my cab threatened to get wedged between two other vehicles. In this way I got safely to Chapuis's workshop—the picture-repairer who also worked for Degas.

When Chapuis had unrolled the picture, he said:

" But, M. Vollard, surely this is the picture the *Sergeant* was taken from, that I re-stretched for M. Degas? He was told the rest of the picture had been destroyed by accident. And you should have heard him on the subject of the legatees! "

When Degas saw the *Soldats épaulant* in my shop, which he recognised at once as having belonged to the same canvas as his *Sergeant*, he was thunderstruck, and found no words to express his indignation but:

" The Family again! Beware of the Family! "

Then recovering himself, he took his stand between me and the picture, and with his hand on it by way of taking possession, he added:

" You're going to sell me that. And you'll go back to Mme Manet and tell her I want the legs of the sergeant that are missing from my bit, as well as what's missing from yours: the group formed by Maximilian and the generals. I'll give her something for it."

So I went back to M. Leenhoff. When I told him the imperative errand I had been entrusted with, he shook his head.

" It looked so tattered," he said, " with the sergeant's legs dangling from it, that I thought it would be better without them, and without the head of Maximilian, which had been destroyed by the dampness of the wall. If I'd thought that a few scraps of torn and mouldy canvas could be of any value, I wouldn't have used them to light the fire with."

All I told Degas was that the missing pieces of the

canvas had been destroyed by the dampness of the wall. But he repeated, " You see, Vollard, how one should beware of the Family."

And by way of protest he had the *Sergeant* and the fragment of the *Exécution de Maximilien* he had bought from me pasted on to a plain canvas, of the supposed size of the original picture, the blanks in the canvas representing the missing parts.

" The Family! Beware of the Family! " he would repeat incessantly, whenever he brought his visitors to look at this restoration.

I remember that on one such occasion, someone asked injudiciously:

" But, M. Degas, didn't Manet himself cut up the portrait you did of him and his wife? "

Said Degas sharply:

" What business have you, sir, to criticise Manet? Yes, it's quite true, Manet thought his wife didn't fit into the picture; as a matter of fact he was probably right. And I made a fool of myself over that affair, for, furious as I was at the time, I took down a little still life that Manet had given me, and wrote to him:

" ' Monsieur, I am sending you back your *Plums*.' . . . Ah! What a lovely painting that was! It was a clever thing I did that day, and no mistake! When I had made it up with Manet, I asked him to give me back ' my ' *Plums*, and he had sold it! "

At the sale held after Degas' death, the *Maximilian* was bought by the London National Gallery, and underwent a further transformation—the two fragments of which it was composed, and which Degas had pasted on to a single canvas, by way of protest, were taken apart again and framed separately.

The whitish streak caused by a crack across the middle of the *Firing Party* had meanwhile been deftly obliterated.

At the exhibition that preceded the sale, I saw a

couple looking with curiosity at the *Maximilian* in its fragmentary state.

" They ought to have given you that picture to restore," said the woman.

The man nodded:

" When you think that from a single leg, which was all that remained of an Old Master after a fire, I was able to reconstitute a period picture: figures, costumes, atmosphere and everything—absolutely everything . . ."

" Yes, and the customer thought his picture even finer than before. . . ."

At this same exhibition there was a copy of the *Olympia* done by Gauguin, which belonged to Degas' private collection. Among the crowd gathered round the picture were two women, one of whom, with a note of anger in her voice, exclaimed: " That's the sort of woman the men desert us for."

At this same sale of Degas' there were, among other works of Manet's, the *Jambon* and a *Madame Manet* in white on a blue sofa—two outstanding pictures which, in 1894, that is to say, more than ten years after the painter's death, were still in the possession of his widow, awaiting a purchaser.

She also retained, at that time, a portrait of herself in a conservatory, and another portrait in which she was seated at the piano. This latter, I fancy, belongs to the Camondo collection. And I am leaving out many that were still to be admired in the little *pavillon* at Asnières, among others a portrait of Manet with a palette, another of Manet standing, and a woman, life-size. To these may be added everything that in those days was referred to as " sketches," things which to-day are the pride of the museums, such as the *Portrait of M. Brun*, life-size, and the *Madame Manet* in pink, with a cat on her lap. Both these paintings were likewise bought at Degas' sale by the National Gallery.

I must also mention another wonderful sketch for

the *Maximilian*, with life-size figures, now in the Boston Museum, which had also lain for a long while rolled up in a corner of the lumber-room at Mme Manet's. If this canvas escaped being cut up, it was doubtless because the figures were thought to be really too little " finished " for M. Leenhoff to retail. Renoir, looking at this *Maximilian*, said:

" It's pure Goya. And yet Manet was never so much himself! "

Among the notable paintings at Mme Manet's there was also a sketch of Faure even more expressive, perhaps, than the finished picture. I remember too a study by Claude Monet of Manet painting in his garden. I wanted to buy this picture, but Mme Manet told me it was not for sale. Some time after, I noted that the place the picture had occupied was empty. Mme Manet had followed my glance:

" I was in need of money," she said. " A German came to see me and took a fancy to the picture. You can understand why I wouldn't sell it to you: I shouldn't have liked M. Claude Monet to see his picture in a dealer's window. But to a foreigner, like that . . ."

The days were yet to come when a picture could be sold in Berlin, bought back in Paris, sold again in New York, all in the space of a few weeks.

I had almost forgotten to mention one of the most important of Manet's works, which remained for a long while in the possession of his widow: the *Bohémiens en voyage*. Mme Manet asked five thousand francs for it, and could not find a purchaser. The wife of a *conseiller général* of the Seine, Mme L . . ., had set her heart on the two children in the middle of the picture. She had several times made an offer for this fragment, which Mme Manet had rejected— without much conviction, the lady seemed to think, for she returned to the assault.

One day she said in my hearing:

"My dear Mme Manet, I've offered you so far fifteen hundred francs: I'll make it two thousand. Come, be reasonable! You're asking five thousand for the whole thing, and I'm leaving you at least three-quarters of the picture!"

And taking Mme Manet's silence for consent, she seized a big pair of scissors which was lying on the table. Mme Manet, seeing the weapon aimed at the picture, sprang up with what alacrity her corpulence permitted:

"Don't you do that! You and your scissors! I should feel you were stabbing my husband himself!"

VII CÉZANNE AND VAN GOGH

The first time I saw a picture by Cézanne was in the window of Père Tanguy's little colour-shop in the rue Clauzel. Two people had stopped outside the window, a gentleman and a workman. " Isn't it shameful," the man in the bowler hat was saying, " to murder nature like that! Trees that can't stand up; a house that may topple over any moment; water the colour of lead! And just look at the sky! If nature was like that, it would put one off ever going out." " Well, it's the other way with me, sir," said the workman. " Every time I look at that picture I say to myself: ' There's a place I'd like to go and fish in of a Sunday! Aren't the blokes jolly lucky that can treat themselves to a well-built house like that! ' I know what I'm talking of. I'm a bricklayer." And the " bowler hat " went away with a flea in his ear. As for me, I regretted bitterly that my small resources as a student would not allow me to buy the painting. I thought to myself: " How nice it must be to be a picture dealer! Spending one's life among beautiful things like that! " And as soon as I had a shop, it was my ambition to arrange an exhibition of Cézanne's works. But first I had to get into touch with the artist. It was particularly difficult to get hold of Cézanne, who would never give anyone his address.

I had heard that he was living for the moment at an inn in the vicinity of Fontainebleau. I made fruitless journeys to no end of little taverns that were said to be specially frequented by artists, till it occurred to me to make inquiries among the colour-merchants in town. One of these explained to me how to find Cézanne's studio. But when I got there, it was only to be told by a neighbour that the painter had moved, as usual without leaving his address. Seeing my disappointment:

"Wait a moment," he said; "I heard one of the removal men say they were going to a street in Paris with the name of a saint and the name of an animal."

With this clue I succeeded at last in discovering the house in which Cézanne lived—in the rue des Lions-St. Paul. His son, whom I saw there, was good enough to be interested in my scheme. But I had great difficulty in organising my exhibition, the canvases having been sent me without stretchers or frames.

A few instances will serve to show how far people were, at that time, from appreciating the work of the "Master of Aix."

Most notable was the indignation of the artists, who not only expressed as much horror as the Philistines, but fearing lest the work should find a market, chose to consider themselves injured in their interests as well as their dignity. The dictum of the art critic of the *Journal des Artistes*, denouncing " the nightmare vision of these atrocities in oils, which nowadays pass the bounds of permissible practical jokes," was one from which not only the public, but even the greatest among the painters hardly dissented.

I had obtained from Puvis de Chavannes, without too much difficulty, a lithograph in black for one of my albums of painter-gravers, and wanted to get something further from him—this time a lithograph in colour.

" I rather like that idea," he answered; " I'll come along to your place and we can choose a subject."

He came in effect a few days later. He stopped in front of my window and looked a long while at Cézanne's *Baigneurs*. Then he went away, shrugging his shoulders, and I never saw him again.

I did, however, receive a certain amount of encouragement, of which the most peculiar instance was the purchase of a picture by a man blind from birth, who was accompanied by his secretary. I learnt afterwards that he was less interested in Cézanne's painting than in the " advanced " ideas he credited him with, as the friend of Émile Zola.

But though certain critics and collectors, and even artists like Puvis de Chavannes, persisted in considering Cézanne's work as no better than a joke, the younger artists were falling more and more under his influence. In 1901 Denis executed one of his most important pictures as a testimony of his admiration for the painter of the *Sainte-Victoire :* his *Hommage à Cézanne,* which is to be seen in the Luxembourg. In the centre is a copy of Cézanne's famous *Dish of Fruit,* which once belonged to Gauguin. On the left Séruzier, the theorist of the group, is holding forth to his friends : Denis, Ranson, Vuillard, Bonnard and Roussel. Odilon Redon and Mellerio have joined them, and I myself have the honour to be present.

When Denis painted this picture I was no longer living at the top of the rue Laffitte, but had taken a big shop with an *entresol* at No. 6, near the Boulevards. To celebrate the opening of my new gallery, I had organised an exhibition of Van Gogh's work, which included more than sixty paintings from his studio in Amsterdam, without counting a lot of his water-colours and drawings. The most important of the pictures, such as the famous *Poppy Field,* was not priced above four hundred francs. But except for the young painters, the public showed little enthusiasm. The time was not ripe. There was a couple, though, who appeared more interested than the rest. The man grabbed the woman suddenly by the arm, and said to her :

" You who always make out that my painting hurts your eyes—well now ! What do you say to *this*? "

The woman, at that moment, was inspecting three portraits of Van Gogh by himself, in each of which one ear was hidden by a lock of hair. I went up to the lady:

"Those portraits," I said, "were painted after Van Gogh had cut off his ear."

"Cut off his ear?"

"He had been spending the afternoon in conversation with a couple of prostitutes. When he came home, he opened his Bible without thinking, and came upon the passage which says that if one of your organs offends you, you should cut it off and throw it into the fire. Applying the text to himself, Van Gogh took a razor and cut off one ear."

"And threw it in the fire?"

"No. He wrapped it in a piece of paper and took it to the ladies' house. 'Give that to Madame Marie,' he said to the maid who opened the door."

"How extraordinary!"

There was another visitor who came back every day towards evening. He would begin by casting a glance at the window, where the *Aliscans d'Arles* was blazing, and then come into the shop and walk round. After a bit he would begin to talk. He was unwearied in his enthusiasm for the *Poppy Field*. One day I missed him at his usual hour. He did not turn up again till several days later.

"I haven't been able to come all this time. My wife has just had a little girl. We are already thinking of her future, and we have decided, by way of dowry for her, to buy things that are bound to go up in value—pictures, for instance."

I saw my *Poppy Field* sold. Instinctively I glanced at it. My man followed the glance.

"If I had money to spare," he said, "that painting would have been in my house by now. But, you see, I have a child on my hands now; I must take life seriously. Fortunately I have a cousin, a professor of drawing of the City of Paris, who will be able to advise us."

It was some time before I saw my man again; and then one fine day he reappeared with a portfolio under his arm. " It's done," he announced. He tapped the portfolio: " The little one's dowry is in here ! " He took out a *Fantasia* by Detaille:

" My cousin managed to get this for me for only fifteen thousand francs. In twenty years' time it will be worth at least a hundred thousand."

About twenty-five years later, the man with the Detaille water-colour came into my shop in the rue de Martignac.

" Now," he said sadly, " the time has come to part with it. My daughter is getting married."

I asked him if he remembered my Van Gogh exhibition, and the " poppy " picture that he appeared to like so much.

" That's a long while ago," he said. " Fortunately I kept my head. What would a picture-dealer give me nowadays for that *Champ de Coquelicots*? "

" Well, my friend, you'd get more than three hundred thousand francs."

" What about my Detaille, then? "

" Your Detaille ! The Musée du Luxembourg has had what was considered his masterpiece—the *Battle of Huningen*—taken up to the garret, and even the rats won't look at it."

One day at my place Renoir saw some charcoal drawings by Van Gogh of farm labourers at work:

" God ! What a fine thing that is ! What would Millet's snivelling peasant look like beside it ! "

VIII MY NEIGHBOURS

One of my neighbours was a brother in the trade, by name Brame. I saw a very elegant individual enter his little shop, and come out again with a number of pictures. " All those pictures! " I said to myself. " All at once, and so quickly! My neighbour's in luck! But then he's got such beautiful Corots in his window." And I concluded sadly, " A pity I can't have a few 1830's too, to attract rich customers! "

In the afternoon I beheld the same gentleman come back to my neighbour's shop. As a matter of fact he could hardly have done otherwise, since, as I soon after discovered, this supposed *amateur* was none other than M. Brame himself, who even in the exercise of his calling wore the *grand air aristocratique* that was his by nature.

I remember a Renoir in Durand-Ruel's window: a woman bathing, supporting her breast with her hand. What a marvel! There was a story to this picture, which I had from the painter himself. One day, at La Celle-Saint-Cloud, he was drinking a *bock* at the café, when the proprietor came up to him, saying:

" I remember you very well. More than ten years ago you took a room in the house . . ."

Renoir jumped to the conclusion that he must have left his bill unpaid.

" . . . and after you'd gone, I found some canvases rolled up in your room. I put them in the attic. Now that you're here, you'll do me the favour of taking them away."

The *Baigneuse* supporting her breast, the *Femme endormie* with a cat on her knees, and other equally important works were all in this roll.

Next door to Durand-Ruel's there was a little shop that did very well: Beugnet's shop, turned so to speak into a florist's by Mme Madeleine Lemaire's pictures. There was something there for every purse, from the little bunch of violets, or the three roses in a crystal vase, to the large decorative panel. It was said that a client of the house, a great admirer of the art of Mme Lemaire, had carried out, at home, an idea of which he was very proud: on the roses, lilacs and carnations of his favourite artist he sprayed the perfume natural to each of these flowers.

What a contrast to the shop retailing these " beautifully imitated " flowers, as Cézanne would have expressed it, was Clovis Sagot's little place—Sagot *le frère*, as they called him, to distinguish him from his elder brother, the big dealer in engravings! Sagot *le frère*, down at the other end of the rue Laffitte, near the church of Notre-Dame-de-Lorette, had opened a little shop where, among others, he showed paintings by Braque, at that time almost unknown. He showed Picasso's paintings too, of his pink-and-blue period. It was there that the Steins found the very fine canvases by Picasso now in their possession. It is strange to think that only a few years before the War, in 1908, a little society, *La Peau de l'Ours*, of which M. André Level was the moving spirit, was able to buy the marvellous *Famille de Saltimbanques* from Picasso himself, for the sum of a thousand francs—a sum which had terrified the collectors of that day. That same picture, when the *Peau de l'Ours* decided to liquidate its purchases, made eleven thousand five hundred francs, and in 1931, at a sale in America, above a million.

In the neighbourhood of the Boulevards there was Gérard too, who specialised in Boudins, Henners and

Ziems. Renoir said to me one day, when I was out walking with him:

" We mustn't forget to look in at Gérard's window. There's a Jongkind there. . . . Such a magnificent sky, and it's nothing but white paper! "

Further up the rue Laffitte there was Diot, through whose hands so many fine Corots, Daumiers and Jongkinds have passed. Behind the shop there was a tiny dining-room without a window, and in the *entresol* three minute rooms in which he lived with his wife and three daughters. Sometimes a customer would look in towards evening and say, " It's dinner-time now, but later on, if my wife doesn't want to go to the theatre, I'll drop in again." And M. Diot would keep a look-out for a tap on his shop window.

From Diot's shop the pictures overflowed into a yard, in which, under a sort of penthouse, were to be seen sketches by Daumier, disdained at a period when " finish " was the thing most sought after. The market value and the importance the least of these things have acquired to-day are common knowledge. It was there that I saw his studies for Don Quixote; one, especially, which delighted Renoir—a landscape in a mere thin wash of umber. And then that wonderful study of *Jesus and Barabbas* that I had once thought of buying. I mentioned this to a friend of mine, a painter:

" Hang it all, Vollard . . . if Daumier were alive, he would throw that rotten sketch in the fire."

And I was fool enough to believe him.

A little before Diot's came the shop run by Tempelaere, in whom Fantin-Latour, who was so long getting known, had found a protector. The painter showed him lasting gratitude, and remained faithful to him later on, when he was successful. Nor would Fantin abandon his little studio in the rue Visconti, the studio of his early, difficult days, which was still dear to his heart.

I had known Fantin-Latour in the days when I was publishing my albums of *Painter-Gravers*. I used to go and see him from time to time. Sometimes I met one of the curators of the Louvre there, M. Migeon. The painter used to like talking music with him. I can still see Fantin, on a little chair before his easel, a skull-cap on his head. At his side Mme Fantin, herself no mean artist, might be working at a piece of embroidery as a change from painting. One day when I was there, " Oh, my God! " cried Fantin, laying down his palette, " I knew I'd forgotten something! " And Mme Fantin, looking at me, explained, " It's always my husband who buys the cheese."

When the painter moved from his old quarter to the *Rive droite*, he seldom went beyond the big Boulevards, on account of the traffic. And if, in spite of his fear, he ventured to cross the road, it was only to visit his dealer friend, Tempelaere, on the other side of the Boulevard.-

Degas considered that Fantin did himself harm by confining himself in this way.

" Fantin's work is very good. What a pity it is always a little *rive gauche*! "

Rive gauche or *rive droite*, Fantin, Degas and Renoir were all alike in this really. With all of them it was always, studio in the morning, studio in the afternoon. I shall never forget the astonishment of a celebrated art critic, who had said to Degas:

" I'll come and see you at your studio."

" Yes," said Degas, taking him by one of the buttons of his coat, " but at the end of the day, when it's dark."

Which shows how little Degas could bear to be interrupted in his work. Now, Renoir did not mind visitors; their presence did not prevent him from going on with his painting. But from that to leaving the studio for the sake of amusement . . .

One day I said to him:

" I know one man who's entirely taken up with his painting, and that's Valtat. He spends his whole life at Anthéor, where there's not a soul to be seen. His only relaxation is shooting."

" What! " cried Renoir, " do you mean to say Valtat goes shooting! He deserts his studio! Suppose one had suggested to Corot that he should go shooting! "

Even at the end of a year's work, when Renoir took a holiday—whether at Varangeville with his friend Bérard, at Essoyes, his wife's home, or later at Magagnosc or at Grasse, before he settled for good at Cagnes—it was still a case of studio in the morning, studio in the afternoon, except that on fine days the studio was the open country.

As for Degas, during the rare holidays he allowed himself, he usually went to Saint-Valéry-sur-Somme to his friends the Braquavals, or else to the Rouarts at la-Queue-en-Brie. He cared for the country only as a place to walk in. He was to be seen marching up and down the garden paths, his eyes protected by large dark spectacles, and taking the greatest care to avoid the flower-beds. As is well known, he hated flowers on account of their perfume.

I surprised him one day when I had gone to see him at the aforesaid la-Queue-en-Brie, in the midst of painting one of those landscapes that used so to stagger Pissarro *père*. The painter was working in the *salon*, with his back to the window.

" But, M. Degas," I said, " seeing the truth with which you represent nature, who would suppose that you do it by turning your back to her? "

" Oh, M. Vollard, when I'm in the train, you know, I do now and then put my nose out of window."

IX THE STREET OF PICTURES

In those days the rue Laffitte was the *rue des tableaux*. If you heard a man say, " I'm going to take a turn in the rue Laffitte," you might be sure he was a collector of pictures. On the other hand, when Manet said, " It's a good thing to go to the rue Laffitte," or Claude Monet asked, " Why go to the rue Laffitte? " they meant respectively that it was a good thing, or that it was useless, for a painter to keep in touch with his fellow-artists.

Degas liked going there when he had finished work for. the day. He went by the omnibus " Pigalle-Halle-aux-Vins," and came back the same way. One day I saw him standing outside Bernheim junior's shop, in which two Corots and a Delacroix were on view. Catching sight of me he came into my shop.

" Tell me, Vollard," he said, " how much do you suppose things like that are worth? "

I had to confess my ignorance.

" Well, I'll have to find out. I'll go and make a bid for them straight away."

He came back a moment later.

" Bad luck! The Corots are sold; but I mean to have the Delacroix! "

And he got it. One day when I had gone to see him at lunch-time, we heard a sound of voices in the hall, and Zoë came hurriedly into the dining-room:

" Monsieur! It's the Delacroix! "

Degas got up with his napkin round his neck, and deserted me then and there.

Cézanne thought that a painter could " profit " by

70

looking at the works of other painters; but then by
" other painters " he meant the Old Masters, and
his rue Laffitte was the Louvre. When he had spent
his afternoon doing a drawing from El Greco, Delacroix, or some other of his favourites, he would say
with pride, " I think I've got on a bit to-day."

Renoir too was to fall under the spell of the Louvre.
After producing masterpieces like the *Loge* and the
Déjeuner des Canotiers, he came out of the museum one
day exclaiming, " With all their blasted talk of
modern painting, I've been forty years discovering
that the queen of all colours is black! Look at Manet,
what he's lost by contact with the Impressionists! "

Degas too reproached Manet for abandoning his
magnificent " prune juice " in order to paint " light."
Yet in Renoir's opinion it was through contact with
the Impressionists that Degas himself attained his
complete development, in those wonderful pastels
that remind one of butterflies' wings.

The rue Laffitte was a sort of pilgrims' resort for
all the young painters—Derain, Matisse, Picasso,
Rouault, Vlaminck and the rest.

I remember the curious appearance of an artist who
took little interest in modern art, but who frequented
the rue Laffitte none the less, in the hope of selling his
wares: Père Méry, an old grey-haired man. Père
Méry had made a speciality of painting little birds:
chicks, ducklings, all the nursery folk of the poultry
world, in fact. He would stand as though rooted in
front of a shop window, a big portfolio under his arm,
waiting patiently for the dealer to beckon him in.
Sometimes, sick of waiting, and discouraged by the
indifference of the dealers, the poor old man would
go off, with his shuffling yet still active gait, to look
for some better judge of " real " and honest painting.
He reproached other pedestrians with walking too
slowly along the pavements, for those were still the
happy days when one had time to dawdle, and might

not infrequently be bumped into by a man reading his newspaper.

Père Méry had discovered a process of "wax painting," which had the property of never changing colour, and not drying till it had been dipped in water. He had published a little book in which he revealed his secret. Unfortunately at the end of twelve months not a single copy was sold, and the painter in a rage destroyed the entire edition. Apart from his studio, the old artist spent a great deal of his time in the *Jardin d'Acclimatation*. Seated on a camp stool in front of the aviaries, he was at pains to sketch their capricious inmates, who at sight of him kept shifting their positions as though to annoy him.

" If only I'd got them at the studio, the wretched creatures," he would grumble, " I'd know how to make them keep the pose."

One day, having asked some people to dinner, he bought a chicken with the intention of using it as a model before putting it in the pot. But the bird would not keep still. From time to time the artist's daughter would peep round the door of the studio: " Hurry up, Papa, it will never have time to get cooked." Upon which, renewed fury of the painter with the fowl. " Just look! " he said, taking me to witness, " the wretched animal keeps fidgeting on purpose! "

It was not only because the *bourgeois* did not care for his painting, that Méry bore them a grudge. His studies of unfledged birds and tailless chicks perplexed them—they were inclined to ask what in the world these creatures were—and Père Méry flattered himself upon painting his models with an exactitude that made any mistake impossible. I pacified him at times by pointing out that townspeople had little opportunity of visiting farmyards, and could not, therefore, be expected to be familiar with his usual models.

One day I noticed a landscape study in his studio:
"You're looking at that painting, M. Vollard.
Well, I wouldn't part with it for fifty francs. I'll
tell you why. I was at Chaville, painting that study,
when an old gentleman walking in the forest came up
to my easel, and asked me to let him look at what I
was doing. 'That's very nice,' he said to me, 'I
am a painter too: my name is Corot.'"

At Méry's death, his studio was sold. Passing a
second-hand dealer's shop some time afterwards, I
came across the little painting again. I thought I
would like to buy it as a memento, and asked the
price. "That's a good thing, you know," the shopkeeper told me. "My wife, who knows all about that
sort of thing, saw a painting in a shop window in
the Avenue de l'Opéra, signed by someone called
Trouillebert, which was not a bit better. I'll let you
have that for ten francs."

Ten francs was the price I got for a little study of
a pot of jam, at my first Cézanne exhibition! It is
true the purchaser did not haggle over it.

But I was not so lucky with other works of Cézanne's,
such as the three big paintings, each of a peasant, in
front of which one visitor had lingered. "There's no
mistaking our peasants of the Midi," he said, turning
to me. A short time afterwards I heard that this
amateur was expected in Paris the next morning by
the eight-o'clock train. By a quarter to eight, in
the midst of a snowstorm, I was walking up and down
the platform of the Gare de Lyon, scanning the
arrivals. At last I saw my man. I went up to him,
and gradually working up to the subject of my
Cézannes, I offered him the three for six hundred
francs.

"I wasn't exactly prepared to buy pictures the
moment I got out of the train," he replied. "All
the same, I'm in a mood for extravagance; I'll give
you five hundred for them."

The price of the pictures to me was five hundred and fifty, so I stuck to my price. But the customer stuck to his offer, and I did not see the colour of his money.

Even when the blessed money has been taken from the purchaser's pocket, even when he is handing it you, it is not safe to say one has it. It is so easy for a hand to draw back! At my first show I had sold a magnificent landscape of Cézanne's for four hundred francs. There was everything in it to please the *amateur*: a river, a boat with people in it, houses in the background, trees. "At last!" the buyer had exclaimed, "here is a picture with a design." Taking out his pocket-book, he extracted four hundred-franc notes and held them out to me. I put out my hand. At that moment the door of the shop opened. The client turned round and recognised a friend.

"I've just bought this picture from Vollard."

"You've done well," said the new arrival. "It's one of Cézanne's best works. It belongs to the period when he was under the influence of Guillaumin."

"So it's a ' *sous*-Guillaumin,' is it? And I've got such characteristic works of all the other Masters. I don't want a pupil's picture."

And back went the notes into the pocket-book.

A few days later, hearing my name mentioned:

"That d——d Vollard nearly had me the other day," he declared. "If it hadn't been for a providential accident, he'd have palmed off a *sous*-Guillaumin on me."

When Cézanne's pictures had gone up a bit, M. Pellerin bought the painting for seven hundred francs. Twenty-five years later he said to me:

"One of your colleagues has been trying to ' do ' me. Would you believe it, he had the cool cheek to offer me three hundred thousand for that Cézanne!"

One of the most picturesque figures in the second-hand trade was Salvator Meyer. Forain did a lithograph of him, holding a picture brought him by an old woman, who stands awaiting his verdict.

Small and plump, with a Greek fez on his head and fireside slippers on his feet, Salvator trotted to and fro among his clients in his shop, talking all the time. While paying careful attention to the "serious" client, he did not despise the customer who had only ten francs to spend. He was very accommodating too. "Goods are meant to circulate," was one of his favourite sayings.

I once unearthed in one of his portfolios a charming page from one of Willette's sketch-books, on which the artist had drawn four different subjects. I kept my eye on this piece till I should have the forty-five francs it was priced at. The day arrived; but it was not without trepidation that I went back to the portfolio. My anxiety, alas, was justified, for just as I was opening it:

"I've got something here for you," said Meyer to a customer. "You who don't care for sketches, I've got four Willettes here, perfectly finished little gems that I've just bought. It's a bargain: two hundred francs."

"They're charming, certainly," said the other, looking closely at them, "but you know, Meyer, I'd noticed them before, in one of your portfolios; only then they were all on one sheet, and you had marked them forty-five francs. Is it because you've separated them that you now want two hundred francs?"

"Ah! that's a bit thick!" cried Salvator, letting one of the Willettes fall, so great was the shock. "Ah! the b . . .! How he must have chortled at having fobbed them off on me for ready money— things he'd bought from me and not even paid for! Bloody ass that I am! Well, it serves me right. It'll teach me not to leave such things lying about in my cheap portfolio. Stuff that came from Dupuis!" And looking again at the drawings: "That's Willette

from the best bin, that is." Turning to his wife:
"Take those up to the dining-room, I'll keep them
for myself."

"Pardon me," said the client, "you've just offered
them to me, and I'm going to have them."

"Have you any more of Dupuis' things?" inquired
M. Manzy, a friend of Degas, who had come in
meanwhile.

"Yes, I have some lying about; but I don't want to
sell them for the moment. What an eye he had, that
man! When he told me the price he was going to put
on his collection, I said to myself, 'It would be
madness to buy.' But it was such beautiful stuff, I
couldn't resist it. And next day it was in all the newspapers that Dupuis had committed suicide. Ah!
that was a death that hit me very hard. Who knows?
Perhaps it was some consolation to Dupuis to know
he had left the things he was so fond of in good
hands."

"And his famous Degas?" asked M. Manzy.
"Have you still got that?"

"I should think so! It's a unique work!" cried
M. Meyer.

And going up the little corkscrew staircase that led
to his *entresol*, he came down again bearing his Degas
in hands that appeared trembling with emotion.
M. Manzy was lavish in his praise, but forbore to
make any offer. From that time forward, each time
they met, it was:

"Well, what about my Degas?"

"Magnificent!"

And then Manzy would turn the conversation. So
at last one day Salvator went himself and "offered"
his Degas to Manzy. The latter, after haggling a bit
for form's sake, concluded the bargain, and they
parted company delighted with each other.

"The great thing in our business," Meyer would
often say to me, "is knowing when to leave go.

There always comes a time when the finest picture has reached its top price."

Meyer's judgment in this respect may have failed him at times, like other people's, but there was no denying his readiness in repartee. I was in his shop one day when a tall, fat man came in, called Larandon, best known for his rather too showy clothes and ill-defined pecuniary resources. His face, ordinarily jovial, was for the nonce rather glum.

" Look here, Meyer," he called out point blank, " I'm told you call me a *maquereau*."

" What? What's that you're saying? " asked Meyer, looking up.

" So-and-so says that you always refer to me as ' that *maquereau* of a Larandon! ' "

" No, no, you've got it wrong," said Meyer, tapping him on the belly. " What I say is ' that GREAT *maquereau* of a Larandon! ' "

" Oh, well, so long as you say it in a *friendly* way, it's all right." And he shook Meyer effusively by the hand.

Dr. Gachet had told me of a whole collection of paintings by Daumier, in the possession of a journey-man-carpenter at Pontoise. The worthy man had accepted some studies, to which Mme Daumier attached no value, in payment of an outstanding bill. Among them, if I remember rightly, was the *Salle d'Attente*, which is now in the Lyons Museum. The owner of these masterpieces kept them under a chest of drawers, because they would have taken up space on the walls.

" My place isn't very big," he would say, " and I've got a wardrobe, as it is. I've got a handsome mirror I bought when I married, and the portrait of my wife done in her own hair. And a lovely old carpet. Yes, really old, my grandmother worked it. Anyway, even if I had room, I'd only put things on the walls that are nice to look at."

One day I ventured to ask him why he didn't get rid of the paintings since they were in his way.

"Well," he replied, "I'd first have to have an offer from an *amateur.*"

I saw at once that a direct offer from a dealer would put him on his guard. Thinking the pictures had hardly been heard of, I was in no hurry to make him the "serious" offer which might have induced him to treat with a dealer. But there is no treasure so well hidden as not to be discovered in time. A dealer, I don't know how, got wind of the matter. Foreseeing, as I had done, the difficulty there might be in treating in person, he had a stroke of genius. He dressed up his clerk to the nines, and hiring a smart carriage and pair, drove up to the carpenter's.

"I've brought you one of the Kings of America," he told him.

On being shown the Daumiers, the accomplice made his pronouncement:

"Ten thousand."

As the carpenter hesitated, the bogus American made a feint of going back to his carriage. The offer was immediately accepted. This price, which in years to come went up more than a hundredfold, was even so a great deal higher than that obtained by Mme Daumier, when a few years earlier she had sold an important collection of studies—a whole removal-van full—for fifteen hundred francs. I remember the outcry in the newspapers at the time against this "odious robbery perpetrated on an artist's widow." As a matter of fact, after hawking his "loot" about all over the place, the purchaser was only too glad to recover his original fifteen hundred francs.

When I heard of the trick my colleague had played so successfully, I said to myself: "Next time I have to do with a reluctant seller, I shall dress up my concierge as an English gentleman." But one does not always carry out one's intentions.

A few years later, after my Cézanne exhibition, I went to see M. Gustave Geffroy.

" Tell me," he said, " shouldn't I lose too much if I tried to sell my Cézannes ? "

I was looking at a landscape for which he had paid three hundred francs.

" That one," I said, " is worth at least three thousand."

" Really? "

I continued my inventory.

" Counting everything, that would make thirty-five thousand francs; without your portrait, of course. If you are disposed to sell, I'm your man."

" Sell them! My Cézannes! I couldn't bear to think of it."

" Well," I said, " if you ever make up your mind to do so, give me the first refusal."

He seemed genuinely pained.

" You are a dealer," he moaned. " You think of nothing but buying to sell again. Now if I were offered a sack of gold . . ."

Not long after, one of my colleagues heard of the Cézannes in Geffroy's possession. To carry the day, he sent him a man of fashion—of the highest circles— a Prince!

With the condescending familiarity of the great, the Prince inquired of Geffroy if he would not sell him his pictures. The man of letters, whose uncompromising republicanism did not prevent him from being dazzled by the sight of a Highness, suggested, stammering, the sum of thirty-five thousand francs I had quoted to him. The affair was concluded on the spot, but in his agitation Geffroy parted at the same time with the most important of his Cézannes, the portrait I had not included in my estimate. And this same portrait, not long after, passed into the possession of an *amateur* at a far higher price than the thirty-five thousand francs paid to Geffroy for the entire collection.

But Gustave Geffroy was not only the art critic-collector who had perceived what a great painter Cézanne was. As a journalist and novelist he had also acquired, in socialist circles, the reputation of a great writer, on the strength of his book *L'Enfermé*, devoted to Blanqui.[1]

No one practised the cult of Blanqui more assiduously than Geffroy. Not only with his pen, but orally, he constituted himself the apostle of the old revolutionary. One day I went to see him at the Gobelins factory, of which Clémenceau, who appreciated his republican loyalty, had had him made director.

" It's the workmen's rest hour," the concierge told me, " so M. le Directeur will be talking to them."

He was right. In one of the allotments belonging to the *personnel*, I found M. Geffroy chatting familiarly with a tapestry worker who was pricking out his lettuces.

The conversation must have centred round Blanqui, and the other had probably been listening with only half an ear to what the author of *L'Enfermé* had to tell him of Blanqui's life—his struggles, his imprisonments —for as I came up I heard the workman say:

" I can see the sort of cove your Blanqui was: another of those profiteers that get themselves stowed away safely in quod, while the rest of the mugs are getting their bokos bashed."

[1] Louis Auguste Blanqui (1805–81), a revolutionary politician and ardent devotee of communism, spent half his life in prison and was twice condemned to death. In his intervals of freedom he held positions in successive revolutionary governments. His election as deputy for Bordeaux in 1879 was invalid owing to his being in prison at the time. He was set free, but died not long after of an apoplectic stroke.

X THE CELLAR

My cellar in the rue Laffitte was divided in two by a partition. One part, which had a ventilator, served as a kitchen, the other, which had no opening, did duty as my dining-room. Here, where there was no communication with the outer air, the heat from the kitchen condensed in heavy moisture.

Renoir, dining with me one night, said, as he picked up his walking-stick that he had stood against the wall:

"There must be a water-pipe leaking somewhere about here."

"Water-pipe leaking? Where?"

"Look at my stick! It's all wet!"

So my domestic arrangements had their drawbacks. But I found it an advantage to have my dining-room under the same roof as my shop, since I needed but the one maid to cook for me and attend to the shop door.

Uncomfortable as it was, my cellar did not damp the enthusiasm of my guests. The fame of its dinners spread even to the foreign Press. The menu consisted chiefly of a dish of which I was rather proud: chicken curry, the national dish of the Island of La Réunion. But since the days of the " Cellar " I have had occasion to sample this dish properly prepared by my countrymen, and I must admit that my reputation as cook was undeserved.

Not so the fame of my guests—Cézanne, Renoir, Forain, Degas, Odilon Redon—to mention only those who have disappeared.

A foreign lady heard of the " Cellar " through Count

Kessler, the well-known German collector of pictures, who sometimes dined there with me. Coming on a visit to Paris from Germany, she jotted down her plans in a notebook, and alongside of " Visit to Maxim's," she wrote " Dine in the *Cave Vollard*." She imagined it to be a restaurant.

As a matter of fact there were times when the " Cellar " might have stood comparison with a Montmartre cabaret. One evening I had a lady among my guests who had just published a volume of verse. After dinner, not without a little persuasion from a kindly neighbour, she got up and declaimed a poem, which threatened to be followed by the whole volume, barring some unexpected intervention. The unexpected happened. While the poetess was pouring out her verses, my cat, who was nursing her kitten, showed signs of uneasiness. The poetess having ceased for a moment, the cat, reassured, started licking the kitten. Alas! the lady did not long remain silent. But she had hardly opened her mouth when the cat flung herself upon her, all her claws extended, and she recited no more that evening.

Another guest had asked to be put alongside Léon Dierx.

" I adore poetry," he told me, " and I should so much enjoy conversing with a favourite of the Muses."

When our poetess had ceased, Dierx's neighbour, addressing him, said:

" I can't for the life of me remember if the beautiful poetry we have just heard is by Lamartine or Victor Hugo."

" Wouldn't Mallarmé be nearer the mark? " whispered Dierx.

" Mallarmé! " cried the other; " I was told he was incomprehensible except to the initiated! "

And with a touch of pride he added:

" Fancy my understanding Mallarmé at the first attempt! "

The lady on the other side of Dierx leaned towards him, saying:

"How exciting the love of a poet must be! To hear the music of poetry when one is losing consciousness of everything else. . . . Oh! Master, do you remember the first woman you ever loved?"

"Do I remember her! She was an old negress on a sugar plantation," replied Dierx placidly.

Another of my guests that evening was a retired Colonel. A few minutes before dinner-time he had come to excuse himself from making one of the party, as he was anxious about his wife's health. I thought myself bound to insist a little, and in the end he decided to stay.

A man with gloomy thoughts should be given a cheerful neighbour. I selected a very oncoming young woman, and paired her off with him.

During the soup the Colonel remained silent. But after the first course he appeared to be getting interested in his neighbour, and by dessert time he was paying her assiduous court. Not far from them sat a friend of mine whose surname was a simple prænomen. The lady addressed him by it familiarly, and this misled the Colonel, who took it for a Christian name, and concluded he must be the husband. From that moment nothing could exceed his attentiveness to the gentleman. When we rose from table, he went up to him and bombarded him with protestations of friendship, even insisting on his coming to stay with him for the opening of the shooting season. The other thanked him politely. Returning to the lady, the gallant Colonel exclaimed:

"I fancy I've made a conquest of your husband."

"You know my husband?"

"I've just been talking to him. He's a delightful man."

"But my husband is in Marseilles. I'm going to join him there to-morrow."

Upon this the Colonel, having no reason to pursue his point further, discovered that it was time to go back to his " poor wife."

I have always appreciated—where others are concerned—the usefulness of being married. If you are asked to do something that bores you: " My wife wouldn't hear of it! " So on this occasion, having wasted powder and shot, the Colonel could retire politely with a " My wife is expecting me." It was the last service, as it turned out, that she was to render him. The model husband became a widower not long after. To his great detriment, be it said; for, having no one left to restrain him, the old soldier began to play the young gallant, and fell into second childhood.

Although I did not exactly keep open house in the " Cellar," my guests brought their friends with them, and I was not always sure of their identity. But a name I am not likely to forget is that of Sister Marie-Louise, whom I had always been very proud of introducing to my guests, till I discovered one day that she had no right to wear the habit. When I apologised to Renoir for having brought him into contact with a false nun, he replied:

" Wherever else I go, Vollard, I can say that I know beforehand whom I shall meet, and what we shall talk about. At your place one does at least meet with the unforeseen."

At one of the dinners in the " Cellar," a charming old lady of seventy begged me to put her beside Forain.

I did so, and when dinner was over I asked her:

" Were you pleased with your neighbour? "

" He was charming! I said to him, ' Master, talk to me of love,' and he replied that love, after a certain age, is obscenity. I shall pass that on. I have his permission to do so."

It was in the " Cellar " that the subject of professional secrecy cropped up one day, I don't remember how. A doctor among the company warned us against the imaginary safety of disguised names, and recalled the well-known story of the abbé who said, " My first penitent accused herself of having deceived her husband." A few minutes later a lady, coming in, cried, " Ah! Monsieur l'abbé, do you remember? I was your first penitent."

" All the same," continued the doctor, " there can be no harm in my telling you a little adventure of mine at a watering-place. One day, quite by chance, I made the acquaintance of a young woman, who told me in the course of conversation that she was a widow, and about to remarry.

" As she was very pretty, I began making love to her. She did not repel my advances. ' I would not deceive a husband,' she said, ' for anything in the world, no matter what his faults might be. I am only listening to you because I am still free. Of course it's understood that once I'm married again, *n.i.*, *ni*, *c'est fini*! '

" I'm telling you this simply as a curious matter of conscience," continued the doctor, " obviously you can never know who was the person concerned."

A few minutes later there was a knock at the door of the shop. One of my friends, with his wife, had come to join us. As soon as the lady caught sight of the narrator:

" Well! " she cried, " what a surprise to find *you* here! Let me introduce you to Dr. X.," she went on, turning to her husband. " You remember my taking the cure at Vichy. This is the gentleman I had the pleasure of meeting there."

The situation was becoming embarrassing. Fortunately a diversion occurred. Two Japanese ladies came in—Mme Itahara and her adopted daughter, Mlle Hama, who kept a little *caboulot* where I had learnt to partake of eels *au caramel*, bean jam, and other specialities of Nippon. I had asked them to come and sing and dance to us. We were all enjoying their performance when someone knocked at the door. It was a messenger from the Grand Hôtel, where a high Japanese dignitary was staying. He explained that the Prince had expressed a wish to " converse " that evening with a countrywoman. " So," he said, " I have been sent to fetch Mlle Hama."

Rather more than an hour later, Mlle Hama came back to us, proudly exhibiting a piece of paper covered with innumerable Japanese characters. This, she explained, was a recommendation from the Prince to an honourable " tea-house " in Tokio, where she intended getting an engagement on her return to the land of her forefathers.

Mme Missia E . . . dined at my place with Renoir, after going on a tour through Holland. She had no very agreeable remembrance of her trip.

" Over there," she said, " the people of the lower class are absolute primitives. I was wearing the simplest of clothes, and yet the women looked at me as though I were some strange animal. You wouldn't believe it, but some of them came and stared me in the face as I walked along the street. Some of them even tried to feel the stuff my dress was made of. Ugh! those women with their fat cheeks and red hands! The very thing for you, Renoir! "

" Not at all," replied Renoir, " I don't only like painting fat stock. Holland isn't really in my line either, nor its painters. For apart from Rembrandt and four or five great Dutchmen . . . Louis XIV wasn't far wrong, when they showed him Teniers' pictures and he said: ' Take away all those ugly apes!' Yet I did once find a marvellous model over there. A regular Madonna! And what a virginal skin! " And turning to his neighbour, the painter Albert André: "You've no idea how lovely that girl's breasts were—heavy and firm—and the pretty little fold underneath, with a golden shadow. . . . I was so pleased with her docility and so delighted with her skin, that caught the light so beautifully, that I half thought of bringing my Dutch girl over to Paris. 'So long as someone doesn't go and seduce her straight away, and she keeps that peach complexion for a bit,' I said to myself. I told her mother, who seemed to be keeping a strict watch over her, that if she would let her come with me, I would see to it that the men had no chance of running after her.

" ' But then what's the use of her going to Paris, if you're going to prevent her from *working*? ' she asked.

" And I tumbled all at once to the nature of my ' virgin's ' occupation when she was not sitting to me."

"Some happenings are clearly supernatural," said a lady at dinner one evening. " Only the other day, I was scolding my son, and he was beginning to answer back, when a violent shock, like a blow from a fist, shook the door in front of which he was standing. I realised at once that it was my dear old friend Papus manifesting his presence. Because a little while before his death as we were talking of the Beyond, he said to me, ' My little one, after I have disappeared, I shall continue to watch over you.' "

One of the persons present, turning to me, remarked:

" It appears that in the Colonies, with the negro sorcerers, the most inexplicable things happen. Come, M. Vollard, you who were born in La Réunion . . ."

" As a matter of fact," I replied, " it was in Paris that I once had an adventure savouring of witchcraft. I had been to the post to send off an express letter. When I got back to my shop, after taking my usual little turn, what did I see? My *pneumatique* on my table. And yet I was perfectly certain I had slipped it into the box. Well . . . I picked it up, and went and

put it carefully into the post-box again. Then I came
home. But damn it all! The *pneumatique* was back
on the table! This time I began to feel a bit nervy.
One of my customers came in at that moment, and I
told him what had happened.

" ' Don't get the wind up, M. Vollard,' he said,
' I'll go with you to the post.'

" We went off together, and my client put the *pneu*
into the box himself. We turned homeward.

" I hope you're reassured now,' said my companion, as we walked leisurely back to the rue Laffitte.

" ' Ah! That's a bit thick, all the same! ' he cried
on entering the shop, more taken aback than he cared
to appear. The *pneumatique* had returned.

" ' Look here, M. Vollard, I'm going to the post
by myself. You stay here. We must really find out
how this damned *pneumatique* manages to get back.'

" Off he went, and came back in a hurry. When he
saw that the letter was not there:

" ' I fancy you've nothing to fear this time.'

" As he spoke the door opened : ' Ne vous dérangez
pas.' It was my *pneumatique* returning, brought by a
little telegraph boy:

" ' That's the fourth journey you've given me.
You must surely know that letters can't be expressed
to Meudon! Fortunately your name was on the
envelope.' "

My guests listened politely to my story, but I could
not help feeling they were disappointed. They had
evidently expected some terrifying account of black
magic—of a negro sorcerer, for instance, sending the
soul of a virgin into the body of a he-goat, and vice-
versâ.

When painters get together they are apt to talk
painting. And ladies are as curious as the other sex
to hear artists discussing their profession. Conversations of this sort were frequent in the " Cellar."

K. X. Roussel, for instance, would lead off with:
" Monet is a Greek."

(Myself) " What do you mean by that? "

" I'm speaking of the purity of his art. Monet
looks at nature with the ingenuous eye of a contemporary of Praxiteles."

" I love Renoir's landscapes," Odilon Redon would
put in. " When Renoir paints trees, you know at
once what sort of trees they are. In a tiny little
painting they've got at Durand-Ruel's, there's a
hedge of dog-roses: one would love to sit beside it.
The whole landscape seems familiar to one. Now,
Monet's triumph is in laying one tone beside another.
But if ever one of these days the colours in his pictures
begin to alter . . ."

Here Redon would stop short, as though embarrassed
at having gone so far. For his modesty did not often
allow him to pass judgment on a fellow-artist.

Delacroix's name having come up in conversation:
" Did you know him, M. Redon? " I asked.

" Only by sight. I came across him now and then;
once, I remember, at a ball at the Hôtel de Ville."

" How is it possible," exclaimed someone, " to like
both Delacroix and Ingres? Delacroix so full of fire,
and Ingres so cold! "

" Ingres cold? " retorted Besnard. " Ingres is
fire itself, controlled passion seeking to conceal
itself."

When Degas was dining with me one night in the
" Cellar," I repeated this saying of Besnard's to him.

" Did you know Ingres, M. Degas? "

" I went to see him one evening with a letter of
introduction. He received me very kindly. Suddenly he was taken with a fit of giddiness, and flung
out his arms as though seeking something to hang on
to. I had just time to catch him in my arms."

I thought to myself: " What a fine subject for a
Prix de Rome painting! Ingres in the arms of Degas!

The last representative of a dying epoch borne up by the herald of a new one!"

One evening, before going down to dinner, my guests were looking at some Cézannes.

"That *Peasant*, now," cried Forain. "You can positively smell his feet!"

Degas was looking at a painting of a white house in the neighbourhood of Marseilles:

"What nobility there is in it! What a change from Pissarro!"

"Come, Degas, don't be unfair!" exclaimed one of his old friends. "You forget that you yourself led me up to Pissarro's *Peasants Planting out Cabbages*, at Durand-Ruel's, and you thought it jolly good."

"Yes, but that was before the Dreyfus affair," said Degas, laughing at his own outburst.

If the impressionists did not easily find favour with Degas, the younger artists, on the other hand, interested him on account of their experiments in design.

I had had a big panel of Roussel's, his *Triumph of Bacchus*, that M. Morozoff of Moscow had bought of me, taken down to the dining-room to be packed. Degas saw the picture standing propped against the wall at the bottom of the staircase. He stopped, and caressing the canvas with his hand, asked:

"Who did that?"

"Xavier Roussel."

"It's noble!"

This reminded me of Cézanne turning over the pages of Verlaine's *Parallèlement*, which Bonnard had illustrated for me:

"That's good. . . . *C'est dessiné dans la forme.*"

Most of the painters who frequented the "Cellar" were known to one another, but this was not always the case with the other guests. One day when I was detained on my way home, all the guests arrived

before me, and it turned out that they were all
strangers to one another. Forain voiced the general
embarrassment. Pointing to the two fetishes from the
Marquesas Islands that stood on either side of the door,
he said dispassionately:

" Those two know each other, anyway."

Among the company, however, was a Nordic lady
whom I did not know myself. Some habitué, no
doubt, had brought her. Pencil in hand, she was
making careful notes of the painters' remarks. Suddenly I saw her pencil stop. Renoir, interrupting a
discussion of some new style of hairdressing, had
exclaimed:

" It's extraordinary what *conneries* women can be
persuaded to stick on their heads! "

The Nordic lady leaned over to her neighbour:

" What is that—' connerie '? "

And seeing the other's air of astonishment:

" The Master said ' *connerie.*' I suppose it *is* spelt
with a ' K '? "

When the meaning of the word was explained to her,
she took it to be a joke on Renoir's part, and moved
with her notebook and pencil nearer to Besnard,
whom one of his friends was trying to interest in a
woman they both knew.

" Mme X. used to have a very pretty nose."

This appeared to leave Besnard quite cold:

" Yes, but it's not enough for a woman to have had
a pretty nose."

But Besnard was in reality the kindest and most
obliging of men. Witness the preface he wrote for
me to Balzac's *Chef-d'Œuvre Inconnu,* which Picasso
illustrated so magnificently. Towards the end of his
life, too, he came to my place, at my request, to look
at Rouault's paintings. Rouault was in Switzerland
at the time, under treatment for serious burns. On
Christmas Eve he had been persuaded to impersonate
Father Christmas, and going too near a lamp had set

fire to the big white beard he had donned for the occasion. His promptitude in rolling himself up in the drawing-room carpet had alone saved him from being even more seriously injured.

Besnard's consent to look at this young artist's work was all the more gratifying as in reality he took little interest in the art of his contemporaries. On this occasion, after having looked attentively at a number of Rouault's paintings which I had arranged on the walls of the dining-room, he took out his watch:

" Three o'clock already! I shall have to leave you. Hurry up and show me the paintings by that Rouault fellow."

One of Besnard's qualities was frankness—a frankness that did not spare his best friends. One day when Frantz Jourdain was attitudinising before Rodin's *Baiser*, praising the happy conception, the magnificent patina, and so forth, Besnard, who was standing beside me, said:

" And you, Vollard, what do you think of it? "

" Oh . . . very good, of course. . . ."

" But surely you can see it's merely two models posing? Those lovers have never slept together, and haven't the slightest wish to! "

Rodin once came to dine in the " Cellar." He kept glancing at a statuette by Maillol that stood on the mantelpiece.

Rodin's presence led us naturally to talk of sculpture.

" If we hadn't got *you*, Master," declared someone, " sculpture to-day . . ."

" And what about *him*? " retorted Rodin, pointing to the Maillol.

Count Isaac de Camondo, the great banker and patron of art, had heard of the " Cellar." The " Parisian " character he attributed to it attracted him, but he evidently imagined it to be a rather

Bohemian resort. One day, however, meeting Claude Monet in the shop:

"What about going to see Vollard's ' Cellar '? " he suggested, and they went down together.

I don't know exactly what he expected to find there. He found nothing but a damp wall.

" It's very nice," he said, hurrying upstairs again.

He never sought to repeat the experiment.

I had the pleasure one day of entertaining Gervex. I had made his acquaintance at Henri Dumont the flower painter's, where he was expatiating on the sculpture of Dardé, a new star of the *Salon du Champ de Mars*.

" He is as much talked of," he said, " as Rostand after the first performance of his *Cyrano*. Our sculptors are all pulling long faces about it."

Gervex, who had very " pally " manners, brought up the subject of my " Cellar "; so I asked him to lunch.

Among the guests invited to meet him was a friend of mine, at whose request I had also invited his chief, the Inspector-General of the Colonial Magistracy. There was also a young actress, and the *Douanier* Rousseau. The Inspector-General proved a very dull fellow. When he left us after lunch, the actress, on being told he was an official of high rank, asked innocently how the Minister could have chosen anyone so foolish. There was no answer forthcoming.

" I mean, what did he do to get his job? "

" What he did was to be a native of the Tarn, like the Minister."

" And what sort of man is the Minister? "

" He is a Senator, and a manufacturer of fezzes. The President of the Council, M. Clémenceau, on taking him into his Cabinet to secure the votes of his group, inquired what he did in civil life, and being aware that the fez is the common headdress of the East:

"' Ah! he makes thingumbobs that the natives wear on their heads, does he? He must know the Colonies, then. We'll pitch him in there.' "

As for Rousseau, he did not utter a single word during lunch. At the end of the meal he took a little note-book out of his pocket and began to draw.

"These white walls are ripping, M. Vollard, with the people lighted up like that! If only I could get that effect into a picture!"

When Rousseau had gone, Gervex asked me:

"Who is he? I didn't catch the name."

"It's the painter, Rousseau."

I could see the name meant nothing to him.

"You haven't heard of the *Douanier* Rousseau?"

Gervex appeared more and more puzzled.

"You know, the customs officer who has started painting."

"And he exhibits?"

"Yes, at the *Indépendants*."

"Good Lord!" exclaimed Gervex. "The *salon* where they exhibited the picture a donkey painted by swishing its tail about after it had been dipped in paint!"

He got up. "Let us be serious. I have a meeting at the *Académie*."

We went up into the shop again. Just as Gervex was about to leave, a woman who was taking her dog for a walk on the pavement opposite caught sight of him, crossed the street and came in. I recognised her at once by her somewhat masculine appearance: it was Mme Louise Abbéma.

"Something rather extraordinary has just happened to me," she said to Gervex. "I had heard that a painting of mine, a group of flowers that I am particularly fond of, had just been sold at the Hôtel Drouot. I found the purchaser was a fairly well-known singer, Mlle Nina P . . ., and I went to ask her to lend me the painting for my exhibition. It was a good thing I went without giving her notice before-hand, for when I was shown into the drawing-room, there was my picture in a magnificent frame, and people standing round admiring it. I went closer, and what do you suppose I saw? My signature had been painted out, and in its place was written ' *Nina à son gros Jojo.*' And 'Jojo' was explaining to the company: 'It's a present from Nina. The last three months she has been behaving in the most mysterious way, always out of the house. "I'm going to my painting lesson," she would say. And this is what she's been at work on for my birthday. An expert was telling me only yesterday it was almost as good as a Louise Abbéma.' "

Just then two of my customers came in. M. Gervex and Mme Louise Abbéma left me, and I never heard how this comic affair had ended, for I had not the cheek to ask Mme Abbéma about it myself.

Cézanne did not often come to the "Cellar." He went out very little. We were dining there alone one day, and I was relating some incident or other I had read in the newspaper, when he suddenly laid a hand on my arm. A moment later, when my servant had gone out of the dining-room:

" I stopped you," said Cézanne, " because what you were saying wasn't proper for a young girl to hear."

" What young girl? " I asked in astonishment.

" Why! Your maid! "

" But she knows all about that sort of thing! You may even be sure she knows more than we do."

"That may be. But I prefer to think she doesn't."

Now, Degas would not even have been aware of the presence of a servant. All he was after in his studies of women was certain gestures; and servant girls did not provide him with these.

One day when I was speaking of his old Zoë, he said to me:

"But you have an old *bonne* too, haven't you, Vollard?"

"Old! She's not twenty!"

"Is that so!—I should have said . . ."

Bonnard painted a picture of a dinner-party in the "Cellar." Forain is there, and Redon, and Count Kessler and some ladies. There is also a severe-looking man, a manufacturer in business in the French Indies.

"You don't seem to be very happy," I said to this man one day, thinking his face looked more than ordinarily glum.

"I'm frightfully hurt. It's enough to disgust one with being a republican! To treat me like that, an old fighter like me . . ."

"What have they done to you, then?"

"Oh! just what one would expect. At the opening of the session of our Council-General in India, there was a doubt as to who would get the majority. Of the twenty-five members of the Council, there were twelve republicans including myself, and twelve reactionaries. The twenty-fifth, an independent, put his vote up to auction. I managed to secure it. The reactionary party bit the dust on the spot. But I had the greatest difficulty in retaining the majority for our side. The day before the meeting of the Council, I shut my man up in my house, so that he might not be tempted to go and re-sell himself to the opposite party. But he contrived to escape. All night long, with a life-saver in one hand and a lantern in the other, I ran about the town looking for him. By the morning I was dead beat; but I had found my fugitive, and did not let him out of my sight again till the meeting. That is what I did for the Republic. And *this* is how it rewards me!"

With thumb and forefinger he seized the lapel of his coat, which was decorated with the *Palmes Académiques*.[1]

"If I were you," I said, "I wouldn't wear that decoration—just to give them a lesson!"

"Not wear it! A ribbon that cost me two hundred rupees!"

"Two hundred rupees to buy a vote! I should have thought that fifty . . ."

"No doubt. But my man owed me two hundred rupees, and that was the only way I could get them back."

One day at lunch I had a very fidgety guest. All at once we heard a sound of canvas tearing. He had sent the two back legs of his chair clean through a big picture that stood behind him. Covered with shame, he poured forth apologies. The company were horrified. I was the only one not to show distress.

"It's nothing," I said.

And the luncheon party went on without further reference to the affair.

On leaving, the awkward fellow was again lavish in his regrets, but I repeated, "It doesn't matter, I tell you." One of the ladies said to me afterwards:

"You were wonderful. How did you manage to keep your temper so beautifully?"

"Oh! it was easy enough."

"Still, a picture of that size . . ."

"Of course, it amounts to something. But . . . the picture isn't mine. Besides, I had warned the owner of it. When he came to ask me to exhibit it, and I said I had no room left on the wall, he simply stood the canvas where you see it.

"'Hang it!' I said, 'if you leave it there it will be *exposé* in more senses than one. There's bound to be an accident to it.'

[1] See Note, *ante*, p. 15.

H

" ' Whoever heard of a picture having a hole knocked in it? ' replied the owner. ' Think of all the masterpieces that have gone safely through revolutions, wars . . .' "

When my man came to fetch his property, I showed him the damage. He looked at the picture, then at me:

" Ah! now, that's splendid! "

" It doesn't seem to worry you," I said.

" I should think not! The picture's insured."

XI ALFRED JARRY AND GUILLAUME APOLLINAIRE

When I look back at those far-off days of the "Cellar," I am reminded of two writers who were destined to die young: Alfred Jarry and Guillaume Apollinaire.

During the War I went to the hospital to see Second-lieutenant Apollinaire, who had been wounded. To get to his room I had to cross the general ward. A blind negro was being led along the rows of unoccupied beds. At each bed he was pulled up, and his guide told him a little story, to which he listened with visible satisfaction.

My curiosity being aroused, I made inquiries, and learnt that the negro had been blinded by a bullet wound in the left temple. His blindness caused him a despair that nothing would calm, till it occurred to one of the hospital attendants to try consoling him by telling him of others more unfortunate than himself. This was why he was being taken, so to speak, on a tour of inspection of the beds. Stopping before each of the imaginary patients, his guide expounded:

"Here is a blind man who has lost a leg. . . . This one has no arms. . . ."

From one amputated member to another they came to the last bed.

"As for this one," said the attendant, "he has only his trunk left."

In the beds next to Apollinaire were two young lieutenants of his own regiment. An orderly-sergeant was with them. "Ask for a dose of castor oil for me," said one of the officers.

99

" I shall have to have an order made out by the M.O., sir, or I shall never hear the last of it. Castor oil is for privates."

" Give me some fruit salts, then," said the officer.

At the mention of fruit salts the orderly-sergeant brought his heels smartly together and saluted:

" Fruit salts are reserved for general officers. Lieutenants, captains, commandants and colonels are given purging lemonade."

He laid the manual on the table. Opening it at random, I lighted on the section, *Bedding*. And I saw that for *messieurs les officiers généraux*, if they are in hospital in Paris, sheets must be changed every thirty days. A *nota bene* stipulated that all months, including February, were to be counted as having thirty days.

The last time I saw Apollinaire was during the epidemic of Spanish influenza, after the War. He had a bottle of rum under his arm.

" Sovereign remedy for 'flu! " he told me. " With this, I don't care a rap for the epidemic."

The Spanish influenza took up the challenge. Two days later it carried the poet off.

Alfred Jarry! There was never a nobler figure in the world of letters. Though very poor, he never made a show of his poverty. He even avoided those he thought capable of helping him. And so scrupulous! I remember meeting him one day on his way to a subscriber to a little review that he edited, to restore the sum of one franc fifty that he had overpaid. To do this he had come all the way from Corbeil on his bicycle.

This bicycle was all that was left to him of a modest legacy which he had spent very rapidly and extravagantly. He also possessed a revolver, and cycling from Paris to Corbeil, where he lived during the summer, whenever he came upon an absent-minded pedestrian, blind and deaf to the bicycle, Jarry, as he drew level with him, would fire.

" But, Jarry, suppose one of them were to kick up a fuss ? "

" A fuss ! What for ? " the author of *Ubu-Roi* would exclaim in astonishment. " By suggesting to the man that he's been attacked, I give him the chance of telling hair-raising tales to his friends."

At the end of the summer Jarry left his troglodyte dwelling, which he always hoped some day to exchange for a tower built by his own hands, to take up his winter quarters in Paris. The first time I went to see him, in a street near St. Germain-des-Prés, it was to ask his opinion on a Latin inscription, for Jarry was a scholar of the first order. When I came to the door of his lodgings, a low door half-way up the stairs, I rang the bell with the conviction that some other door I had not noticed would open. But the little door it was that opened a few inches. The top of it reached to my chest.

" Bend down so that I can see who you are," said a voice from inside.

When I had succeeded in squeezing into the place, I stared in astonishment at Jarry's hair, which was cut *en brosse* and was all white at the ends. I was not long in realising that the white came from the ceiling, which was high enough not to inconvenience Jarry, but not sufficiently high to keep his hair from touching the whitewash.

Jarry explained that his landlord had divided one of the flats horizontally in two, for the use of tenants of small stature. The author of *Ubu-Roi* lived here with two cats and an owl. The bird, too, must have had a white top to its head, for constantly perched as it was upon its master's shoulder, as the latter moved to and fro it swept the ceiling with its crest.

I have already mentioned Jarry's dislike of owing anybody anything. In the same way, if he had done anyone an injury, he would not rest till he had made up for it. One day he fired a pistol into a hedge, and a lady shot up from behind it in a fury:

"Sir! My child is playing about here, and you might have killed him!"

Said Jarry gallantly:

"Madam, I would have given you another!"

XII CONNOISSEURS AND COL-LECTORS—I

Born under the sign of the Crescent, M. de Cam-ondo's forefathers had not hesitated, on entering Europe, to abandon slippers and fezzes for boots, bowler hats and, in course of time, the nobiliary particle. But neither jacket, bowler hat, nor even a subscription to the Opera and a racing-stable sufficed to exhaust M. Isaac de Camondo's zest for the career of a gentleman. He felt bound to exhibit a taste for art. And with that *flair* that he showed not only in affairs of finance, the banker of the rue Gluck realised that the connoisseur of painting who would not appear out of date, owed it to himself to take notice of the Impressionists. At the same time, if M. de Camondo was to consent to " go in for " the art of the vanguard, it must be done without breaking with tradition. So that before the *dignus entrare* was pronounced, the paintings were subjected to the severest scrutiny. This scrutiny took place on a Sunday, after a luncheon to which those painters were invited whose pictures the host was not in the habit of buying; a circumstance which, in his eyes, conferred a guarantee of impartiality on their opinions. At coffee-time, therefore, together with the liqueurs and the cigars, the servants carried round the pictures which had been submitted.

One Monday I had gone to inquire if a painting of *Women bathing*, by Cézanne, that I had sent in a few days before, was being kept. I was shown into a room which served as the *salon des refusés*, and there

I saw my picture. In a neighbouring room I heard two menservants chatting:

"Did you hear that bloke yesterday, when he was looking at that picture of naked women in there, saying: 'What a lovely bit of china!' 'He's a bit balmy, t'other one,' I says to myself. Well, when I was taking the tyke for a walk this morning, I stopped outside the antique shop at the corner of the street, to look at a big blue dish they've got in the window. It's amazing, my boy! Now that I've seen the picture again, it looks like a bit of china to me too."

At that moment M. de Camondo came in with a tall young man, whom he led straight up to the Cézanne:

"I wanted to show you this painting before sending it back. Would you believe it, a critic said, here, only yesterday: 'What a lovely bit of china!' Everyone knows it isn't Cézanne, but Renoir, who used to paint on china."

M. de Camondo paused a moment; then he added:

"Just because I like to get expert opinions, some people imagine I buy with my ears. You can tell all those smart fellows that I've quite good eyes to see with too."

M. de Camondo became aware of my presence.

"Ah! there you are, M. Vollard."

And pointing to the Cézanne:

"What exactly does your picture represent?"

"Why! women bathing!" I replied, taken aback.

"Ah! really! Women bathing! Would you mind telling me what they're bathing in? Women bathing! Where there isn't a drop of water!"

And turning to the individual who was with him:

"Who was it now that said, 'Nothing overhears so much rubbish as a picture'?"

One day M. de Camondo came to my shop with a tall man whose outrageously Parisian manners betrayed the foreigner. From the deference shown him by M. de Camondo, I realised that my visitor was a man of note. I heard: " Oui, monseigneur. Non, monseigneur . . ." After a bit I discovered that this personage was none other than His Majesty Milan, ex-King of Serbia.

Wishing to appear *au courant* of everything that was new in art, he had asked M. de Camondo to take him to all the haunts of " advanced art." I was at that time holding an exhibition of Cézanne's works.

On entering, His Majesty mentioned having seen a large composition in my window a few days earlier, which he wanted to look at more closely.

It was a picture by Henry de Groux, representing corpses of kings being carried away in baskets, from beneath the covers of which dangled crowned heads, and hands gripping sceptres. In the centre of this composition were removal-men brandishing a banner inscribed " *Mort aux Vaches !* "

His Majesty fixed his eyeglass in his eye, and contemplated the painting with extreme attention. All at once he frowned.

Modelling his expression on that of his companion, M. de Camondo ejaculated:

" Fancy allowing the work of such anarchists to be exhibited ! "

The king roused himself from his contemplation.

" Your Henry de Groux, M. Vollard, is not a conscientious artist. He calls his picture *Mort aux Vaches*, but there is not a single figure of a *sergot* in it."

" But," I replied, ignoring the signs M. de Camondo was making to me, " he's not referring to policemen in this case, but to kings."

" How very curious," observed His Majesty; " I have not come across that meaning in my lexicon."

King Milan took a little notebook from his pocket, which bore the title, *Parisian Expressions most in Use*.

Opposite the word "*vache*," which was explained as "*agent de police*," he wrote: "is also said of a king." Then he announced:

"I am an eclectic: I will buy this picture."

Eclecticism, with His Majesty, meant collecting, indifferently, ballet-girls by Degas and by Carrier-Belleuse, of whom he spoke to me that day with enthusiasm.

A week later, again escorted by M. de Camondo, King Milan came back to my shop. Behind them was a hotel porter carrying de Groux's *Mort aux Vaches.*

"I've been thinking it over. A king can't have a picture of that sort in his house," he said to me. "You see, we have to set an example of respect."

I thought with vexation that he was going to ask for his money back. But my royal visitor had not yet the assurance of the "old connoisseurs." He had merely come to ask me to exchange the picture.

His Majesty asked to have all his purchases sent to his hotel. Having a great desire to see how a king lived, I decided to take them myself, and presented myself next day at the Hôtel du Bas-Rhin, in the Place Vêndome.

I was at once shown into the royal apartments. Soon afterwards a footman, who was looking out of a window into the street, gave a whistle. Another footman ran to the entrance door and glued his ear against it. All at once he flung open the folding doors, and His Majesty, in a frock coat and light grey top-hat, made his entrance. When the door had been closed again, the king took off his hat and stuck it on the valet's outstretched fist, as though it were a hat-peg. From that moment my respect for King Milan increased by leaps and bounds. Imagine my feelings when I beheld an individual all bedizened with gold presenting his correspondence to him on a silver salver! I have always been

dazzled by gold lace, by all that glitters on sleeves
and headgear, and I could not help thinking that if
I had been the king, I should have worn the magnificent gold-embroidered garment myself, and given
the frock coat to the Chamberlain.

King Milan, catching sight of me, called out:
" Do you know Abel Faivre? I've got one of his
finest drawings here." With an agility that was
astonishing in a man of his corpulence, he climbed
on a chair and ran his hand along the top of a wardrobe. When he came down off the chair, the sleeve
of his frock coat had got dusty. He took off the
coat and went down on all-fours in his shirt-sleeves.
Running his hand under the wardrobe, he pulled out
an Albert Guillaume. The fact was, the taste that
King Milan proclaimed for " advanced " art was not
concerned with the works of the leaders as such. It
included in a general way everything that was in
the fashion. Thus for him Abel Faivre and Degas,
Cézanne and Albert Guillaume were all bracketed
together as " advanced " painters.

He was certainly sincere when he said it was a
pleasanter job to be a Parisian than a king. But
in time, seeing that the king behaved like everybody
else, Paris ended by losing interest in him. Even
M. de Camondo substituted the appellation " *mon
cher comte* " for that of " *Monseigneur*." (The king
travelled under the name of Comte de Takovo.)

One day somebody told me he had been present
at a dinner in honour of King Milan at M. de Camondo's. " They gave us a dish of eggs, mauve
eggs, the preparation of which had apparently necessitated two days' work." The speaker had also
admired a pie, an incomparable dish, to the making
of which went I know not what bird that could
only be procured at the price of gold. I saw this
gentleman again later. A few days previously he
had again dined with His Majesty at M. de Camondo's.

" Well," I asked him, " did you have the famous mauve eggs and the pie? "

" No . . . we had a very . . . very simple dinner."

I gathered that the vogue of the august guest was decidedly on the wane.

After the death of the ex-king, all that remained of his collection came back to Paris, and was sold at the Hôtel des Ventes. On this occasion the Press of the Boulevards extolled, for the last time, the " eclecticism " of King Milan.

M. Denys Cochin was the type of the genuine *amateur* who buys pictures with no thought of the profit to be made on them. In other words, he bought for pleasure. It was an expensive pleasure, for no sooner had he bought a picture than another would tempt him, and then there would be an exchange, with adequate compensation—adequate, that is, for the dealer. And the more ardently M. Denys Cochin had desired a thing, the sooner he fell in love with another; much like children who, when they have been given some long-coveted toy, throw it aside almost at once.

I had a painting of Cézanne's to sell on commission— an *Interior*—for a private owner, anxious to sell, but unable to make up his mind as to the price. M. Denys Cochin admired the picture each time he came to the shop.

" Promise me," he said repeatedly, " to let me know directly your *amateur* comes to a decision."

At last I was able to report:

" My client wants an offer made him. He is coming to me to-morrow."

" I'll give so much. I was going away for a couple of days, but I'll put off my journey."

Two days later, as soon as the shop was open, M. Cochin turned up.

" What about the picture? "

" It is yours."

" Let's take it round to my place at once! "

We got into his carriage.

All at once he said to me:

" It's a fine picture, isn't it? "

I fancied I saw a shadow pass over his face. The nearer we drew to his house, the more thoughtful he appeared, and he kept repeating:

" It really *is* a fine picture."

In his drawing-room we tried the picture first on one wall and then on another:

" It's certainly a very fine picture," he said again; " but just look! It doesn't go with anything here, neither my Delacroix nor my Courbet, and as for the Manets . . . You can see for yourself. . . . Really, I don't see where I can put it. What a pity! "

" That's all right," I said; " I'll take it back."

And I packed up my Cézanne.

" As I was passing Hessel's," remarked M. Denys Cochin, " I caught sight of a painting that looked to me very good. Come and look at it with me."

I cried off, under pretext of urgent business. I did not want Hessel, supposing M. Cochin took the picture and got fed up with it next day, to think I had been running it down. By and by, towards lunch-time, M. Denys Cochin came in with a picture under his arm.

" I couldn't resist the temptation," he said. " Isn't it a lovely thing? "

I agreed with enthusiasm. It was a delicious Renoir.

" I'm not going home," continued M. Cochin. " My wife is in the country. Let's go and have lunch together."

On our way to the restaurant he repeated:

" I'm very pleased, Vollard. This Renoir delights

me more every minute. It's a bore—I'd have loved to spend the afternoon at home with my pictures, but I've got to go to the Chamber of Deputies. Ribot made us promise to be there. He's got a question to put."

" M. Ribot is a very eminent man," said I.

" And so delightfully simple! I went to see him the other day at his Longjumeau estate. He showed me an old seat propped against a weeping willow, with envelopes and wrappers strewn all over the ground. 'That's my study,' said the President modestly."

During lunch M. Cochin cast a glance from time to time at his purchase, which he had placed opposite him on a chair.

" It's a fine piece of work, isn't it? " he asked me suddenly, in a voice that I thought had a tinge of anxiety in it.

I assured him it combined force and grace to an unusual degree.

On leaving M. Cochin, I went back to my shop. Two hours later he turned up again with what looked to me like a picture under his arm. I was not mistaken.

" I just ran home for a moment," he explained. " Would you believe it? The Renoir wouldn't do either. It held its own all right, but the pictures alongside, no! So, as I had seen a little Delacroix, a few days ago, in the rue de Sèze . . . Fortunately it wasn't sold. How do you like it? "

" A jewel! "

" Isn't it? But I must be off. I ought to be at the Chamber by now. I promised Ribot."

At that moment M. de Camondo came into the shop. M. Denys Cochin showed him his new purchase, and he was loud in its praise.

M. Denys Cochin, thoroughly pleased:

" I was beginning to wonder if the picture, splendid

as it is. . . . Well, now I'm completely reassured. I must fly to the Chamber."

None the less, before the day was out I was to see M. Cochin once again, laden as before with a picture.

"You see, Vollard," he explained, showing me a little Manet. "After I left you I saw this little marvel at Durand's. I couldn't resist it. And they let me have it for my Delacroix. . . . And yet I was awfully taken with that, too!"

He stood a moment contemplating the Manet:

"You'll think me absurdly changeable, Vollard, but now I think of it, I'm not sure I don't rather regret the Delacroix."

He looked at his watch:

"Durand-Ruel is still open . . . I'll go and look at the picture again."

"Were you pleased with M. Ribot's speech?" I asked.

"Good Lord! Ribot! I'd clean forgotten him. . . . Oh, well, never mind. Between you and me, you know, I knew every word he was going to say beforehand. Greatly applauded, of course. As for having the slightest influence on anybody in the Chamber! But you must let me go, or I shall miss my Delacroix."

During the War a tragi-comic adventure befell M. Denys Cochin.

One day the police of France and Spain were simultaneously alarmed. A telegram from Paris to Madrid had just been intercepted, worded as follows: "Accept hundred and twenty thousand for head of the Queen," and signed *Denys Cochin*. Was not this part of some anarchist plot, and was not the name of the eminent statesman a red herring drawn across the track? The actual facts were these. At Durand-Ruel's, some time before, M. Cochin had been held, like a pointer at gaze, by Goya's *Portrait of a Queen*, which he bought there and then. But afterwards he had discovered that the Goya " did not hold its own " with his other pictures. He gave it to be re-sold to a Spanish dealer, who took it away with him to Madrid and had just found a purchaser for it.

I have said that M. Denys Cochin bought for pleasure. I might add that he was never mistaken in his choice. All his pictures were of the first order. What an incomparable museum might be created with all that was once in his possession! Delacroix's *Corinne chez les peuples pasteurs*, Manet's *Exécution de Maximilien* and the *Serveuse de bocks*, now in the Mannheim Gallery, Corot's *Vue de Rome* and *Eglise de Vézelay*, and Manet's *Course de Taureaux*, too, " the finest that painting has ever given us," as Renoir used to say to me. And then all his Cézannes: *Figures, Still-lifes, Landscapes*. And the Gauguins and the Van Goghs. I was almost forgetting Corot's wonderful portrait of a woman, so long unheeded, and made famous by the sale on which M. Denys Cochin decided during his lifetime. Cruelly hit by the deaths of his two sons and his son-in-law who had been killed in action, and greatly weakened besides by ill-health, his pictures, that he had loved as a child loves its playthings, no longer " amused " him. He decided to part with them.

An imposing figure among collectors was that of Chauchard, the owner of the *Grands Magasins du Louvre*, " L'Empereur du Blanc," as his friends called him. I never, it is true, had occasion to approach him, but I knew him so well from the confidences of his habitual guests, that I cannot resist the temptation to let him figure in these recollections.

" Chauchard, you beat everything! God made the seasons, and it would need a miracle to change them; but you can displace them or unite them at will! "

This was the sort of thing that greeted him in his dining-room, where flowers and fruit brought from all the countries of the sun turned winter into summer.

This chorus of praise, however, could not always stir the host from a brown study. His thoughts perhaps were busy with the Louvre, that he was thinking of enriching with some fresh jewel: *La Vache*, by Troyon, Théodore Rousseau's *Chataigniers*, or Millet's *Angélus*.

Or another problem might be haunting this noble Mæcenas. Determined to leave his habitual guests an ineffaceable memory of himself, he had planned that at their last, supreme gathering around his bier, each of them should have the privilege of carrying one of his pictures at the head of the funeral cortège.

To his residuary legatee, the Minister Leygues, would fall as by right Millet's *Angélus*, which, on account of the price he had paid for it—four millions of our francs of to-day—seemed to him incontestably the finest of his pictures. But his other friends too—ambassadors, captains of industry, kings in exile—must each have a picture assigned to them, in strict accordance with rank, to carry on the day of the funeral.

Left to himself again, Mæcenas, with a pot of glue in one hand and the photographs of his friends in the other, would start reapportioning for the umpteenth time his Corots, his Meissonniers, his Jules Duprés, his Bastien-Lepages, his Cabanels, Courbets, Detailles, without ever solving the riddle: Who was to carry the Corot? Who the Cabanel? At last one day, as he swore aloud in his perplexity, a parrot, flapping its wings on a perch, let fall in a nasal voice a phrase it had heard its master ejaculate many a time in a rage: " Chauchard, you're a bloody fool! "

Some time later, when I had become a publisher, I heard that the *Magasins de la Samaritaine* had dis-

I

tributed a calendar on New Year's Day, on which one of Renoir's pictures was reproduced in colour. This reproduction was said to be perfect; peculiarly successful. Being interested in new processes of engraving, I went to the *Samaritaine* to ask if it would be possible to have one of these calendars. They promised to look for one. When I returned, I was told the calendar had been sent out several years previously; only one copy had been found, and that in rather bad condition. The head of the department added that the owner of the *Samaritaine*, M. Cognacq, was anxious first to know why I was so keen on possessing this almanack, and would like to see me on the subject. On the day appointed, while waiting to be received by him, I was wandering about the shop, when my attention was attracted by an old employé who was picking up all the pins and bits of string that he found on the floor. Whilst I watched this performance absent-mindedly, my imagination was at work elsewhere. M. Cognacq was evidently interested in Renoir, I thought, since he had had one of his pictures reproduced. And I began building up all sorts of plans. At last they brought word that M. Cognacq was ready to see me, and I was shown into his office. Imagine my surprise! Whom did I see behind a vast work-table? My old employé of a moment before, busy sorting out the odds and ends he had just harvested. Without interrupting his work, he expressed his astonishment that an out-of-date calendar should be of any use to me.

"It is my copyright," he pointed out to me; "its reproduction is forbidden."

"Oh, but I merely want," I said, "to examine a process which I have been told reproduces perfectly."

"If that's all . . ."

He ordered a copy of the calendar to be brought. I saw that the reproduction of the Renoir was neither better nor worse than most of the colour-prints intended for publicity purposes.

I thought it a good opportunity to mention my Renoirs, Degas and Cézannes.

"Excuse me," he said, "either one thing or the other. Either you are making some sort of suggestion with regard to my shops, in which case I will tell them to take you to my head buyer; or else you are thinking of my private collections, and for those I have my regular agents. M. J., their chief, is the person you should see."

This failure did not tend to encourage me in my approaches to the magnates of the drapery business. It was quite by chance that I once again found myself face to face with one of the richest of these Crœsuses. I am referring to the director of the *Galeries Lafayette*.

I had bought an umbrella at this shop that I wished to change for one with a different handle. The salesman in the department spared me no questions: What day did I buy the umbrella, why was there no ticket left on it, etc., when suddenly I heard:

"What! M. Vollard, you here?"

The speaker was none other than the president of the Board of Directors of the *Galeries Lafayette*, M. Bader himself. He continued:

"The 'slump' is evidently not affecting *your* Treasury, since I see you are making a purchase. . . ."

These few words were sufficient to show me that I could hope for no more from M. Bader than from M. Cognacq. There remained only to secure a new umbrella. Transformation scene! The salesman suddenly became most attentive. Handing me another umbrella, he could think of nothing to say, in his perturbation, but:

"Thank you, Monsieur. . . . Pleased to meet you."

XIII CONNOISSEURS AND COLLECTORS—II

At Paul Alexis's house one day I saw a *Landscape under Snow* signed by an unknown artist— Montillard or some such name—and Paul Alexis said:

"As you go in for pictures, you might do worse than take that one."

"How much?"

"Two hundred and fifty francs."

"Right!"

I was preparing to carry off my purchase when he stopped me:

"Allow me to remove the frame."

"I beg your pardon! It was only for the frame's sake that I bought it. I don't mind leaving you the painting."

"But I want the frame too, you see."

"What made you put a picture like that into such a valuable frame?"

"A picture like that, you say? The man who painted it is not a mere nobody. He used to belong to the Impressionist set. He knew Cézanne and Pissarro intimately."

I began to feel interested in Montillard. A man who had known Cézanne and Pissarro might have some of their works in his possession.

"What has become of your Montillard?" I asked Paul Alexis.

"I fancy he's still living at Gif."

I went to Gif next day, and ran the old painter to

earth. I told him I had heard through his friend
Paul Alexis that he had frequented painters I myself
had known, and some of whose works I possessed:
Cézanne, Renoir, Guillaumin and others. We chatted
for a bit, and the worthy man went over his remin-
iscences.

"I suppose," I ventured, "you must have got a
few paintings by your old friends—Pissarros, for
instance, and Cézannes . . ."

"Of course. I've got some Cézannes, and some
Pissarros and Vignons. Would you like to see
them?"

"Very much. You are not thinking of selling
them?"

"By Jove, yes! Would you buy them?"

"I don't say I wouldn't."

He went into the next room and brought back
about ten paintings.

"Give me twelve hundred francs, and you can
have the lot."

I agreed without delay.

At that moment a woman's voice called to him.
He went into the other room, and I heard these
words:

"You've got the money?"

"I've got the money, and he didn't haggle. It's
well above the last price-list."

I was thoroughly puzzled. What could this price-
list be? I had never heard of anything of the kind.

While Montillard was rolling up the canvases, I
threw out a feeler:

"By the by, if you have the price-list handy, I'd
like to look up Sisley's work."

He took from his pocket a printed slip resembling
a newspaper "galley," and I read:

"*The Impressionists : Latest Prices.*—Renoirs are
going down. No demand for Sisleys. A few Pissarros and one Cézanne offered at ten per cent.

below. Nothing doing on the Vignons. A little business on the Monets."

" Where can one subscribe to this list? " I asked in the greatest astonishment.

" An old friend of mine who works for the Press gives it me."

When I got back to Paris, I went to the picture repairer.

" I found these paintings at Gif," I told him.

" At Gif, did you? I've got a customer there—a journalist. He's been gassing to me for the last five or six years about some pictures by Cézanne and Pissarro belonging to a friend of his. ' I've thought of a dodge,' he said to me once, ' for getting them cheap, one of these days, and I fancy I shall soon be able to bring them to you to stretch.' It would be rather a joke if these were the very ones! "

Imagine the scene when the wily friend arrived, with quotations even more lamentable, no doubt, than the last! What a fool he will have looked when Montillard announced triumphantly: " Only fancy! Some idiot . . ."

A few weeks later, at a picture dealer's, I saw a man in a great state of agitation. I was told he was Aurélien Scholl.

" What's the matter? " he was asked.

" Would you believe it? Some brute, taking advantage of an old artist's foolishness, has just robbed him, literally robbed him, of a whole lot of Cézannes and Pissarros! It's abominable! "

In picture dealing one must go warily with one's customers. It does not do, for instance, to explain the subject, or show which way up a picture is meant to be looked at. A collector once sent me a photograph of a picture: " I would like a companion piece," he wrote, " to this charming Spanish land-scape I once bought from you. I have never seen the atmosphere of that country so well rendered." And he gave the dimensions of the canvas. I remembered quite well having sold him the picture, but I had never been sure what it represented. The photograph did not tell me much more. I did not know which was the right side up. I ended by going to a painter and asking him if he had a companion piece to the landscape.

"But it's not a landscape, you know, it's a man playing a guitar."

Which reminded me of the story of the *Scène de Personnages*—wasn't it by Luc Olivier Merson?—which, hung upside down in the *Salon*, was taken for a landscape and obtained a high award.

There is also the *amateur* who likes a picture because of its title, even if the title has nothing to do with the subject; an example of which is afforded from high quarters. We all know the illustrious sculptor— "the greatest of modern times," according to his admirers—who called a study of a foot "*Rêve enchanté*." Rodin, apparently, knew to what extent a title may enhance the appeal of a work of art.

While on the subject of titles, I might recount the extraordinary *avatars* undergone by a picture of Cézanne's.

I was holding an exhibition of this painter's work, including a picture of a shepherd and some naked women in a landscape. By mistake, the picture happened to be in a frame from which I had forgotten to remove the label, and this read: *Diana and Actæon.* In the Press notices, the picture was described as though it had really been meant for a *Diana bathing*. One art critic praised the noble attitude of the goddess and the modest air of the virgins surrounding her. He particularly admired the gesture of the attendant nymph at the entrance to the glade, who with her uplifted arm bade the intruder begone.

" This is not," he added, " the ' Begone! ' of the coy maiden, signifying ' Don't take me at my word,' but truly the ' Begone! ' of the offended virgin."

Some time afterwards I was asked to lend Cézanne's picture of the *Temptation of St. Anthony* to an exhibition. I had promised the painting, but could not send it, as it had been sold in the meantime. In its place I sent the pseudo *Diana and Actæon*, after removing the unfortunate label from the frame. But as the *Temptation* was expected, no one thought of rectifying the title in the catalogue, and on the strength of the printed word an influential art review described the picture as a *Temptation of St. Anthony*. Where others had seen the noble attitude of a goddess, the art critic now discovered the bewitching yet perfidious smile of the daughter of Satan. Actæon became a pathetic St. Anthony. The repelling gesture of the outstretched arm changed to a seductive invitation, and so on. On the last day of the exhibition the collector who had refused the picture when it was called *Diana and Actæon* came to see me. He had in his hand a copy of the review in which the glowing article had appeared. " I've just bought that *Temptation*," he said. " Its realism is admirable."

When I asked Cézanne what the subject of his picture really was:

" It has no subject. I was merely trying to render certain movements."

Here is a still stranger adventure in which Cézanne's paintings played a part.

I showed one of my clients two Cézannes, but he refused them off-hand :

" I'm sick of these pictures with blank patches in them."

A few months later he begged me to go and see him.

" I've just come from Budapest," he informed me.

" Six days in the train is pretty stiff! But I've brought back these two marvels."

I recognised my two pictures that he had turned down not long before.

The collector continued:

" They knock yours to bits, don't they? It was a dealer in Berlin who acted as go-between. Your colleague in Budapest was very obliging. He took a Renoir of mine in exchange, and in cash not even the double of what you wanted for your two sketches! There are blank patches in my pictures too, I grant you. But in the things you showed me they were due to lack of finish, whereas the blanks in mine are ' intended.' Anyway, it's easy to see, we'll compare them one of these days."

I told him I had sent my pictures abroad on commission, and had just heard they had been bought by a Parisian on his way through.

" It would be really rather funny if it turned out to be one of your own customers who had seen them at your place and not recognised them," he said. And as I smiled: " Come now, you may as well tell me the truth. . . ."

An old customer from the provinces came into my shop, looked at a few pictures and said suddenly:

" I've just seen a Pissarro in Durand-Ruel's window: a haystack. It's a subject I haven't got among my pictures by that painter."

" Have you asked the price of it? "

" Oh, no! What's the use, in a shop like that? A picture of that quality is bound to be too dear for me. All the same, I may tell you I don't despair of coming to some arrangement with Durand."

A few days later he came back.

" What do you think Durand is asking for that Pissarro? Two thousand five hundred francs! "

" Two thousand five hundred! By Jove, now's the

time to buy up Pissarros, then. . . . A great painter, Pissarro, you know. . . ."

But the *amateur* cried angrily:

" I don't gamble in pictures. I love painting for its own sake. All the same, when a painter begins to go down like that . . . The minute I get home, it will be Down with my Pissarros and off with them to the Auction Rooms."

On the other hand, there are collectors to whom their pictures are the most precious things in the world.

I remember one who in the course of a serious illness fell into a sort of prostration from which nothing could rouse him. A medical luminary, consulted as a last resource, did not attempt to mince matters.

" I am afraid there is really nothing more to be done. If this condition continues, we must expect a fatal issue very shortly. Only some unexpected event, some very strong emotion, for instance, might provoke a favourable reaction."

" Suppose we suddenly announced that *Maman* is at death's door," suggested the family doctor. " He is very fond of his mother-in-law." And bending over the patient, he shouted:

" Your mother-in-law has just had a stroke! "

The patient received the announcement with the utmost indifference.

" No reaction, Madame! Your husband will pass peacefully away," said the consulting physician to the wife standing by the bedside.

" Listen, Doctor," she said at a venture; " I'm not sure that really his pictures don't come first with him."

" Ah! He has a passion for *something*? In that case we might attempt . . . Had he a favourite picture? "

" Yes, Doctor. . . . Look, those *Sunflowers* by Van Gogh over there. . . ."

" All right. We'll pretend we're going to sell them."

A well-known dealer, let into the secret, came to see the Van Gogh, valued it, discussed it, took it down. As he appeared to be going off with it, the patient suddenly showed signs of violent agitation, sat part way up in bed, and fell back sobbing.

" He is saved ! " cried the physician.

XIV CONNOISSEURS AND COL-
LECTORS—III

One day the bell rang at my flat in the rue de Gramont. I opened the door and found a gentleman very much out of breath after the ascent of my four flights of stairs.

"I want to see some pictures," he told me, "but I'm in a great hurry. I'm leaving for Nice in an hour's time. The Carnival begins to-morrow, and I don't want to miss the opening."

We dashed off to my shop, which was only a few yards away. I was about to parade my Renoirs and Gauguins and Daumiers—he had given me some indication of his tastes on the way—when:

"First of all," he said, "you must show me round the corner. When my bladder is too full I haven't all my wits about me."

These preliminaries had taken up a quarter of an hour. It would take him another quarter to get to the station. We still had half an hour, during which he purchased a respectable lot of Manets, Gauguins, Daumiers and Renoirs. He paid me something on account and dashed back to his car. An accordion-player in the street was dragging out a refrain. My client got into his car, beating time to the tune with his head. Someone to whom I mentioned this said:

"He must have been a Viennese. Music always acts like magic on them."

The address he had left me proved my informant to be right.

At the end of a few months, having heard no more, I wrote to remind him that I was to send him his pictures as soon as I had his cheque. He wrote me the most friendly letter back, full from beginning to end of praise of the charm of Paris. But not a single reference to his purchases. I tried again two or three times, and each time his reply suggested a purchaser trying to get out of his bargain.

I had nearly made up my mind to go and see on the spot what was happening, when the pictures I had sold him suddenly went up a great deal in value. I hastened to tell him this good news, suggesting that he had better not delay any longer in settling his account, since he was making such a good thing of it. He replied that he was coming to Paris, and we would lunch together.

We had an excellent lunch at Larue's. My Viennese was accompanied by a very pretty woman, who from the first was particularly nice to me. They took me with them to the theatre in the evening, and after the theatre we had to have supper. My host was becoming more and more open-hearted.

Suddenly he got up, and seizing both my hands, cried:

" Listen, dear friend, I can't bear the idea of doing you an injury by taking advantage of the rise in price of my pictures. I would much rather cancel the bargain."

I was certainly not prepared for this announcement. Did he imagine I had invented the rise as a trick to make him pay up?

" I shouldn't like you to sacrifice yourself out of kindness to me," I replied. " Please think it over."

" I've made up my mind."

" Well, if you really wish it . . ."

And I asked for writing materials.

I had my cheque-book with me, and I returned my client the sum he had paid me on account. He pocketed it with the pleased expression of a man who has just swindled his partner.

But he soon discovered that the swindler is liable at times to cheat himself. A few days later one of my colleagues said to me:

" I've just met a Viennese who is furious with you. He goes about telling everybody that you've cheated him, and that he won't be doing business with you again in a hurry."

I was reading in my shop when a gentleman came in. As he remained silent, I went on with my reading. I have been described now as lying in wait behind my door, ready to pounce on my client, now as practically shoving out any impertinent creature who may have come with the intention of buying. Neither of these attitudes has ever been mine. I do not hurl myself at the customer, neither do I turn him out. I merely ask him what he wants. Seeing this new-comer glance from time to time at the street, I ended by asking him if he was waiting for somebody.

" I'm waiting for the rain to leave off."

At the first fine interval he went away. I was surprised to see him again the next day.

" Do you know who is the greatest painter? " he asked me abruptly.

And as I stood speechless, he flung at me:

" Steinlen is the greatest painter. Have you any of his pictures? "

I showed him a few pastels. He bought them there and then. Then he asked:

" Could you get me some more? "

" Come back this evening: I may have some by then."

The *amateur* shook hands with me effusively. In the afternoon I went to see Steinlen. He was smoking his pipe. The portfolios beside him were stuffed with drawings. I bought the lot.

On my return to the rue Laffitte, I found my

amateur walking up and down outside the door of the shop.

"Have you got some?" he asked. "I'll take the lot," and laden with his purchase he went off delighted.

Next day he came back.

"I've made a great discovery. It isn't Steinlen who's the greatest painter, it's Maurin. Have you any of his work?"

"I've got a few things."

He seized greedily on those I showed him, and declared insatiably:

"Now I want some more."

"I fancy I can lay my hands on some. Come back in two hours' time."

I went to Maurin and took all he had. When I got back to the shop, my customer, who was waiting for me, paid me the sum I asked without so much as opening the parcel of paintings I had brought.

A few days later I had a visit from Maurin. He said:

"I can accept any amount of orders now, for I've discovered a dodge for turning things out very quickly. I just draw the outlines, and then by a process I've invented, I powder the colour and spray it on to the drawing." He would not give me any details till he had taken out his patent.

It was some time before I saw my *amateur* again; then suddenly one day he turned up. He said to me rather mournfully:

"Maurin is decidedly not the greatest painter. But then who is the greatest painter, really?"

"To tell the truth," I replied, "it is impossible to settle who is the greatest painter. There are 'the greatest painters'—Cézanne, Renoir, Monet, Degas . . ."

He stopped me.

"When I hear too many names at a time," he said, "it makes my brain seethe."

And he fell into a profound reverie.

"Rabelais," I suggested, breaking the silence, "recommended the use of dice in cases of doubt."

"My sister made me swear," he replied, "never to touch cards or dice."

"But if we put the names in a hat and drew lots, that wouldn't be gambling, would it?"

He thought my idea excellent, and took some little slips of paper on which he wrote the names I dictated to him: Cézanne, Renoir, Degas, Monet, Gauguin, and some others he had made a note of himself: Latouche, Ziem, Charles Jacques. After we had thoroughly shaken up the bits of paper in the hat, one of them came out with the name of Van Gogh on it.

Our surprise was great, since this name had not been put into the hat. But the explanation was very simple. My customer had picked up from the table, without thinking, a label bearing Van Gogh's name, and had put it into the hat with the others. He decided to let Van Gogh count as well.

"I hear an inner voice telling me to follow what chance has determined. My sister advised me always to listen to my inner voices."

And he chose some fine Van Goghs.

He decided to draw lots again. This time it was Cézanne's name that came out. I had a good many Cézannes.

He took thirty of them besides the Van Goghs.

He promised me as he went away to come back soon.

He did not come back. A few years later a Dutchman passing through Paris said to me in the course of conversation:

"We've got a fellow in the lunatic asylum at the Hague whose history is really curious. By avoiding society, going to bed early and never speaking to anybody, he had acquired the reputation of a profound thinker. His sister entrusted her fortune to him to look after. After spending some time in Paris, he came home with packing-cases full of pictures, but only four florins in his pocket. The purchases were submitted to experts and the man was medically examined. The experts were unanimous in declaring that the old pictures merely showed him to be a perfect ignoramus in art, but the modern paintings—the Cézannes and the Van Goghs—could only have been bought by a madman. The mental specialists having confirmed the conclusions of the experts, the connoisseur was immediately shut up."

Aha, thought I, that must be my man.

It was. On the death of this singular individual his family hastened to liquidate the whole stock of paintings, which the law had not allowed them to touch during his confinement. At the sale, one of the Van Goghs fetched thirty-five thousand francs. The Cézannes had been carefully laid aside, so as not to frighten the public. But a little painting, dating from the Master's youth, got slipped in among the others, and fetched fifteen thousand. It was then decided to bring out the whole collection. The collectors fought over it, and the sale produced over two millions.

The news got about, and turned people's heads to such an extent that they began to fancy madmen must have a peculiar *flair* for pictures likely to go up in price. It sounds hardly credible, but a group of connoisseurs collected a capital sum which they put at the disposal of some half-witted creature, and despatched him to Paris accompanied by a delegate of the group, whose function it was to be to send home the pictures selected by the lunatic. But the latter spent more time in resorts of pleasure than in the painters' studios. At that game the credit at his disposal was soon exhausted, and the venture came to an end.

K

Here is another example of the notions people entertain about painting that " sells." This time it was not a question of buying pictures, but of manufacturing them.

A child I knew grew up a " natural." The parents were worried about their son's future, till someone suggested they should encourage him to paint.

They were flabbergasted, of course.

" But I assure you, at the auction rooms nowadays it's the pictures by ' loonies ' that fetch the highest prices ! "

One difficulty arose: the lad was possessed by a spirit of contradiction. So they schemed to put canvases, paints, and brushes within his reach, with strict injunctions not to touch them. The unruly youngster immediately seized the canvases and covered them with paint. When his output was considered sufficient, the parents went to the director of a gallery reputed to be " in the forefront," and said to him:

" We've come to show you some lunatic painting."

But the dealer took one glance at what they had brought him:

" Look here! D'you take me for a fool? This isn't lunatic painting. Lunatic painting is when you don't know if it's a portrait or a landscape or a still-life. Whereas look at all this! Everything here is perfectly recognisable! What do you expect me to do with that? "

The couple were thunderstruck.

" Christ! " exclaimed the father, " that's nearly fifteen hundred francs' worth of paint and canvas gone down the drain! "

XV CONNOISSEURS AND COLLECTORS—IV

One of my Russian clients asked me off-hand where he could be sure of buying a good umbrella.

"I'm just going to the *Printemps*," I told him, " to buy some handkerchiefs. Come with me, you'll find what you want there."

After they had shown him every sort of umbrella, he chose one at last and asked the price of it.

"Thirty-five francs."

"Is that your lowest price?"

"Everything here is at a fixed price. We don't bargain."

"Come! You'll surely let me have it for twenty-five?"

Mute astonishment on the part of the assistant.

"If I went up to thirty francs?"

The salesman waved the suggestion aside, took back the umbrella and was about to restore it to its place.

"So thirty-five francs is really your lowest price? All right then, I'll take it."

I reported this scene to a native of Moscow:

"Your client is not a real Russian," he said. "The Russians one sees in Paris are either sons of the people, who don't visit picture-dealers, or else men of the world, who know perfectly well that one doesn't bargain in shops."

"Yet he speaks Russian very well."

"That doesn't prove that he's a Russian. Shall I tell you what? Your man is a Pole."

I learnt later that he was a Dutchman who had been

131

brought up in Russia. When I saw my Muscovite again, I informed him of this.

" Didn't I tell you he was a Pole? " said he.

From which I gathered that to a genuine Russian, any man who talks Russian without being a native is a Pole.

The purchaser of the umbrella did at least know what he wanted. Your genuine Russian may not even do that. Maurice Denis was going to Moscow to set up some decorations he had been commissioned to execute for the great collector, M. Morosoff. A younger brother of Morosoff's was just saying how much he was looking forward to meeting the painter, who was expected next day. He was playing with a revolver that was lying on the table as he spoke. Suddenly he cried:

" I say! Suppose I were to shoot myself? Then I should know straight away what comes afterwards."

And putting the weapon to his head, he blew his brains out.

And that was the end of M. Morosoff's brother, who suddenly discovered he was more curious about the things of the next world than the paintings that so passionately interested his brother and his friend Stoukine. But that is another story.

One day a hotel porter entered my shop. He came to announce a customer who was on the look-out for pictures " like that." And he indicated some *Nudes* by Cézanne which were in the window. The next day he came back in attendance on a Little Russian, a certain Count Snasine, who, when he saw the Cézanne *Nudes*, shook his head in disdain.

" Too coarsely painted. I want some high-class *cochonneries*." [1]

[1] Among the peoples of the East, any representation of nudity is considered indecent, hence my Russian termed a painting of the nude a *cochonnerie*. Others besides Orientals are of the

I replied that I did not keep that sort of thing, and advised him to go to the Musée du Luxembourg, where there were plenty of pictures that might put him in the way of finding what he wanted. He came back full of enthusiasm. He had been particularly struck by a work that was just in his line: Bouguereau's *Mater Dolorosa*. He asked me to summon this artist to my shop, with sketches representing his " most refined *cochonneries*." I explained that the painter in question commanded very high prices, and was not in the habit of putting himself out.

" Never mind, then," said he, " I'll go and look him up."

I was rather curious to know who this strange votary of " refined *cochonneries* " might be. By way of drawing him out a bit, I told him I had Russian customers: a rich merchant . . .

He interrupted me.

" I'm not a merchant, I'm a nobleman. I go in for philanthropy. My father was a philanthropist; I am following my father's example."

The Russian went away, and I did not expect to see him again. But after a time he came back to the shop. He told me he had been turned out by Bouguereau, who called him a " *vieux cochon*," but that a copyist in the Museum had told him of a painter who did pictures of nudes quite as finished as M. Bouguereau's. This was a certain Cabanel, whom he had finally been taken to see. This Cabanel had received him in the most charming fashion, and had shown him, in effect, some very finished nudes. They

---

same mind. The Conseil-Général of La Réunion awarded a scholarship to a young painter who, to show the progress he was making, had sent in a painting of a naked woman lying down. The picture was hung in the Sessions Hall of the Conseil-Général. When my father saw it he cried: " What! They have hung up that *cochonnerie* ! It must be taken down at once ! " It was a copy of a picture by Bouguereau.

had done business together. I did not spoil his pleasure by telling him this must have been a bogus Cabanel, since the real one had long been dead.

He was so pleased that he was determined at all costs to have me dine with him.

" I've discovered in this Paris of yours a little . . . what do you call it? Ah, yes, I know . . . a little *bistrot*."

And he insisted so long that I felt it would be rude to refuse.

But my host could not remember the address of the *bistrot* in question; he said he would come and fetch me next day.

As we were getting into our cab:

" Rue Cambon," he said to the driver, " I'll tell you when to stop. It's a tiny little *bistrot*."

This " tiny little *bistrot* " proved to be the famous Café Voisin, where my host had engaged a table. At dessert, he suggested spending the rest of the evening at some show or other. What was the most fashionable theatre? I mentioned the *Variétés* at a venture. The Russian called the porter and sent him to take three stalls.

The porter came back. There were no seats left.

" But I must have them! I'll pay whatever they want! "

The argument was no doubt decisive, for the porter shortly after brought us the three tickets.

On arriving at the theatre, I was making for the cloak-room, but my host stopped me:

" Too long, the cloak-room."

And when we were in our seats, I realised that the third was to put our coats on.

I shall never forget that evening. The vacant seat was the cynosure of the spectators who had been given uncomfortable *strapontins*. At the beginning of the performance they took it to be engaged, and expected the occupant to arrive at any moment.

But after the first interval, as it still remained empty, over and over again the whole row had to stand up to let someone move down to the coveted place. And each time the Russian would say, politely but firmly:

" This seat is engaged."

And he would point to the coats and hats laid between us.

When we came out—the deuce if after all that I can remember the subject of the play—I thanked the ostentatious gentleman for the evening I had spent with him.

" And it was a good idea, wasn't it, having a seat to put our coats on, and rest our elbows? "

XVI THE STEINS AND OTHER AMERICANS

One morning, in the rue de Gramont, I was visited by a very distinguished-looking lady.

"I am the Marquise de S . . .," she told me, "I have come to ask you to do me a very great service. I have a great wish to see the Matisses and Picassos that belong to the Steins. I have been told you know them well."

"You need no introduction, Madame," I said; "they are the most hospitable people in the world, the Steins—the two brothers and the sister, Miss Gertrude Stein—their door is open to the public every Saturday from nine in the evening onwards."

"So I have been told. But to-day is Monday, and I have to leave for Rome the day after to-morrow at the latest. And I don't want to leave Paris without having seen the Steins' Picassos and Matisses. At a tea-party at the Ritz the other day people were talking of the Picassos, and I sat there looking like a fool."

She hesitated a little, and went on:

"I am great friends with the Italian Ambassador. Don't you think that if I were to get him to approach the American Ambassador . . ."

"I know that people have tried these arrangements between ambassadors before, but without success."

"In that case there's nothing for it. I must put off my journey."

On the following Saturday, at her request, I accompanied the Marquise de S. . . . to the Steins'.

Outsiders might easily have imagined themselves

in a public gallery; no one paid any attention to them. People came in and out, and Leo Stein never moved from his favourite position: half-reclining in an armchair, with his feet high up on a shelf of his bookcase.

" Excellent for the digestion," he declared this to be.

People who came there out of snobbery soon felt a sort of discomfort at being allowed so much liberty in another man's house, and did not come again. Only those who really cared for painting continued to frequent this hospitable house.

When I recall those old times, I see on the walls of the rooms at the Steins' paintings by Matisse and Picasso—certain *Nudes* by Cézanne and the marvellous portrait of Mme Cézanne in a red armchair. This painting had once belonged to me, and I had lent it to a retrospective exhibition of the " Master of Aix," organised at the *Salon d'Automne* of 1905. Every time I went to the exhibition I saw the Steins, the two brothers and the sister, seated on a bench in front of the portrait. They contemplated it in silence till the day when, the *Salon* being closed, Mr. Leo Stein came to bring me the price of the painting. He was accompanied by Miss Stein. " Now," said she, " the picture is ours! " They might have been ransoming someone they loved.

Miss Gertrude Stein's is a very attractive personality, in which the artist predominates. She writes for her own pleasure; if fame has come to her, it is certainly not because she has sought it. There is nothing more lively, more fascinating than her conversation. Her eyes sparkle with intelligence. Their expression at times is mocking, but the mockery is tempered with indulgence: if a spice of it creeps into her speech, it is rounded off by a gay laugh at her own expense.

To see her with her dress of coarse velveteen, her

sandals with leather straps, and her general air of simplicity, one would take her at first sight for a housewife whose horizon is restricted to her dealings with the greengrocer, the dairyman and the rest. But you have only to encounter her glance to perceive in Miss Stein something far beyond the ordinary *bourgeoise*. The vivacity of her glance betrays the observer, the investigator whom nothing escapes. Yet one cannot withhold one's confidence from her, so disarming is the laugh she seems constantly to turn against herself.

Recently someone said to me:

" I've been reading Miss Stein's description in the *Nouvelle Revue Française* of X.'s studio.[1] There is not a single allusion in it to the painter's art; she merely notes down the objects that meet her eyes: a chair here, an easel there; on the wall a framed picture; a statuette on a bracket. . . . It's as dry as a bailiff's inventory! "

I should have no right to complain of such a method —I myself have always scrupulously refrained from playing the critic—but it cannot even be said to be Miss Stein's. She gives us far more than a frigid enumeration. For instance, incapable though I am of putting a name to any character in a *roman à clef*, in the silhouette Miss Stein has drawn of me I recognised myself at once, as the fellow leaning with both hands on the doorposts, glaring at the passers-by as though he were calling down curses on them. That is a thing *seen*. How many times have I not regretted that nature has not endowed me with an easy-going, jovial manner!

Another American collector:

Mr. Barnes comes to see you. He gets you to show him twenty or thirty pictures. Unhesitatingly, as they pass before him, he picks out this or that one. Then he goes away.

[1] *The Autobiography of Alice B. Toklas*, Chapter II.

In this expeditious fashion, which only a taste as sure as his made possible, Mr. Barnes brought together the incomparable collection which is the pride of Philadelphia.

Another American collector to whom artists owed a great deal was Mr. John Quinn. During the War, Mr. John Quinn busied himself generously in making the United States purchase the works of French painters. A lawyer of repute, he placed his legal knowledge at their service as well. He intervened in particular, and not without success, in their differences with the American Customs. An example of these disputes was the action brought against the sculptor Marcoussis on the subject of a bronze, entitled *Oiseau*, which the Customs officials declared to be a piece of raw metal. They suspected a trick to escape the duty payable on unworked metal.

In another case, during the course of a discussion at the American Consulate as to the difference between artistic and industrial work:

" Would you mind standing up? " said the painter Georges Rouault to an official in whose office he happened to be.

The astonished official stood up.

" Look at your chair. The wooden disc on which you sit is pierced with holes. They are all identical; that is industrial work. If those holes had been made with a hand tool, no two would be alike. That is the difference between the work of art and the work of a machine."

Mary Cassatt once said to me:

" I've been talking to Mr. Havemeyer about you. So do put all your best things aside for him. You know who I mean by Havemeyer? "

Did I know! Havemeyer, the sugar king! Only a little while before I had read in the papers that a serious drop in sugar having occurred in the American market while Mr. Havemeyer was away, the latter had rushed back to New York, and his return had sufficed to restore sugar to its former firmness. The sugar king! While selecting the pictures I thought worthy of being submitted to him, I kept saying to myself, " If I had his power I would dazzle the world not by my magnificence, but by the simplicity of my life. For instance, I wouldn't have a yacht. I wouldn't have special trains made up for me. I wouldn't hire an entire palace. I wouldn't encumber myself with a numerous staff, as it appears the magnates of petroleum, cocoa, paper and chewing-gum do." I had got thus far in my meditations when a very shabby cab (it was in 1898) stopped at my door. A gentleman, very simply dressed, got out and entered the shop. I cursed the intruder. Suppose Mr. Havemeyer were to arrive suddenly, and I had to keep him waiting while I sold an engraving perhaps! As a matter of fact, it was some Cézannes that the stranger wanted to see. He chose two, and gave me his card. It was Mr. Havemeyer.

What surprised me even more than the unpretentious garb of this wealthy client, was the spirit of strict economy he showed in everyday life. On his travels his staff consisted of a lady's-maid for his wife. I even heard the latter mention a ticklish piece of mending she had to do. Mr. Havemeyer, whom I accompanied one day when he was going to see a picture, stopped outside the Opéra Comique, saying:

" I have to buy some tickets. I am going to the theatre this evening with my wife and a friend."

When we got to the booking-office:

" Three orchestra stalls," demanded the sugar king.

" Everything is taken, monsieur, we have only boxes left."

" Give me three box tickets."

" The boxes we have left have four seats, and we don't let them separately."

" Very well. I'll come back some other time."

And turning to me: " You see, there are only three of us; I should have paid for one seat for nothing."

This is not to say that Mr. Havemeyer could not spend large sums upon occasion. He could be extravagant now and then, but he liked to feel the extravagance was justified. This was not the case when I offered him two Cézannes, one being the portrait the artist painted of his sister, which is so curiously like an El Greco. Mme Havemeyer had been arrested by this picture.

" How much? "

" Ten thousand francs."

" Why ten thousand, when you are only asking seven for the other picture, which is just as important as this? " she asked.

" It's true," I said, " the two pictures are equal in a sense. But you must admit that in the portrait of the sister there is that indefinable thing, *le charme*."

" So you want me to pay extra for LA *charme*? " said Mr. Havemeyer.

Not long after, the picture was purchased by another king of industry, a French king this time, the king of margarine, M. Auguste Pellerin. When she heard of the sale, Mrs. Havemeyer could not help reproaching her husband with having let the Cézanne slip. To make up for it, on the evening of her birthday, Mr. Havemeyer came home with a Lawrence.

" Do you really like this picture? " his wife asked him. " It seems to me so very inferior to the Lawrence we were offered the other day."

" I know it is," replied the sugar king, " but this picture was such a bargain at a hundred thousand francs! "

But careful and calculating though he was, and on his guard against LA *charme*, Mr. Havemeyer was himself not proof against a sudden infatuation.

One day I was showing him some pictures.

" How much is that Cézanne? " he asked all at once, looking at the *Aqueduc aux pins parasols*.

" Fifteen thousand francs."

" I'll have it."

Then, as though to excuse his haste in buying it, he said, turning to his wife:

" Doesn't the background remind you of the fresco we admired so much at Pompeii? "

He went on gazing at the Cézanne, murmuring:

" I wonder what there is in it that reminds one of so many things? "

Mr. Havemeyer was usually advised in his purchases by Mary Cassatt. She had persuaded him that he could make no better use of his money, since his pictures were to enrich the artistic heritage of the United States. I particularly remember two pictures by Goya that she made him buy when he was on a trip through Spain: a woman with a ring on her finger, and, best of all, *The Balcony*.

I said to an American lady, a client of mine:

" If this goes on, we shall soon be obliged to go to America to see the best European pictures."

" That's true. . . . We can buy . . ."

" Yes, you'll be able to fill your skyscrapers with them; but what you haven't got is a house that goes back even so far as four or five hundred years."

The American lady looked thoughtful for a moment.

" An old house? " she said. " But that's quite easy; I can buy one and take it over with me to America."

" Of course you can carry off a heap of stones; but the soul of the house, can you take that with you too? "

" The soul of the house? What is that? "

" If you prefer it, the atmosphere with which it is suffused, the site with which it is incorporated, and from which it is inseparable, everything that gives it its peculiar character, its charm, its face so to speak; the very moss, for instance, that makes the roof green every spring. Those are things you cannot transplant. You may remove the house; but no matter where you take it, it will look like a stranger in a foreign land."

Three months later my American invited me to her country house in the neighbourhood of Paris. I was very fond of the place, with its wide views from the verandahs of the house. But what a shock I got that day! An enormous building—an old château of some sort—had sprung up, obstructing the entire view.

"Oh! dear Madame! How awful to have this in your way! After the marvellous view you used to have!"

The American smiled.

"You were talking to me about houses four or five hundred years old. Well, that castle is eight hundred and forty years old, guaranteed on the bill. It was quite easy to get. I just telephoned to my agent: 'I want a château eight hundred years old. Buy.' And in no time the men were at work digging up and pulling down, and numbering the stones. And I said the tiles were to have their moss on them too. Come and look. . . ."

And she carried me off.

"Don't tell me my château isn't very fine!"

"Obviously it must have looked very fine where it was. But don't you think yourself that it looks very unhappy at finding itself here?"

"Of course it hasn't got—what was it you called it?—its atmosphere. We call that the architecture of the site. Well, we've thought of that too. All our plans are laid, and once the château is in America . . ."

"What! Are you going to have it retransported over there?"

"I must. I did mean to keep it here. I was going to send another to America, an older one still. I've been offered a still older one, guaranteed on the bill. But, you see, I sent the photograph of this castle to my son James. James goes in for art, and he thinks it's just too fascinating! He wants this one and no other. He can't come to France, because he's seasick. So I've promised to send the castle to America. It's just as easy as moving it here. Once the stones are numbered and packed in boxes, the dear old place could go round the world. But it had to come here first. I'm giving a party, with a sort of play staged in an old *castel*. As soon as the show is over, the whole thing will be taken down, numbered and repacked; and my architect has given me a written engagement that in five and a half months from then the château will be put up again on James's estate, on the shores of Lake Michigan."

After a pause the American continued:

" And as for what you call atmosphere . . . the architect has got hold of the wind that blows over there, and the song of the nightingale, and the chirping of the little crickets and the sound of the Angelus bell."

Calling a servant, she made him bring her a phonograph, from which the above-mentioned noises were heard to issue.

" The wind isn't a success," said the American apologetically; " I've ordered them to register it again."

XVII GERMAN CRITICS AND COL-LECTORS

It is a fact that any new thing born of the French genius meets with indifference, not to say hostility, at home.

Any audacity is regarded with suspicion, whether it be in literature, music or painting. With regard to modern painting I have related the obstacles Manet, Cézanne, Degas, Renoir, Gauguin and the rest had to surmount before they made any impression on their countrymen. A singularly paradoxical situation: the Frenchman, who is argumentative by temperament, becomes a conservative when confronted by any new trend in art, so great is his need of certainty, and so afraid is he of being taken in. The German, on the contrary, while bowing instinctively to anything in the way of collective discipline, yet gives enthusiastic support to every anticipation of the future.

Take Paul Cassirer with his Berlin Gallery, that might be a prolongation of the rue Laffitte, and the famous Berlin painter Liebermann, who hangs our finest Impressionists on the walls of his studio; take the directors of the National Museums, always at work enriching their collections, and the most famous of the Berlin collectors, who are to be seen at the big sales at the Hôtel Drouot, sending up the prices of the whole modern school as well as of its glorious predecessors, Ingres, Corot, Delacroix. It has always been so, since the days of the great Frederick himself, who held our Watteau in such esteem.

Then there are the German art critics, such as

Meier Graefe, who fought so often and so courageously for the triumph of French art. Right in the middle of the War there was an exhibition of German book-binding in Switzerland, and there, clothed in the most sumptuous morocco, were my editions of *Parallèlement* and *Daphnis et Chloë*, illustrated by Bonnard, which the bibliophiles across the Rhine had piously welcomed at the very time when my publications found so little favour in France. On this occasion Meier Graefe said unhesitatingly in the *Frankfurter Zeitung* that a book like *Daphnis et Chloë*, in which everything was so perfectly balanced—paper, type and illustrations—could never be achieved in Germany. "Nor by anyone else in France either," he added, as if to excuse his own country. But the books Bonnard illustrated later proved him wrong in this.

When my edition of *Daphnis et Chloë* came out in 1902, Count Kessler puffed the book most ardently among his friends. He even acquired such a taste for fine editions that he decided to publish a book him-self, destined to be followed by many others. The book was printed on a paper manufactured by Maillol himself: the famous *papier de Montval*. And when the artist said one day that he was afraid the linen might preserve traces of the chloride used in the bleaching, and that the paper made from it might turn yellow, Count Kessler thought nothing of going himself into the depths of Hungary to get linen made by peasant women who did not know the use of chloride.

Speaking of M. Kessler, I remember a dinner-party to which he had also invited a very pretty German Baroness, whose name I forget. It was at the *Tour d'Argent*, a restaurant which, in spite of being so much frequented by foreigners, had preserved a thoroughly French character. It is true that wherever there is good wine one feels one is in France; and the cellars of the *Tour d'Argent* enjoyed a great reputation. I can still see the head waiter, the famous Frédéric, bowing before the Baroness, and congratulating himself on meeting the granddaughter of Count Münster, whom he had often had the honour of serving. I had felt a certain apprehension at the idea of the *canard au sang* (I don't like the sight of blood) for which the establishment was famous, but I must confess I thought it very good. There was only one fly in the ointment: I like head waiters to be clean-shaven and to have short hair. Now, Frédéric's hair was long, and he was very stubbly about the chin.

There was also a distinguished German among the guests, a Baron von Bodenhausen. He was a tall, powerful fellow whom I could better have imagined in officer's uniform, sword in hand, marching his men at the goose-step. Count Kessler had converted Baron von Bodenhausen to modern art, so I had occasion to see him several times at my shop. One day we were talking of Frémiet's statue of Jeanne d'Arc, and my brother reminded us of Michelet's saying, that the real miracle accomplished by Jeanne d'Arc was the reconcilement of all the French in the face of the enemy. At these words Baron von Bodenhausen, who was admiring a Cézanne, turned round all of a piece and shot an angry glance at my brother. I said to myself, " Why should he take offence at the name of Jeanne d'Arc? After all, he's not an Englishman." When the War broke out in 1914 I understood Baron von Bodenhausen's annoyance at the bare idea of the reconciliation of the French in the face of the enemy.

And now, to give some idea of the mentality of my German customers, here is an amusing trait.

One day a couple came to my shop, asking to see my Gauguins. All at once the lady discovered she had lost her hatpin, and asked if there was a shop in the neighbourhood where she could get another. " We have a *Bazaar* near here," I replied, " my servant will take you there." When they returned, the maid took me aside and said, " Monsieur had better be careful. The lady found a pin she liked very much, but when she saw the price she said, ' One franc ninety-five! That's too dear,' and she took one at eighteen sous." Yet those were the people who bought a hundred and fifteen thousand francs' worth of pictures from me.

XVIII BEFORE MANET'S *OLYMPIA* AT THE LOUVRE

One day at the Louvre I saw a visitor standing before Manet's *Olympia*, in whom I recognised the painter Charles Toché. I went up to him and reminded him that I had often heard him speak of his relations with Manet.

" How did you come to know him? " I asked.

" I was in Venice, eating an ice at the Café Florian, when the great painter, whose elegant figure was familiar to me, came and sat down near by. His wife was with him, and I was struck by her majestic bearing. Her sunshade fell down and I stooped to pick it up. Manet thanked me: ' I see you're a Frenchman. *Mon Dieu*, how this place bores me.' Madame Manet smiled at me. Her rosy, childish face beamed from under an enormous hat. ' Edouard likes joking,' she said. ' He's playing the Parisian.' "

" M. Toché, tell me about that famous picture of Manet's, *Les Pieux du Grand Canal*."

" I shall not forget Manet's enthusiasm for that motif: the white marble staircase against the faded pink of the bricks of the façade, and the cadmium and greens of the basements. Oscillations of light and shade made by the passing barges in the rough water, that drew from him the exclamation, ' Champagne bottle-ends floating! ' Through the row of gigantic twisted posts, blue and white, one saw the domes of the incomparable *Salute*, dear to Guardi. ' I shall put in a gondola,' cried Manet, ' steered by a boatman in a pink shirt, with an orange scarf—one of those fine dark chaps like a Moor of Granada.' Some of the guests of the villa Medicis were listening to Manet from a neighbouring boat. At these last words they sniggered. I heard the word ' *pompier.* ' "

" There is a story in the Bible of children who laughed at a prophet and were devoured by a bear. A marine monster should have arisen from the depths of the canals . . ."

" Oh, well! it came to the same thing in the end. The Bear Oblivion has devoured the painters of that period, in which Manet said he felt like a dog with a tin can tied to its tail."

" Evidently," said I, " Manet bore the jeers of his contemporaries with more philosophy than Cézanne, who was known to say, ' Don't they know I'm Cézanne? ' "

" That depends. Mme Manet told me that a great, or rather a famous, art critic, a friend of the family, had once been so bold as to refer ironically to one of her husband's pictures in the Press. Two days later, Manet went out early, saying he was going to do a sketch in the Bois de Boulogne. On his return he announced that he had just run his sword through the wag's shoulder."

We sat down to chat at our leisure.

" To come back to that picture of the Venetian barge-posts," said M. Toché. " When the picture was finished, I was really astounded. One could not imagine anything more true, better situated in the atmosphere. Replying to a remark of mine, ' It was not at school,' Manet said, ' that I learnt to construct a picture. On my first day at Couture's they gave me an antique to draw from. I turned it about in every direction. It seemed to me most interesting head downwards. Anyway, after two or three attempts I gave up trying to get anything out of the antique. But I learnt a great deal during my voyage to Brazil. I spent night after night watching the play of light and shade in the wake of the ship. During the day I watched the line of the horizon. That taught me how to plan out a sky.' "

" How did Manet paint? I remember Cézanne saying, ' Manet spatters his tones on to the canvas.' "

" That expresses it. It was not at all a linear process, but with rapid individual touches he scattered shadows, lights, reflections over the canvas with astonishing sureness, and his lay-out was made.

" I remember dining with him in a little restaurant opposite the Giudecca. The table was laid in an arbour covered with vines. A little opening in this arbour framed the lovely church of San Salvatore, whose pink tones contrasted with the glaucous green of the water and the black spindle-shapes of the gondolas. Manet observed and analysed the different colours taken on by each object as the light faded. He defined their values and told us how he would try to reproduce them, steeped in this ashy twilight greyness. Suddenly he got up, and taking his paint-box and a little canvas, he ran down to the quay. There, with a few strokes of the brush, he set up the distant church."

" Any picture by Manet certainly suggests brush-strokes put down definitely, once for all."

" Wait a bit! That was what I thought before I had seen him at work. Then I discovered how he laboured, on the contrary, to obtain what he wanted. The *Pieux du Grand Canal* itself was begun I know not how many times. The gondola and gondolier held him up an incredible time. ' It's the devil,' he said, ' to suggest that a hat is stuck firmly on a head, or that a boat is built of planks cut and fitted according to geometrical laws! ' "

I could have listened all day to M. Toché.

" One day," he went on, " I was expatiating on the possibility of combining poetry and reality in a picture, when Manet exclaimed, ' If that ass of a Courbet were to hear you ! His idea of reality was . . .

Well, look at his *Burial at Ornans*, for instance, in which he has succeeded in burying everybody, priests, gravediggers, mourners and all. The horizon itself is six feet underground.' "

" Really, was Manet so hard on Courbet? What did he think of his fellow Impressionists? "

" Monet alone found favour with him. He called Cézanne ' a bricklayer who paints with his trowel.' And Renoir he looked upon as a decent sort of chap who had taken up painting by mistake."

A few days later, M. Toché and I met again.

" You tell me you often had the chance of seeing Manet at work? " I said, eager to hear more.

" In Venice I used to go and join him almost every day. The lagoons, the palaces, the old houses, scaled and mellowed by time, offered him an inexhaustible variety of subjects. But his preference was for out-of-the-way corners. I asked him if I might follow him in my gondola. ' As much as you like,' he told me. ' When I am working, I pay no attention to anything but my subject.' Now and then he would make a gesture of annoyance that set his boat rocking, and I would see his palette knife scraping away with ferocity. But all at once I would hear the refrain of a song, or a few notes whistled gaily. Then Manet would call out to me, ' I'm getting on, I'm getting on! When things are going well, I have to express my pleasure aloud.' "

" M. Toché, how do you account for Manet, the bantering Parisian, the true *boulevardier*, having such a passion for Spain and Italy? "

" He liked Spain much the better of the two. ' Spain,' he said to me one day, ' is so simple, so grandiose, so dramatic with its stones and its green-black trees. Venice, when all is said, is merely scenery.' "

" But the great Venetian painters . . ."

" One morning I was looking with him at the *Glory*

of Venice, by Veronese, in the Ducal Palace. ' There's something about that that leaves one cold,' he said. ' So much useless effort, so much wasted space in it. Not a shadow of an emotion. I like the Carpaccios, they have the naïve grace of illuminations in missals. And I rank highest of all the Titians and Tintorettos of the *Scuola di San Rocco*. But I always come back, you know, to Velasquez and Goya.' "

" What did he think of Tiepolo? "

" Tiepolo irritated him. ' These Italians bore one after a time,' he would say, ' with their allegories and their *Gerusalemme Liberata* and *Orlando Furioso*, and all that noisy rubbish. A painter can say all he wants to with fruits or flowers, or even clouds.'

" I remember wandering with him round the stalls of the *Pescheria Vecchia*, under the bridge of the Rialto. Manet was intoxicated by light. He bubbled over with delight at the sight of the enormous fish with their silver bellies. ' That,' he cried, ' is what I should have liked to paint if the Conseil Municipal of Paris had not refused my decorative scheme for the Hôtel de Ville. You know, I should like to be the St. Francis of still life.' Another time we went to the vegetable market. Manet, a slender figure in blue, his straw hat tilted to the back of his head, went striding over the heaps of provisions and vegetables. He stopped suddenly before a row of pumpkins, the kind that grows only on the shores of the Brenta. ' Turks' heads in turbans! ' he cried. ' Trophies from the victories of Lepanto and Corfu! '

" When Manet had been working hard, he would set out, by way of relaxation, to ' discover ' Venice. Madame Manet would accompany him, and they would wander through the most tortuous of the little streets, or, taking the first gondola that came, explore the narrow *canaletti*. Manet was mad on old tumble-down houses, with rags hanging from the windows, catching the light. He would stop to look at the

handsome shock-headed girls, bare-necked, in their
flowered gowns, who sat at their doors stringing beads
from Murano or knitting stockings of vivid colours.
In the fishing quarter, at San Pietro di Castello, he
would stop before the great piles topped with enormous eel-pots made of withies, that the light turned
to amethyst. He marvelled at the children, burnt
golden by the sun, shaking off their fleas on the crumb-
ling steps of the old staircases and quarrelling among
themselves, their faces smeared with polenta and
water-melon. The afternoon would end up with
visits to the second-hand dealers, in whose miserable
booths there was no hint of the sumptuous antique
shops that were to arise on the same sites fifty years
later. Nothing delighted him so much as to ferret
out an old piece of lace, a finely-worked jewel, a
valuable engraving.

" He would often arrange to meet me during the
evening. Venice is particularly pleasant in the
evening, and Manet liked going out after dinner.
He became talkative on these occasions, and did not
scruple to tease Mme Manet in my presence, usually
on the subject of her family, and particularly of her
father, a typical Dutch *bourgeois*, sullen, fault-finding,
thrifty, and incapable of understanding an artist.
But a fisherman had only to start singing a barcarolle,
or a guitar to throb, and instantly Manet would fall
silent, caught by the charm of nocturnal Venice. His
wife, who was an excellent pianist, expressed the
delight it would be to her to play Schubert, Chopin or
Schumann in such surroundings. So with her consent
I laid a little plot. One evening after dinner I invited
her and her husband to come for a trip on the water.
I had our boat rowed towards a canal beside the Bridge
of Sighs. There a wide barge was moored, of the
kind used for household removals. I had had a
piano put aboard her, concealed by rugs, and Mme
Manet, as arranged, had been complaining of the

rocking of our gondola, and I suggested we should get into this other boat, which was much steadier. We started off in the direction of San Giorgio Maggiore. Suddenly, under Mme Manet's fingers, a melody arose. It was a romance of Schumann's. That moment, Manet told us later, left him with the most delicious impression of his whole stay in Venice."

"What a relaxation Venice must have been for Manet, after the busy life of Paris!"

"In Venice he thought of nothing but painting. What a number of plans he made that were never to be realised! There was that Sunday in September, for instance, when I accompanied him to Mestre, where regattas were being held in the lagoon. Each racing gondola, with its rowers clad in blue and white, seemed a fold of an immense serpent. Lying on the cushions of our boat, a rug over his knees, one hand dragging in the water, Manet, from under his wife's parasol, described to us the plan of a picture he would like to paint of this regatta. Manet, who was considered an extravagant innovator at the École des Beaux Arts, had thought out this composition according to such classical rules that the statement he made of it to us would, I fancy, have delighted Poussin. I noted down with the greatest care the incomparable lesson that I had just heard.[1]

[1] This is the note, which M. Toché kindly allowed me to copy:

I. With a scene like this, so disconcerting and so complicated, I must first select the characteristic episode, delimit my picture by an imaginary frame. The most salient things here are the masts with their multi-coloured bunting, the green, white and red of the Italian flag, the dark, undulating line of the barges laden with spectators, and the arrow-like line of the black-and-white gondolas fading away into the distance, with, at the top of the picture, the line of the water, the goal set for the races and the ethereal islands.

II. I shall first try to distinguish the different values as they build themselves up logically according to their several planes in the atmosphere.

III.   The lagoon, mirror of the sky, is the parvis of the barges

" This must have been one of the last things Manet enjoyed in Venice. Not long afterwards he came to my room early one morning, and I was struck by his dejected air.

" ' I have been recalled to Paris,' he told me. ' My life here was too pleasant, I suppose. Who knows what fresh worries await me over there? ' I accompanied my delightful new friends to the station. On the way, Manet gazed once more, intently, at the Grand Canal, the rose-coloured palaces, the old weathered houses, the gigantic piles looking like bagwigs as they emerged from the slight fog. Up to the moment when he got into the train, Manet said not a word."

" But you saw him again in Paris? "

---

and their passengers, of the masts, pennants, etc. It has its own colour—tints borrowed from the sky, the clouds, the crowd and the other objects reflected in it. There can be no question of wire-drawn lines in a moving thing such as this, but only of values which, rightly observed, will constitute the real volume, the unquestionable design.

IV. The gondolas, the various barges with their mainly sombre colouring, and their reflections, constitute the foundation I shall lay on my parvis of the water.

V. The figures, seated or gesticulating, dressed in dark or brilliant colours, their parasols, their kerchiefs, their hats, form the crenelations, of differing values, which will provide the necessary foil and give their true character to the planes and the gondolas which I shall see through them.

VI. The crowd, the competitors, the flags, the masts, will be built up into a mosaic of bright colours. I must try to catch the instantaneousness of the gestures, the shiver of the flags, the rocking of the masts.

VII. On the horizon, far up, the Islands. . . . The sails in the furthest distance will be merely hinted at in their delicate, accurate colouring.

VIII. Lastly, the sky, like an immense glittering canopy, will envelop the whole scene, playing its light over figures and objects.

IX. The painting must be light and direct. No tricks; and you will pray the God of good and honest painters to come to your aid.

" I did not come back to France till four years later. Then I went to see him in his studio in the rue de St.-Pétersbourg. Everything there was of a monkish simplicity—not a useless piece of furniture, not a knick-knack, but everywhere the most brilliant studies on the walls and easels. At the end of the room, on the mantelpiece, a plaster cat, with a pipe in its mouth."

" Had not Manet another studio in the rue d'Amsterdam? "

" Yes, a most picturesque one, in a sunny courtyard. You came in by a vestibule whose walls were smothered in a profusion of sketches. On a number of little tables there were bunches of flowers arranged in water-bottles or ordinary tumblers. The well-known portrait of Antonin Proust stood on an easel. Studies of women in light-coloured dresses, with big hats on their heads, were ranged along the wooden staircase, painted red, which led to the studio proper. Sheets of paper, covered with strokes of charcoal or pastel, covered the floor. On the walls were some big pictures half begun. A horsewoman's black hat standing out from the white canvas, a horse's head with an anxious eye, a pink sunshade, and so forth. Like certain sketches by Velasquez and Goya, these gave me a sensation of vibration and of life that the finished picture does not always produce."

" Did you see Manet during the last years of his life? "

" A few weeks before his death I went to the rue d'Amsterdam. I found the great artist alone, sad and ill. ' I am working,' he said, ' because one must live.' When I assured him that all lovers of painting believed in him as much as ever, ' Splendid! ' he replied. ' But alas! can faith without works be considered a sincere faith? It is true that my tailor admires me! And then there is Faure. How they slated me for the portrait I did of him as Hamlet!

They said the left leg was too short. But when a figure is rushing forward, how can the two legs be like those of an infantryman standing at attention? And the sloping floor? By Jove, I'd like to know what the official drawing-masters would do to give the illusion of Hamlet running towards the spectator.' Manet had risen. He shrugged his shoulders, rammed his flat-brimmed hat on his head, and said to me, with a smile that drew up the corners of his moustache, 'Let's drop all that! We'll go and have something at Tortoni's.' He felt one of his pockets. 'Good!' he said, 'I have my sketch-book. There's always something to jot down in the street. Look here.' And he showed me a charming study of legs, pinned to the wall. 'A waiter was opening a syphon the other day, at the café. A little woman was going by. Instinctively she picked up her skirt.' "

XIX THE STUDIOS OF MEISSONIER AND OTHERS

(a) *Meissonier*.

I was at Lewis Brown's when someone turned up, with a picture under his arm.

" Another find? " asked Lewis Brown.

" Wait and see."

The new-comer unwrapped the picture and said: " What do you think of this study of horses? "

Brown looked at it.

" You think it's a Meissonier? "

" Just so. And I've been mad to find out for certain, ever since I fished it out yesterday at the *foire du Trône*. It isn't signed, but still . . . My wife's quite crazy about it! "

" I didn't know your wife was interested in painting."

" She knows a lot about its value. At Georges Petit's she saw a Meissonier that wasn't up to this one, and they wanted fifty thousand for it. . . . What a pity there aren't a few figures in it besides the horses! "

" I wonder . . ." murmured Lewis Brown. " Supposing your *machin* was not by Meissonier? "

" You don't mean it? "

" I'm giving no opinion either away. At first sight, from the way the paint's put on, and the drawing . . . I should be tempted to say it was. But we can soon make sure. Come along to Meissonier. He is a very decent chap. If your picture is by him, I will ask him to sign it."

I expressed a wish to see this famous painter's studio.

159

" That's easy enough.   Come with us."

On arriving at Meissonier's, we were asked to wait. On an easel there was an almost finished painting; and underneath it hung a great magnifying-glass as though inviting the visitor to examine the fineness of the work.

My attention was soon attracted by the strange task which was being performed in a corner of the studio by one of the Master's pupils.   Armed with a rake like a croupier's, he was engaged in levelling, on the floor, a layer of sparkling white powder that looked like boracic acid.

" I'm preparing," he said to Lewis Brown, " the field of battle that M. Meissonier is about to paint."

He opened a box and took out guns, little trees, ammunition-wagons, soldiers and horses, that he ranged in battle formation in the frosted square. Taking a spray, he pressed the rubber bulb and projected a cloud of liquid gum over the whole of the little army, which he dusted afterwards with a powder of a duller white.

To Lewis Brown, who was looking on with curiosity, he said:

" How difficult it is to mix gum arabic rightly! If there's too much, the spray won't work.   If there is not enough, the rice powder won't stay on."

" Is that rice powder? "

" One could use boracic acid everywhere, of course. It would even be simpler to have only one white instead of two.   But the Master likes tackling difficulties."

Meissonier came in:

" Brrr! " he said, casting a glance at the work of his assistant, " what a fine winter landscape!   It almost makes my fingers ache. . . . Ah!   The brutes! "

Two big flies, fascinated by all this white, had settled on one of the cannons.   From a little table

Meissonier took a sort of revolver. He aimed at the insects, and fired. A chemical odour diffused itself.

Meissonier turned to Lewis Brown.

" When I painted my *Retreat from Russia,* instead of boracic acid I used caster sugar. What an effect of snow I obtained! But it attracted the bees from a neighbouring hive. So I replaced the sugar by flour. And then the mice came and ravaged my battle-field, and I had to finish my picture from imagination! It almost looked as though I should have to wait for the snow to fall if I wanted to paint a winter land-scape."

" Monet," said Lewis Brown with an ingenuous air, " can only paint from nature."

Meissonier made a peremptory gesture:

" Don't talk to me of your Monet and all the gang of the *jeunes.* The other day I saw a picture by someone called Besnard in which there were violet-coloured horses. Let us talk seriously."

" Let us talk of your art, my dear Master," said Lewis Brown. " I have come to see you, as a matter of fact, on the subject of a picture which might be by you, and which has been found by my friend S . . ."

Meissonier looked at S . . ., then at the painting, and said:

" I congratulate you! You've got hold of a very good thing. It is actually one of the best imitations of a Meissonier that I have seen. Just a little some-thing more, and I should be taken in myself."

I put in timidly:

" But it is that ' little something ' which constitutes genius."

The Master smiled at me. He returned the picture to the disappointed purchaser, and patting him on the shoulder, said:

" Don't take it to heart! As it is, the picture is very good. It is quite worth a good Detaille."

M

(b) *A Visit to Gervex.*

Gervex had been associated with the principal painters of his time, particularly Manet. He had also lived a long while in Russia, where he had been received at Court, and I imagined he must have brought back a number of interesting recollections. I was soon disappointed, for Gervex had preserved hardly any. But I found the man himself such agreeable company that I was delighted when he invited me to come and see him again.

One day in his studio I met a very elegant person who began to talk at length of " his " art. Like Gervex, he was a Commander of the Legion of Honour. From his tone of assurance I imagined at first that he must also belong to the " Institut." But from Gervex's introduction, I learnt that he was that very individual painter of armour and textiles, M. Jacquet. Going up to an easel on which stood the life-size portrait of a woman in a muslin dress, so transparent that she appeared almost naked:

" A lovely skin," said M. Jacquet. " The man who has that on the wall of his bedroom will be able to do without a woman in his bed."

" That," said Gervex, " is the portrait of the wife of one of my admirers."

" The deuce! " said the other. " He doesn't have a bad time of it, that admirer of yours. And he allowed her to sit like that? "

" It is not her body. I merely did a little study of her head; my model sat for the rest."

" And your *amateur* was pleased? "

" Rather! He asked me at once for the model's address."

Gervex appeared to be cogitating. He continued:

" I feel perpetually torn between truth to nature and decorative effect. And nature always wins the day. What one needs is honesty. And when one has conscientiously put down what one sees—as I have done here—the picture will assume a decorative value as well."

"That's jolly well not the case with your friend Clairin," said Jacquet. "I have just seen a *Nude* that he is putting the finishing touches to . . ."

Gervex (*indulgently*): "Clairin is not without talent, and if he did not waste so much time in society . . ."

"He's working, you know, at the moment, at a portrait of Sarah Bernhardt: his concierge is sitting for it, in some of the actress's old clothes. 'I am incapable of doing anything out of my head,' he said to me, when I looked in during the sitting."

"I suppose," said Gervex, "he didn't show you, at the same time, a study of Sarah that he once began, and then abandoned? A Sarah in something of the pose of the *Olympia*, also with a negress, a bouquet and a cat; only Clairin's cat is white."

"When I was in the Louvre the other day," replied Jacquet, "I passed by the *Olympia*. Between our-selves, if a woman like that were to walk the streets, one wouldn't give her three francs. But, by the by, Gervex, wasn't it you who put that chap's foot in the stirrup, by getting him into the Salon?"

"Let us be fair. When Manet started painting, he had such marvellous greys. Of course, if you compare him with Velasquez and Goya . . ."

"I had a good look at the Velasquez on my last journey to Madrid. Don't you think one might go one better than that? Imagine a painter with the reds of Carolus, the bluish-white of Henner, and for arma-ture the drawing of a Jean-Paul Laurens . . ."

He was interrupted by the arrival of Mme Madeleine Lemaire. After the usual salaams, she turned to M. Jacquet, saying:

"I was with your friend Lobre a minute ago. He told me you had just got an important commission from a rich silk merchant. My congratulations!"

" It's for a replica of the picture I got my gold medal for, in the old days. Would you believe it, my client's mistress considers that in my painting to-day I make concessions to Impressionism! And yet she's quite an intelligent woman."

" Yes," put in Gervex, " she has a fine bottom. . . ."

" So now," said Jacquet, " I shall have to fish out all my bitumens, all the messes I used to daub on my canvases in the old days."

I could not help thinking of Picasso, to whom I had passed on a request for a replica of one of his earlier pictures, *L'Enfant au Pigeon.*

It was in the days when his pictures would not sell, and the price offered was a substantial one. But Picasso looked at me in surprise.

" But I should have no pleasure in copying my own work, and how do you suppose I can paint without enjoyment? "

Another day, when I got to Gervex's, I found him quite upset, as the result of a singular adventure. Two days earlier, during dinner, the maid had come in to say that " someone wanted to see Monsieur."

" Tell him to come back to-morrow," said the painter.

But he changed his mind, thinking it might be an American, and told her to show the visitor into the studio, whither he betook himself.

Twenty minutes passed and Mme Gervex, feeling anxious, went into the studio. She saw her husband at bay in a corner of the room, and in front of him an individual armed with a cudgel, shouting:

" I shall not go away till you have taught me to draw."

With great *sang-froid* Mme Gervex said to her husband:

" Why won't you teach Monsieur to draw? "

And turning to the stranger:

" Only, Monsieur, you must first put your name down. The register is in the concierge's lodge."

They all three went downstairs. Mme Gervex made the visitor, now very meek, go in front of her. All at once he made a dash for the *porte-cochère* and vanished.

Next day, the police having been informed, an *agent* kept careful watch before the building.

Towards evening the peculiar stranger again presented himself, and they tried to arrest him; but he succeeded in escaping. Running after him, they came up with him in a hovel, where an old woman cried out on seeing them:

" My God! What has he done now, Monsieur l'agent? My boy hasn't got all his wits about him, but he's quite harmless; it's only when he is crossed that he gets angry."

Gervex, however, was not satisfied with this assurance, and the concierge was given instructions accordingly. So that a few days later when Forain came to call on Mme Gervex, he was held up and informed, " If Monsieur has come for the drawing course, it is suspended till further orders."

(c) *Henry de Groux.*

I met the Belgian painter Henry de Groux at his fellow-countryman's, Félicien Rops. De Groux had just exhibited, in the " Salon des Indépendants," his astonishing picture, *Robbers of the Dead after the Battle of Waterloo*. The man was tremendously picturesque. With his frock coat, his felt hat with its wide flat brim, his red neckcloth, the gold rings in his ears, he was just like some character of Balzac's. He cared for nothing but painting. He would have painted no matter where, in a garret, in a cellar. He was all his life the prey of colour-merchants, frame-makers, all the artisans and tradesmen connected with painting. They furnished him with the paints, canvases and

frames he needed, but they carried off his pictures as
security.   When he had pledged a canvas at which he
wished to go on working, he was obliged to run off now
to the frame-maker, now to the colourman or the
stretcher-maker, and beg his creditor for a corner to sit
and paint in.

He was as simple as a child.   He had only to be
told that so-and-so bought pictures, and he would rush
off at once to one of the detainers of his works, and
announce joyously, " I've found a purchaser for my
picture! "

But it might happen that other creditors besides the
depositary had rights to the picture, and each of
them wished to be present at the negotiations.   In
which case the presumptive buyer would be visited
by Henry de Groux wreathed in smiles, with a painting under his arm, followed by the representatives of
the frame-maker, the colourman and the stretcher-
maker. . . .

If the affair failed—and it failed almost invariably—
de Groux bore no grudge to anyone.   At most, upon
leaving the house, he would turn towards the windows
of the *amateur* and, taking his bodyguard to witness,
exclaim:

" That chap is a dirty dog!   I should have hated to
think my picture was in his house."

But a man cannot live on invectives.   In his days
of penury de Groux would remember that he had
friends.   He would take a fiacre and go and try to
touch them.   He was lucky if, at the end of his collection, he had enough to pay the cabman, without
having to leave him his famous silver-headed walking-
stick in pawn.

Speaking of this walking-stick, I really thought one
day that de Groux had suddenly gone mad.   I was
strolling with him near the Palais Royal.   All at
once he flung himself upon a passer-by and snatched
away the walking-stick that he was carrying under his

arm. The man ran off with de Groux after him, lashing him on the back and arms. A few moments later he came back, quite out of breath.

" The fellow had stolen my walking-stick. But I was sure I should find it again! "

His optimism never deserted him. He found himself one day at Marseilles without a halfpenny in his pocket. He was standing in ecstasy before the gateway of an old hôtel, when someone came out and accosted him.

" You are looking at my door? I am the owner of the house. Would you like to look over it? "

De Groux pleased his host so much that the latter entertained him for several months. When they parted, a little tired of each other, the painter found a lodging on board an old boat.

" I knew everything would turn out all right," was all he said.

One morning when I was at his flat in Paris, he wanted to show me a big pastel. He stood it against a door.

" Take care! " I cried. " That door might open."

" No fear! It is blocked up."

" But you know," I said in jest, " one sometimes thinks a door is blocked up and then . . ."

At that very moment the door flew open. The pastel was flung to the ground, and in its place stood the artist's little daughter, petrified with astonishment.

" See how lucky I am! " cried the painter as he picked up his picture. " There's only the glass broken."

(d) *Monet.*

On the first day of my Cézanne exhibition, a very stout man with a beard came into the shop. He looked a typical gentleman-farmer. Without haggling he purchased three of the most important paintings. I imagined I had to do with some provincial collector.

It was Claude Monet. I saw him again more than once on his way through Paris. What was most striking, in a painter of his celebrity, was his extreme simplicity, and the fervent admiration he expressed for his old comrade of the heroic days of Impressionism, Cézanne, still so little known. But the incomprehension of the public extended at that time to much better-known artists, to Monet himself in particular. During the exhibition of the *Nymphéas*, at Durand-Ruel's, which was so successful, a man came into my shop and said :

" Monsieur, I have just been admiring the pictures on show at your neighbour's. I wanted to ask M. Durand-Ruel about them, but they tell me he is in America. But perhaps you know this M. Claude Monet? "

" I do."

" I supply the biggest dressmaking firms in New York with hand-painted materials. That will show you that I am on the look-out for real artists. What I have just seen at Durand-Ruel's pleases me. Of course there are a few little things that won't quite do, but thanks to my experience in the matter, the artist will soon improve. Do you know where he lives, this M. Claude Monet? "

Now what do you think of that?

I had the honour of being received by Monet at Giverny. I had been looking forward to all the paintings by himself that I should have the good fortune to see. But there were very few, and I expressed my astonishment at the fact.

" But you see, there is no room left," said the Master.

It was quite true. The house was large, but the walls of all the rooms were covered with paintings by Monet's friends. I told him one did not often see pictures of such rare quality in the hands of even the best known collectors.

" And yet I only take what I can get cheap," he said. " Most of the paintings on these walls had been lying about for a long while in shop-windows. In a sense I bought them by way of protest against the indifference of the public."

I was looking at the picture, *La Famille Monet*, by Renoir.

" Manet," said Claude Monet, " wanted one day to paint my wife and children. Renoir was there. He took a canvas too and began painting the same subject. By and by Manet drew me into a corner and whispered, ' You're on very good terms with Renoir and take an interest in his future—do advise him to give up painting! You can see for yourself that it's not at all his job' ! "

(e) *Pissarro*.

The first thing that struck one in Pissarro was his air of kindness, of sensitiveness, and at the same time of serenity, a serenity born of work accomplished with joy. And yet what a life of vicissitude was his, from the moment when he left his island of St. Thomas to come and settle in France! He suffered poverty, the common lot of all the painters of that period when pictures were not selling. And he had a great many children. Mme Pissarro tilled the ground herself to feed her family. Then came the " *Année Terrible*," the Commune. The painter, after being turned out of his studio, came back to find it destroyed. His paintings, which represented a considerable amount of work, had disappeared! But in spite of so much wasted effort he would not yield to discouragement and went on producing painting after painting. Looking at those landscapes that exhale the very scent of the fields, those quiet peasant women bending over their cabbages, those placid goose-girls, who would guess that most of those canvases were painted during the period of the artist's worst calamities?

On his way back from Durand-Ruel's, Pissarro would often stop at my place for a chat. With what openness of mind this old man, with his great white beard, judged his fellows, Cézanne, Renoir, Claude Monet! He was interested in all the experiments which at that time were exciting the artists. He was curious about every form of art. During one of the last visits he paid me, he spoke with rapture of a page of an old book. He was studying it from the standpoint of a typographer of the days when linotype did not exist.

His sons all became artists, as was only to be expected. One of them, Manzana Pissarro, became one of the masters of decorative art. The eldest, Lucien, fell under the spell of bibliophily. He turned printer, illustrator, publisher. The first work that came from his press, *La Reine des Poissons*, disheartened me by its perfection; but in the end it helped to spur me on to attempt publishing myself.

(f) *Sisley*.

Of all those who have been called the great Impressionists, the least fortunate was Sisley, whose paintings are so sought after to-day. All these men, at a certain time, suffered the cruellest privations; but the Master of Moret never even knew the most modest competence. The first time I saw him was when I went to beg him to do me a colour lithograph for the album of painter-gravers that I was preparing. He accepted with the most perfect good grace and gave me a *Goose-girl*.

His end was terrible: he died of a cancer of the throat. He endured his disease with a courage which won the admiration of all, and displayed to the end an optimism that nothing could impair. After his last operation, one of those interventions that surgeons perform, as they say, to please the family, he wrote to one of his friends: " I am suffering even more than before, but I know that it is going to cure me. I am seeing pink butterflies."

(g) *Guillaumin*.

Guillaumin, of all the great Impressionists, has lagged most behind in the matter of prices. For though Sisley's paintings have gone up since his death, Guillaumin's are still suffering from the lack of demand that has been the lot of so many great artists. And yet what works the painter of *La Creuse* has left us!

Forced at the outset to accept an administrative post in order to live, Guillaumin devoted all his free time to painting. I can see him at his easel, in his studio in the rue Servandoni. When I told him I hoped to bring him some purchasers:

" Look here," he said, " I hope they're not the sort of people who buy just to cover their walls? "

I reassured him. His face brightened.

" Then I shall look out for them. They are my friends already."

(h) *Signac*.

I was a long while getting to understand Signac. Having heard *pointillism* described as " painting in petit-point," I had taken it for some sort of lady's needlework, and I used to pass by the Seurats and the Signacs without looking at them. It was not till I had had it explained to me that *pointillism* meant the division of tones, that I discovered Signac for myself.

Here is a reminiscence connected with this artist.

I had just sold one of his pictures.

" What are you going to do with that painting? " I asked the purchaser.

" Hang it on my wall, of course! "

" In that case," I said, " I must warn you that you are looking at it upside down."

I turned the picture the right way up.

" How curious! " cried the *amateur*. " Like that the picture means nothing to me. I'm half inclined to give it back to you."

He kept it, however. Once again I had been shown that it does not do to tutor one's customers. As a matter of fact, was not the purchaser of the Signac right, without suspecting it, to think a picture so good when it was upside-down? I saw Lewis Brown one day, looking at a *Hunting Scene* he had just bought, upside down. And as I appeared surprised:

" It's the best way," he said, " to judge of a picture."

(i) *Maximilien Luce.*

What a curious character as a painter was Maximilien Luce, and what a good fellow! Although he did nothing to push himself, and moreover professed the most violently anarchist theories, he had his customers. As a matter of fact, a purchaser who is frightened may sheer off for a time, but he will always come back if the painter interests him.

At the time when Luce was beginning to be sought after, I had in my window a picture of his representing a cathedral. A lady who was passing stopped to look at the painting, and asked me:

" How much? "

" Eight hundred francs."

" Eight hundred francs! That's not a great painter's price."

And she went away, saying to the friend who was with her, loud enough for me to hear:

" All the same, I did like that picture very much. But one must be sensible. If one began buying pictures by second-rate painters . . ."

Some of Luce's comrades were complaining one day, in his presence, of the difficulty of " arriving."

" Hang it all! " cried Luce, " one doesn't paint for the sake of ' arriving,' but for one's pleasure."

(j) *Gauguin.*

To see him, with his great height and arrogant bearing, a fur cap on his head and a cloak thrown round his shoulders, followed by a little half-breed Indian girl dressed in brightly-coloured finery, one would have taken Gauguin for some Oriental Prince. The story of this coloured girl, straight from the Malayan Isles, is worth telling.

An opera singer, Mme Nina Pack, was on friendly terms with a rich banker who had business relations with the traders of the Malayan Isles. The singer happened to say before the representative of one of these, "I would love to have a little negro girl." A few months later a policeman brought Mme Nina Pack a young half-breed, half Indian, half Malayan, who had been found wandering about the Gare de Lyon. She had a label hung round her neck, with the inscription: *Mme Nina Pack, rue de la Rochefoucauld, à Paris. Envoi de Java.* She was given the name of Anna. Some time later, in consequence of a little domestic drama in which Anna was implicated, she was dismissed. She came to me, as I had known her at her employer's house, to ask me to find her a good situation. I judged her qualifications as a housemaid to be very middling, and thought she stood more chance of succeeding as a model. I told Gauguin about her.

"Send her to me. I'll try her," he said.

Anna pleased him, and he kept her. She was the cause of Gauguin's memorable battle with the Breton peasants, who threw stones at the poor girl, accusing her of being a witch. In the course of the fray the painter had his foot broken. He never got over this accident.

Redon was very much struck by the diversity of Gauguin's gifts. One day when some workmen had been repairing a stove, he said, showing me a piece of sheet-iron:

" Give it to Gauguin, he will make a jewel of it."

It was a fact that Gauguin turned everything that fell into his hands—clay, wood, metal and so forth—into little marvels.

The dilapidated exterior of the house where he had his studio reminded one of a barn; but once inside, one might have been in a palace. The miracle was achieved by the paintings with which the artist had covered the walls. He had given the place of honour to the two painters he liked best: Cézanne and Van Gogh. Three Van Goghs hung above his bed: in the middle a landscape in a mauve tonality; to right and left, *Sunflowers*—the same, I believe, that were so much admired at the Degas sale—and opposite these, a still-life by Cézanne, the very one that led Huysmans to talk of " lopsided fruit in drunken pottery."

Towards 1898, when Gauguin, then in Tahiti, was in such pressing need of money, his friend Chaudet offered this picture to all the collectors at six hundred francs. Nobody would have it. At last somebody decided to buy it, but demanded the frame, which was of carved wood, into the bargain. This painting passed later into the hands of Prince Wagram. At present it belongs to the Pellerin collection, and when an amateur who does not mind what price he pays, wants a still-life of Cézanne's found for him, he never fails to add, " it must be as good as the one which belonged to Gauguin."

Degas ranked Gauguin very high. He only reproached him for having gone to the ends of the earth to paint.

" Cannot one paint just as well in the Batignolles," he would say, " as in Tahiti? " But Gauguin was so little appreciated that one can understand the need he felt to escape from his contemporaries. Like Cézanne, Gauguin had at first imagined he would conquer their hostility if he could succeed in being admitted to the official *Salons*. Like Cézanne too he met with refusal after refusal at the hands of the juries. It was only through a trick on the part of a friend, the master-ceramist Chaplet, that he was enabled at last to see one of his works in the *Salon*. But under what conditions! Chaplet, who had fired one of Gauguin's earthenware pieces, the *Oviri*, in his kiln, exhibited it in his own show-case. But of course the artist's name was visible on the terra-cotta. This was still too much for the *officiels*. It was only upon Chaplet threatening to withdraw his own work that the *Oviri* was allowed to remain.

One can imagine the sort of reception Gauguin was likely to get from the curator of the Musée du Luxembourg, M. Bénédite, who considered his professional duty forbade him the faintest indulgence towards an art that had not obtained the hall-mark of the Institute. Gauguin was the victim on two occasions of M. Bénédite's scruples: at his return from Tahiti, when he offered him the finest of his paintings from his exhibition at Durand-Ruel's for his museum; and when, backed by Degas, he came to ask him for a commission for a fresco. Bénédite started up in amazement:

" But fresco-painting is done on a wall! "

Which in Bénédite's mind evidently signified that a wall cannot be stored away in the attic like a mere painting, when the artist's patron has disappeared.

Gauguin was to have his revenge—thirty years after his death, it is true. When a plaque com-memorating the centenary of his birth was placed on the house where he was born, there were gathered together in his honour the Curator of the Museum of Fontainebleau, the President of the Municipal Council, on behalf of the City of Paris, M. Maurice Denis representing the Académie des Beaux-Arts; and lastly the Minister of National Education, M. de Monzie, who spoke in the name of the Government. Recalling the saying of a critic that Gauguin's art had everything against it—women, collectors, museums—M. de Monzie pointed out that to-day museums and collectors were proud to possess even the smallest of Gauguin's works, and that the women had begun to powder their faces with the ochre with which Gauguin painted the flesh of his Tahitians.

It is curious, in this connection, to note the difference of the reactions provoked in France and in other countries by anything connected with art. I remember that when a picture of Manet's was to be bought by the Mannheim Museum, even the workmen esteemed it a point of honour to contribute. With us an occasion of that sort leaves factory hands indifferent.

Alongside the birthplace of the painter of Tahiti, there was a milliner's shop, of which the two sales-women, from the doorstep, seemed to be following the ceremony with lively curiosity. A customer, coming up, asked what was happening. The milliners looked at one another, and one said, " We don't know . . . apparently it's a Minister speaking." Soon after, I listened to two peaceable *bourgeois*:

" Who was this Gauguin, exactly? "

" Didn't you hear? He was a sailor."

" Didn't they say he was a stockbroker too? "

" I don't know, that must have been a brother; they talked of another Gauguin too, who was a painter."

A comic incident marked the beginning of the ceremony. Among the people who had gathered round the little platform on which the orators spoke in succession, was a hawker, carrying a parcel of braces and suspenders on his shoulder. As he could see little of what was happening and could not hear the speeches, he thought there must be another hawker there, puffing his wares like himself. He inquired of his neighbours, " What's the mate gassing about? What's he trying to fob off on them? " and then, catching sight of the police, he made off himself without waiting to be told.

(k) *Degas and the model.*

I was just ten when I first saw some of Degas' horses in the Museum of La Réunion. An event had just occurred which had caught my childish fancy. The curator of the museum had received a box from France containing the egg of an Æpyornis. As a matter of fact, it was only an imitation. I had hastened to be present at the unpacking. Among the paper which had been packed round the object, I perceived a picture of horses torn from an illustrated review. I thought these horses as fine as those that I used to admire, every year, at the races. Ah! that Réunion race-course! A plain, surrounded by hills on which was ranged the whole populace: Chinese, Indians, Arabs, Negroes, clad in brightly coloured stuffs. I have always had such a lively memory of this bewitching *décor* that the hippodromes of France leave me cold. One day, turning the pages of a review, I came across the same one that had struck me so forcibly in my childhood. This time I looked carefully at the artist's name: it was Degas. I mentioned my discovery to Lewis Brown:

" By Jove! Degas is the greatest of them all. His studio is quite close by. But you've seen Degas once as it is. Yesterday, when we were starting out together, the person with big black spectacles, to whom I said good-morning as we passed."

I got into touch with Degas myself not long after. I had given the frame-maker Jacquet some planks of foreign wood from the Exhibition of 1889. I intended having frames made of them. One day Jacquet said to me, " You know, M. Degas is always scheming out frames. He has seen your wood, and told me to ask if you would let him have it." Here was an opportunity to approach the " terrible " painter. I replied that I would not take any money for it, but that I should be delighted to accept the smallest sketch of

N

his in exchange. Degas agreed. That was how I made my way into his studio.

When he moved from the rue Ballu to settle into the rue Victor Massé, everything for which there was no room in the new flat was taken up to the studio. Consequently the most heterogeneous objects were to be seen there side by side. A bath, little wooden horses with which the artist composed his pictures of race-courses, so marvellous for their colour and movement. Easels too, with canvases half-finished on them, for after he had started an oil-painting, he soon gave way to discouragement, not being able to fall back, as he did with his drawings, on tracing after tracing by way of correction. I remember too a tall desk at which he stood to write. Once an object had found its way into the studio, it never left it, nor changed its position, and gradually became covered by a layer of dust that no flick of a feather duster came to disturb. The painter would have been very much astonished if he had been told that his studio was not perfectly tidy. One day I brought him a little picture that he had asked to see. As I undid the parcel, a scrap of paper, no bigger than a confetti, flew out and settled in a seam of the floor. Degas pounced on it: " Do take care, Vollard ! You will make my studio untidy."

When I arrived, the painter was working on one of his pastels, those marvellous things that have been compared to butterflies' wings. I mentioned this in the hearing of the painter La Touche.

" Couldn't you," he said, " try to find out from Degas where he gets the pastels which give him those shades that no one else can obtain? "

When I saw Degas again, he happened to have a box of pastels in his hand, and was spreading them out on a board in front of the window. Seeing me watching him :

" I take all the colour out of them that I can, by putting them in the sun."

" But what do you use, then, to get colours of such brightness? "

" Dead colour, Monsieur! "

When I reported this to La Touche, the way he looked at me showed me clearly that he thought I was laughing at him.

They were speaking of a former dancer in Degas' presence:

" You must have known her, M. Degas? "

" She even sat for me. I painted her waking up. There was nothing to be seen but her legs feeling about through the opening of the bed-curtains for her slippers, which had been thrown on an Oriental carpet. I even remember the reds and the yellows. I can see her two green stockings too. I wanted to keep that painting, but it appeared to please the poor girl so much that I gave it to her. I have been told that she became a pupil of Joseph Bail."

I asked the painter to tell me a little more about this person.

" I see what you're after. You want to buy her portrait from her. I fancy it will be difficult. She was so fond of it, and now-a-days she must be secure from poverty."

Degas was not mistaken as to my intentions. But it was first necessary to find the retired dancer. I set about it without delay and ended by discovering where she lived. I went to her house. My old overcoat, which I could not part with on account of the affection I always have for my worn-out clothes, must have made a bad impression on the maid who opened the door, for she would not let me go further than the hall. I explained as well as I could what I had come for. Evidently I did not make myself sufficiently understood, for, from the place to which I had been consigned, I heard her announce to her mistress: " It's a shady-looking man. He says he's come for Madame's legs and stockings."

" Chuck him out, Angèle! "

I did not wait for the housemaid to communicate this reply to me, but decamped there and then.

On my return home, I wrote to the lady to explain the misunderstanding, and told her the real object of my *démarche*. The next day she came to my shop.

" So there's a sale for Degas? " she asked me point-blank.

" Certainly! "

" They're all alike, these artists! One never knows where one is with them. And yet he seemed a decent fellow, that one! . . . Why didn't he tell me his painting would be valuable some day? "

" So you haven't got the painting any longer? "

" Of course not, I've covered it up. One day when I had to copy an ' Interior ' by my professor, Joseph Bail, as I had no canvas handy, I took that one and painted over it. But I've brought you something that will take the place of it. Only I warn you I want a decent price for it."

She opened her hand-bag and took out a little exercise-book with the margins filled with scribbles, among which it was possible to distinguish outlines of soldiers and horses.

" It's a drawing-book of Detaille's! You know who I mean? He gave it to me himself, saying, ' I was nine years old when I did those drawings. I have been keeping that book like a treasure; I refused it to a cousin of the Tsar's, and my friends had made me promise to give it to the Louvre. But as you've been nice to me, I'll make you a present of it.' "

Greatly to the lady's surprise, I showed no enthusiasm for this incomparable relic. Delighted to learn that Detaille had not always been as wooden as his figures, I dismissed this touching pupil of Joseph Bail's.

(1) *Mary Cassatt.*

Mary Cassatt! At the time of my first attempts,

when I used to ask myself anxiously what the morrow would be like, how often did she get me providentially out of a difficulty!

" Have you a picture for the Havemeyers? "

It was with a sort of frenzy that generous Mary Cassatt laboured for the success of her comrades: Monet, Pissarro, Cézanne, Sisley and the rest. But what indifference where her own painting was concerned! What an aversion from " pushing " her work in public. One day at an exhibition, they were fighting for and against the Impressionists. " But," said someone, speaking to Mary Cassatt without knowing who she was, " you are forgetting a foreign painter that Degas ranks very high."

" Who is that? " she asked in astonishment.

" Mary Cassatt."

Without false modesty, quite naturally, she exclaimed, " Oh, nonsense! "

" She is jealous," murmured the other, turning away.

Mary Cassatt owned a place at Mesnil-Baufrêne where she used to spend the summer. It was there that she died in 1926. The entire village followed the funeral procession. None but old Mathilde, her devoted maid, and a few intimates, knew the whole extent of her generosity, for Mary Cassatt accompanied her acts of beneficence by a dry, almost distant gesture, as though she felt shy of doing good.

In the cemetery, after the last prayers, the pastor, according to protestant custom, distributed to those present the roses and carnations strewn upon the coffin, that they might scatter them over the grave. Looking at this carpet of brilliant flowers, I fancied Mary Cassatt running to fetch a canvas and brushes.

XX CÉZANNE'S HOME AT AIX

I once visited Cézanne in his native town, after the exhibition of his pictures at my little shop in the rue Laffitte, and at this distance of time I still remember vividly the thrill of seeing all those "Cézanne" landscapes filing past my carriage window on the journey from Marseilles to Aix.

Another vivid memory is of Cézanne at his easel, painting away enthusiastically at some canvas that he would quite likely destroy a moment later in a fit of temper. Witness his *Paysan*, all riddled with knife-thrusts, and the *Still-life* that I saw from the studio-window, dangling from the branch of a cherry tree.

Whenever I think of Cézanne I am reminded of that studio, whose walls were hung with reproductions attesting the painter's love of the Masters—Luca Signorelli, El Greco, Tintoretto, Titian, and nearer to our own day, Delacroix and Courbet—poor reproductions, mere halfpenny prints, but sufficient to transport the artist into the atmosphere of the museums.

Cézanne's classical culture, his passion for Baudelaire, his anger at encountering a contemner of anything he admired, and his sudden change-over to the sensitiveness and ingenuousness of a child, were unforgettable characteristics of the man. Once, in my presence, he was upbraiding Zola, lately dead, for having dared to reproach Corot with painting nymphs instead of peasant-girls in his landscapes. Suddenly, at the height of his fury, he turned to me with a quiver in his voice, and said, "Forgive me, M. Vollard, I love Zola so much, really."

It was at an hotel in the Cours Mirabeau that I put up at Aix. I can never recall that town of a hundred fountains without seeing its " Cours Mirabeau " all bathed in sunlight, and the charming patterns of light and shade under the plane trees. I have specially pleasant memories of the hours spent in the *Café des Deux Garçons* with the poet Joachim Gasquet, the leader of the intellectual youth of Aix. It was here that I first heard of autonomism. But the autonomists of Provence did not, like those of Brittany, go in for bombs; their worst excesses went no further than upsetting an inkpot on the head of King René. Some young hot-heads were annoyed with him for having given his duchy to France, and thus degraded to the rank of a banal department an ancient province proud of its past.

I shall never forget lunching at Gasquet's, and the shock of pleasure I felt on going into the dining-room. On the walls were three Cézannes: the *Femme au Chapelet*, which passed later into the collection of Jacques Doucet; a *Cornfield*—a purely classical composition; and the famous *Sainte Victoire*, since purchased by Courtauld, the famous London collector. Cézanne, wishing to be " hung " at any cost, had sent these two last-named magnificent paintings to an exhibition organised by an amateur society of which he was a member. The pictures could not be refused, since the rules gave each member the right to send in two paintings. But the organisers thought it their duty to apologise for the discredit this cast on a respectable art show.

The luncheon was excellent. Demolin was there, a young writer of Aix, who showed the most brilliant promise, and another young man, of whom Gasquet thought a good deal, but whose name I do not remember. At dessert, our host gave us the first reading of one of his most recent poems, which was generously applauded,

As we were leaving the table, the maid announced: "Monsieur Cézanne." With the painter was Gasquet's father, a retired baker and convinced Royalist. His son "staggered" him, but worried him even more. He felt much the same apprehension as Cézanne's father, who used to admonish him: "My child, think of the future: *on meurt avec du génie et on mange avec de l'argent.*" Hearing his son singing the praises of so many great writers of the past, he could not but question the wisdom of choosing a trade that involved competition not only with the living but with the dead. These enthusiasms of "Joachim's" did not displease Cézanne, but prepared as he was to begin his own work over and over again, he may well have wished the poet would control the youthful ardour with which he poured out his verse like a bird in song.

Cézanne, as he came in, glanced at an illustrated review of modern art, in which, at the head of an article on the Provençal masters, were the portraits of Puget and Daumier.

"Do they so much as know, at Marseilles, that Puget and Daumier are their countrymen?"

"As Cézanne is ours!"

Cézanne shot a severe glance at the interrupter. Probably he did not much relish the compliment, coming as it did from one of his fellow-townsmen, of whom he was accustomed to say that they were "not up to much."

When, shortly after, Cézanne got up to go, Gasquet let fall the name of Baudelaire. And the painter, who could not hear the name of his favourite poet without quoting from his poetry, began:

> Au dessus des étangs, au dessus des vallées,
> Des montagnes, des bois, des nuages, des mers,
> Par delà le soleil, par dela les éthers,
> Par dela les confins des sphères etoilées, . . .

When Cézanne had ended, there was a silence that

no one dared break. There was a general feeling of discomfort. Then Mme Gasquet, getting up, went to the piano and played a Beethoven sonata, which Cézanne applauded generously, although his leanings in the way of music were towards military bands and barrel-organs.

Plato suggested that poets should be crowned with roses and then re-escorted to the gates of the Republic; he did not recognise the potential value of a poet at the critical hour when the defenders of the citadel need bracing. A trench comrade of Gasquet's once said to me, " When that chap came along, we were in mud up to the belly—and in a hell of a funk ! . . . He spouted some verses of Calendal to us, and it put heart into us again at once. The sky was no longer black; we could have sworn we heard the cicadas chirping."

Cézanne did a portrait of Gasquet, now in the museum at Prague. The poet's former professor of philosophy, M. Dumesnil, saw this painting in my gallery, and after looking at it for a long while, said:

" How strange ! I thought I had plumbed the soul of my pupil, and yet this portrait shows me a Gasquet I did not know. I see now that the real Gasquet was not the ingenuous creature I took him for."

I cannot leave the subject of Aix without mentioning a few of the people I met there—the J. . . family in particular, who owned such magnificent Cézannes, and left them lying about at the top of the stairs alongside the most heterogeneous objects: birdcages, chairs with broken seats, cracked chamber-pots, things of no value, but promoted to the rank of household gods for their former share in the family life. And then the countess who relegated her Cézannes to the attic, while refusing energetically to part with them: " I am not a shopkeeper, Monsieur ! "

" But supposing there are rats in the attic ? "

" Never mind, they're *my* rats ! "

And lastly, all those fools who believed firmly that the apparent infatuation of Paris with Cézanne was merely its latest joke against the provinces, and accepted blindly what Cézanne said of himself when he deplored his incapacity to " make things look real," or when he assured a lady water-colourist of Aix who was asking his advice, " But, Madame, if I were as clever as you, I should have been accepted by the *Salon* long ago."

No wonder then if all these people thought Cézanne was taking advantage when he sent in two of his paintings to an exhibition by the Society of Amateur Painters of Aix. On that occasion, as on so many others, it was his art that enabled him to endure the vexations and mortifications that his paintings brought upon him.

" You know, M. Vollard, I believe painting is what does me most good," he said to me one day when he was talking of the " pretensions of idiots, intellectuals and rogues."

It is hardly necessary to add that he avoided all contact with them, even with other artists (*les " Ôtres "*). So great actually was his suspicion of other people, that on meeting a comrade in the streets of Aix whom he had not seen for thirty years, when the latter after the first effusions asked him for his address, he replied evasively:

" I live a long way off . . . in a street. . . ."

XXI SOME MORE IMPRESSIONISTS

(a) *Renoir at Essoyes*.

Renoir had a little house at Essoyes, his wife's native place, where he used to spend the hottest months of the summer. What delightful moments I have spent in that place, an old peasants' house, with thick walls, surrounded by a garden planted with fruit trees!

When the autumn came, one of his friends expressed his astonishment that he should linger there, instead of returning to Paris before going to the Midi, where his infirmities constrained him to spend the winter.

"Why should I go to Paris?" replied Renoir. "I don't want central heating when I can have a good wood fire to sit by. The butter here is perfect, and the bread better than any you can get in Paris. And then the good little *vin du pays*."

I remember that wine, and a certain *marc* which was worth all the old Armagnacs. Alas! I shall never again drink either the wine or the *marc* of Essoyes; for the region has been included in the Champagne zone, and all the harvests are bought up by the manufacturers of sparkling wine.

What pleased me particularly at Essoyes was the river, which added so much to the charm of the landscape. Renoir, when he could no longer walk, often had himself carried down to the water's edge.

During one of my visits to the place I asked what were the local curiosities. They hastened to tell me of the tomb of the former owner of the *Magasins du Louvre*,

Commander Hériot. The latter's one ambition in life, it appeared, had been to achieve a magnificent and original burial-place. Commander Hériot, who prided himself on having ideas, had hesitated between two notions: a low, square monumental block, and a tapering pyramid. But he died before coming to a decision, and his family felt it their duty to carry out his wish. After many tergiversations, they decided to amalgamate the two schemes. The result is, possibly, a very fine funeral monument. On one of the sides of the monument is an inscription enumerating the principal merits of the commander, and informing us that his brother, who had the edifice erected, is a Chevalier of the Legion of Honour. On the day when I was shown this work of art, I saw an old peasant woman on her knees before the tomb. As she passed by me afterwards:

"Was Commander Hériot a relation of yours?" I asked her.

"Oh, no, Monsieur. What an idea!"

"Then why were you praying by his tomb?"

"Well, you see, Monsieur, no one ever visits it. So when I've finished cutting grass for my rabbits, I say a *Pater* and an *Ave* before it. How can a rich man like that be so forgotten?"

(b) *Forain.*

I saw Forain for the first time about forty years ago. I was studying law, and even then everything connected with art attracted me. My correspondent in Paris, a planter from La Réunion, had said to me:

"Here's a louis. You who are always talking painting, go and find me a print, a little drawing, anything you like so long as it's . . . well, you know what I mean. . . ."

I should not have had the cheek to do it on my own account; but as I was acting for another, I risked it and went to Forain, whose drawings I had admired in

the *Courrier Français*. I told him the errand I was
entrusted with. He smiled, opened a portfolio and
gave me a wash drawing of a woman preparing to
waylay an invisible client.

" Marvellous! " exclaimed my correspondent when
I handed him the drawing. " How did the fellow
get hold of it! I could swear that was the woman I
met the other evening in the rue Notre-Dame-de-
Lorette. And yet I was pretty sure we were alone."

I explained that it was the artist's job to give the
impression of reality, of the thing seen.

" How I regret not being an artist! " he murmured.
" Fortunately there are other satisfactions in life."

All the same, he could not get his Forain out of his
head.

" You know," he confided to me one day as he was
contemplating his drawing, " it must give you a
devilish lot of pleasure to be able to suggest a thing
like that! If I had my life over again, I believe I
should learn to draw."

Degas thought a great deal of Forain. The esteem
he felt for his talent prevented him from being annoyed—and with Degas this was almost unbelievable—
when Forain came late for dinner. But Degas remained uncompromising on the subject of flowers.
Though he tolerated them in a garden, he tabooed
them relentlessly in the house.

One day, coming to lunch with Forain and finding
no one in the salon, Degas went into the dining-room.
There was a bunch of flowers in the middle of the
table. Furious, he picked it up and, traversing the
flat, went and laid it in a corner somewhere. The
hostess's cousin, coming into the dining-room, cried:

" They've forgotten the flowers, and M. Degas is
lunching with us! "

After looking everywhere, the housemaid ended by
retrieving the nosegay, and put it back in its place.

When they went in to lunch, Degas, who was giving Mme Forain his arm, left the room precipitately. They dashed after him. He consented to return, but they had first to swear that he should never again see flowers on the table.

Like Degas, Cézanne had a great admiration for Forain. In his studio in the rue Hégésippe Moreau there were all sorts of satirical drawings of the " Doux pays " pinned on the wall.

" I like having them to look at," I heard him say to a visitor who showed surprise at seeing Forain beside Luca Signorelli and Poussin.

Forain's output was immense: paintings, drawings, etchings, lithographs, besides a whole lot of little compositions in sepia, after the manner of the eighteenth century, that the painter kept jealously in his portfolios.

Though from the first a master of his craft, he thought nothing of making twenty or thirty studies to catch a single attitude, a single gesture. I remember being struck, as a result of this, by the intensity of movement he succeeded in imparting to the figure of a man who, with his hand clapped to his cheek, was reeling under the impact of a box on the ear.

Not many people knew Forain in his capacity of gentleman-farmer. I went to see him at his estate at Chesnay, and came upon him as he stood looking at a bull that was being led by a farm-hand.

" Are you going to do a study of that magnificent beast? " I asked him.

" No. I'm showing him at the Comice Agricole. My farmer assures me that we shall get a first prize."

(c) *Odilon Redon.*

Second-rate artists imagine that the great works of the masters are achieved by means of tricks. La Touche, as I have related, wanted to know the processes employed by Degas. In the same way an

estimable critic, M. Roger-Milès, exclaimed one day
in my hearing:

" That devil of a Redon! How does he get those
deep blacks in his lithographs, and that velvety look of
his charcoal drawings? "

I passed the question on to Redon, who laughed:

" Tell Roger-Milès that it's by eating beefsteak and
drinking real wine."

Redon belonged to the days when people still cared
for wine. He knew something about it, for he was a
native of the Bordeaux country, where his family
owned vineyards. One evening when he was dining
with me, he said to me:

" Your wine has a bouquet! Did you choose it
yourself? "

" Of course! "

" I did not know you were such a connoisseur. . . ."

" The patent of connoisseurship you are awarding
me, I obtained once before at the Hôtel Drouot from
a qualified *gastronome*. He was congratulating me on
my purchases at the sale of the Grand Véfour cellar.
' It's very simple,' I told him. ' I was behind you. I
watched your manœuvres with your silver cup and your
little cubes of cheese, and I had two cases of the same
wines you chose knocked down to me.' "

Redon considered himself under an obligation to his
purchasers. Unlike Degas, he did not look upon
pictures as " necessaries of life." " Those who buy
my work," he would say, " are the friends of my
mind." From that to believing that they liked him
for himself there was but a step, and Redon was not
long in taking it. One day I gave him an order for an
album of lithographs: the *Apocalypse*. He asked for
ten copies for himself, adding, not without a certain
pride:

" I always keep ten copies of my prints for my
amateurs . . . I want their collections to be complete."

" With pleasure," said I. " But won't you commission me to sell them to them? I can guarantee to get you twice the money."

" They would be so hurt if I did not sell them my lithographs myself and if I changed my prices. Besides, I have nothing to complain of. When I think of poor Bresdin who couldn't get even five francs for one of his drawings . . ."

It was because of this species of ingenuousness that Redon's works remained so long at such low prices. A hundred francs for one of his magnificent drawings, and seven francs fifty for a lithograph! The " patrons " of those days paid him dearer in admiring speeches than in hard cash. One of them, a celebrated hosier of the rue du Sentier, actually hit on another advantage to be got out of his relations with artists. Having bought something from Redon, he said:

" You won't mind coming to fetch your hundred francs? "

And as though by chance he appointed a day which was his wife's " at home " day.

" A cup of tea? " suggested the astute spouse of the dealer in cravats.

The latter was thus enabled at small cost to satisfy the vanity of his " lady," who could now flatter herself that she had an artistic salon.

This exploitation of the painter lasted until the day when a picture dealer of the rue de la Boétie, who had bought a few Redons, had the idea of putting them up for sale at ten times the sum the artist had hitherto accepted. The Redons were snapped up as soon as shown. The dealer's example was rapidly followed by his brethren, and when soon after I met the Comte de P. . .

" Just fancy," he said, coming up to me. " In the rue de la Boétie the other day, I was looking at one of those bunches of flowers that Redon himself used to let me have for two hundred francs. Some sort of half-breed came in, and was not the least surprised to be asked three thousand for it! "

Redon was more astonished than delighted at this rise in the price of his works.

" Would you believe it? " he said to me. " They are offering me such sums now that I hardly feel it honest to accept them. Besides, all these purchasers now-a-days—do they really care for what they buy? I feel homesick sometimes for my old *amateurs*. They kept me a bit short, it is true, but they said such nice things to me! . . . Still, if she wants to buy carnations, my wife isn't obliged to skimp on something else now."

Flowers! Even in the days when the couple were worst off, there was always a bunch of them in the studio. Though, as a matter of fact, the sight of flowers alone was not enough for Redon. He liked pleasant faces to look at as well. And Mme Redon, always anxious to please her husband, was careful to invite pretty women to her parties.

Redon prized intellectual culture. He considered it necessary to everyone, and particularly to the artist.

" One day," he told me, " when I was going to see one of my friends at the ' *Ruche* '—you know that haunt of artists—I had an inquiry to make, and I stopped in front of a ground-floor studio. Through the open door I could see a little donkey serving as a model to a painter. Beside the painter sat a young woman doing some embroidery. Just like a Primitive picture. On a table there were some tulips, and a book with a worn binding that showed it had been often read. I said to myself, " That looks promising! "

(d) *Whistler*.

It was not without hesitation that I went one day and knocked at the door of Whistler's studio, in the hope that he would give me a lithograph for my album of painter-gravers. The famous artist was

o

said to be unapproachable. He received me, however, in a way that touched me infinitely, coming as I did, young and quite unknown to him, to beg the collaboration of a Master whose smallest engraving was worth a fabulous price.

There was not a picture to be seen in his studio. I threw out a few timid hints for the artist to show me some. But that day he could think of nothing but a lawsuit that had been brought against him. Whistler had asked a price for a portrait, which upon reflection he considered insufficient. The painter's client refused to raise it, and Whistler destroyed the painting. The painter considered he had the right to do this, since he had repaid the cheque received in payment; but his client retorted that before returning the amount of the cheque, Whistler had cashed it, which implied, in his opinion—and it must have been that of the Tribunal—acceptance of the price. Whistler was furious. He expounded to me at length the reasons which, according to him, gave him the right to destroy any of his works if he chose. I was about to leave, when he said to me:

"Will you stay to lunch with me? You can share my cutlet."

I accepted with joy, expecting wonders of a lunch with Whistler. Many were the legends about him. It was said he had an Indian servant, a Chinese cook. They spoke of the luxury he displayed in London, and his mania for having everything to harmonise, even the colour of the dishes with that of the food they contained. I was prepared for an omelet in a blue dish, followed by a langouste on a green one. Suddenly there came a knock at the door.

"Now we will have our lunch," said Whistler.

An old woman came in. She was carrying a basket in which were the promised cutlet, a dish of spinach and a few potatoes. She spread a cloth on a little table, and the painter, as he had offered to do, shared his cutlet with me. The spinach was cold.

" You must heat it up," said Whistler to the servant.

She put the dish in front of the fire, and when the painter went to pick it up, he burnt his fingers.

" That's too much ! " cried the painter. " The dish is red hot, and the spinach is as cold as ever."

" China is a bad conductor of heat," I said diffidently.

Whistler called the servant back :

" I have just burnt myself with your dish, and the spinach is still cold. I don't suppose you even know why."

Dumbfounded, the old woman stared at her master.

" I will tell you why," said Whistler. " Your spinach is cold because china is a bad conductor of heat. Do you understand ? "

Speechless, the servant threw a black glance at me, as though to say, " Who is this fellow that's letting me in for all this jaw ? "

(e) *The " Nabis."*

Bonnard, Denis, Ibels, Piot, Ranson, Roussel and Vuillard had made friends at Julian's studio. The Hebrew word *nabi*, which signifies " prophet," was given to their group by one of their comrades, a certain Cazalis, who was working at Hebrew under Professor Ledrain. Of course none of these young painters considered himself a prophet. But though they were attracted by Impressionism, they aimed at finding a mode of expression of their own. They were not alone in feeling this need of a renewal. Other young painters, seeking a scientific technique, were trying to adapt to painting the recent discoveries of Chevreul in his researches on light (hence the theory of complementaries already foreseen by Delacroix). For these painters, the combination of colours takes place in the eye; only pure colours, therefore, should be laid on the canvas. This was Neo-Impressionism. The precursors of this new school, Seurat and Signac, did not despair of bringing their glorious elders over to their side. Someone succeeded in leading Degas up to the *Atelier* that Seurat was exhibiting at the *Indé-pendants*. But bored with the theories on the evolution of painting that were being unfolded to him, Degas turned round abruptly, and pointing out a picture at hazard, cried:

" Why shouldn't *that* be the painter of the future? "

It was a painting by the *douanier* Rousseau.

The *nabis* lunched together once a month in a little wine-shop in the Passage Brady. I heard a funny story about this *bistrot* from one of its frequenters. As the key of the lavatories was often lost, the proprietor had tied it to a marrow-bone. Every minute there was a shout for the " marrow-bone," which provoked general hilarity. This peculiarity had ended by giving its name to the dinner, which had become the *Dîner-de-l'Os-à-Moelle*. At these *agapæ* the talk was mostly of painting. The theorist of the group was Séruzier, the *massier* of the studio to which the *nabis* belonged.

Séruzier, who spent his holidays one summer at Pont-Aven in Brittany, came back in a state of frantic enthusiasm.

" I met a painter of genius over there," he told his comrades, " a man called Gauguin. He showed me what painting should really be: ' If you want to do an apple, do a round.' "

And Séruzier exhibited triumphantly a little daub he had painted according to the principles of the " Master of Pont-Aven." Truth to tell, the *nabis* remained at first a little cold with regard to this work, which Séruzier called *The Talisman*. But if Gauguin had no direct influence upon them, at least the new ideas that his disciple brought back from his conversations with him gave the *nabis* to think, until such time as each of them found his own direction.

About 1893 I was put in touch with the *nabis* by Maurice Denis, who had noticed the little exhibition of Manet's drawings I was holding at the time. Thanks to this meeting I obtained pictures from Bonnard, Denis, Roussel and Vuillard, and entered into cordial relations with them which permitted me to call upon their talent when I started as an art publisher.

Other young artists, though they did not belong to the group of the *nabis*, exhibited with them, notably the painter Valtat and the sculptor Aristide Maillol.

It was through Renoir that I came to know Valtat.

" I was in Brittany," Renoir told me, " when I saw a young artist, one day, putting the last touches to a study. I was struck by the happy harmony of colour throughout his painting. It was Valtat."

As for Aristide Maillol, he had started as a painter, but not being able to afford canvas and paints, turned to sculpture, an art in which he soon became a master. He began by carving statuettes in wood, on account of the cheapness of the material, and at the same time he tried his hand at tapestry-work, delightful embroideries in wool dyed with colours prepared by himself.

There was also a young Swiss artist, Félix Vallotton, who came to join the *nabi* group. He showed much talent in his wood-engravings, cut with a penknife, which were reproduced in the *Revue Blanche* beside drawings by Bonnard, Vuillard and Roussel.

Later on, without entirely giving up engraving, Vallotton started painting. The probity of his drawing led to his being dubbed *le petit Ingres*. His conscientiousness in matters of art was no less rigid, and a rather funny story was told in this connection.

He was painting the portrait of a middle-aged lady, a countrywoman of his, and he declared in the course of conversation that a painter should never " gloss the truth." So when later on he had occasion to say to her, " Don't change your position . . . smile . . . so that I can see your teeth," " They are not my teeth, M. Vallotton," said the lady. And blushing, she removed her denture.

I had bought one of the earliest works of this painter, a big painting of women bathing which I was to lend to an exhibition of *Nudes*. The exhibition over, various circumstances had prevented me from going to fetch my painting, when one day someone said to me, " As I was walking through the Bastille quarter, I saw a picture through an open window that looked very much like your Vallotton."

I went to the gallery where the exhibition had been held, and claimed my picture, which was not to be found. But it was explained to me that the gallery had changed hands. By good luck the concierge, who had helped with the removal, remembered that the former owner, upon leaving, had told the removal man he could keep everything that was left—a few broken chairs, a damaged safe, some old crockery and lastly a big painted canvas that had made everybody roar with laughter. Fortunately the concierge knew the address of the removal man, who lived, in effect, in the Bastille quarter. I went there in all haste, and found my picture.

" My wife wanted at first to use it in place of the oilcloth on our dining-room table," the fellow said to me, " but it wasn't soft enough. I couldn't get rid of it, even for five francs; nobody wanted it in the quarter. So then, as the paper had peeled off in one of our rooms that is rather damp, we hung the canvas on the wall till my boy should have time to put a layer of paint over it, the same colour as the room."

I gave ten francs and got my picture back.

Séruzier was as it were a link between the *nabis* and Gauguin, whose theories he expounded with conviction.

One day, on the Grands Boulevards, I heard my name called. I turned round: it was Séruzier.

"You are alone?" he asked. "Shall we go a little way together?"

And at the end of a few minutes:

"You see that woman in a violet coat, there, in front of us. When I stopped you she was in the some plane as yourself. With your brick-red overcoat—you can't think how the two colours screamed at being coupled together. Positively it made me ill."

Séruzier's attachment to Gauguin was such that one day when Maurice Denis happened to say he was looking for a model to sit for Castor in *The Daughters of Leucippus*, Séruzier, who was as handsome as a young god, exclaimed suddenly:

"If you like, I'll be your model. The five francs for the sitting can be sent to Gauguin, who is dying of starvation."

Here is a little incident that will show how much Gauguin's painting was at first misunderstood, not only by the native Bretons, but by Parisians. Gauguin had offered one of his paintings, a marvellous still-life, as a birthday present to *la mère* Gloanec, the proprietress of the hotel where he lodged. A Parisian municipal official who happened to be at the hotel, declared, when he heard the name of Gauguin, that he should go away if a painting by " that swine " were seen in the room. So to enable Mère Gloanec to hang up the picture without losing a customer, it was attributed to Emile Bernard's sister, who was staying at the hotel with her brother. This was how a picture by Gauguin came to be signed *Madeleine B.* It is now the property of Maurice Denis.

I went to Pont-Aven in the hope of acquiring some of Gauguin's paintings. At Mère Gloanec's tavern, where I went first, there was nothing to buy. But once I had settled in there and made my intentions known, information began to flow in. People vied with each other in setting me on the track of a *châtelain*, a public official, even a fisherman, who had known Gauguin, and with whom I stood a chance of finding some of his canvases. I was sent on endless walks, along impossible roads. No doubt the budding reputation of the artist in Paris had arrived amplified in Brittany, for the prices asked for the least of his pictures were greater than I could afford. I had come back to Paris empty-handed, therefore, when in a picture-dealer's window I saw a Gauguin every bit as good as those they had wanted five hundred francs for in Brittany. I asked the price. They told me, " Three hundred francs."

(f) *Other " Jeunes "—Matisse, Vlaminck, etc.*

After the great Impressionists, and again after Van Gogh and Gauguin, people said, " Painting is now played out." But Bonnard, Maurice Denis, Roussel and Vuillard appeared and gave them the lie. " We were wrong," said the croakers, " but this at any rate is the end." Yet to refute them, and to prove that there *is* no end to art, still another generation of painters sprang up. Derain, Marquet, Matisse, Vlaminck, to mention only a few.

I had already met Vlaminck by chance, without knowing it. One day in the rue Laffitte I had passed a tall, powerful fellow whose red scarf, knotted round his neck, might have suggested some militant anarchist, if, from the way in which he was carrying a canvas, I had not immediately recognised him for an artist. As far as I remember, the picture in question represented a sunset which appeared to have been squeezed out of tubes of paint in a fit of rage. The effect was startling. The man with the red scarf had kind, peaceable eyes, but one expected to hear him bellow,

" If anyone laughs at my painting, I'll bash his
face in." One could not help jibbing a bit at a
painting like that; all the same, there was something
exciting in it that made me wish to get into touch
with its author. What was my surprise the day
Matisse took me to Vlaminck's studio! Here was the
painter with the red scarf. This time he was wearing
a wooden tie of his own invention, the colours of
which he changed to suit his fancy. The landscapes
covering the walls of the studio were so many chal-
lenges to the *bourgeois* whose idea of nature is of
something tame and tidied up. Nevertheless, far
from being put off by this *outrance*, I bought everything Vlaminck showed me. I did the same with
Derain. But Derain, after giving me all the paintings
on the walls of his studio, took one back again: a
copy of a Ghirlandaio. What an admirable transcription! I remember Degas' anger when he saw
an admirable coloured lithograph by Auguste Clot
of one of his own works: "What? They have
dared . . ." And almost immediately after: "All
the same, he's a clever fellow, the wretch that did
that!" I fancy that Ghirlandaio, too, would have
admired such a replica of his work.

At a later date I asked Vlaminck and Derain to go
and paint for me in London. I was bitterly reproached
at the time for having taken these artists " out of
their element " by diverting them from their usual
subjects. Now that time has done its work it is easy
to see, on putting the French paintings beside those
done in England, that a painter " who has something
to say " is always himself, no matter in what country
he is working.

Matisse has been a disappointment to those who
like an artist to stick to the same manner all along.
Forsaking those greys that please his admirers so
much, he suddenly turned to the most brilliant

colours; for instance, in the *Portrait of a Woman* that he showed at the Salon d'Automne, and which marks a new stage of his talent. Although the artist's audacity did not go beyond the bounds of pure classicism, these bright colours brought him under suspicion of compounding with the "*Fauves.*"

Nothing more was needed to put the president of the Salon d'Automne, M. Jourdain, on his guard. He wished to appear friendly to the new trend in painting, but as a prudent leader he practised a certain opportunism, taking care not to break too openly with academic art, which still enjoyed the favour of public opinion. So, in the constant apprehension lest one of his " colts," taking the bit between his teeth, should compromise him in his official capacity, he decided that Matisse, with this *Portrait of a Woman*, was " playing the modern " with excess. He begged the jury to refuse the painting " in their friend's interest." It was accepted nevertheless.

" Poor Matisse ! " moaned M. Jourdain. " I thought we were all his friends here ! "

Among the young painters who were seeking their way, mention must be made of Charles Dulac.

I came to know Charles Dulac in 1890 when M. Henry Cochin, the erudite translator and commentator of Dante, arranged an exhibition at my place of the works of the young mystic painter so much admired by Huysmans. I chiefly remember a pool, with majestic swans floating on its pale surface. Dulac, a Franciscan soul, conceived of a work of art as a flight towards God. And following the example of Fra Angelico, before taking up his brushes he would kneel in prayer, awaiting inspiration. It was the general opinion, however, that the two painters had only this act of piety in common.

The Director of the Beaux-Arts, M. Roujon, opened the exhibition, the honours of which were done by

M. Henry Cochin. When the official had meted
out the customary praise, he took me aside and
said:

"I was told I should meet M. Cochin at your
exhibition."

"You have just been talking to him."

"That's not M. Denys Cochin. I know him well."

"But it is not M. Denys Cochin who has organised
this show, it is his brother Henry."

"Ah!" said M. Roujon, "I thought it was M.
Denys Cochin who protected young painters. . . ."

M. Henry Cochin, who was watching us, came up,
saying:

"May we not hope, M. le Directeur, that you
will retain one of these fine paintings for the
Luxembourg?"

"I should not hesitate certainly if it depended
solely on me," replied M. Roujon.

"At any rate," M. Cochin went on, "since you
appreciate Dulac's talent, we shall count on your
supporting him."

"Alas!" said M. Roujon, "there are two men in
me: the artist and the official."

And pointing to a landscape in which a sky of an
anæmic pink was reflected from a sea of silver grey:

"As an artist, of course, I am very sensitive to all
these experiments in colour. But you must see that
a Director of the Beaux-Arts is bound to follow public
taste, not to precede it."

XXII TWO SCULPTORS: MAILLOL AND RODIN

(a) *Aristide Maillol.*

"One day when I had been to see Maillol at Marly-le-Roi," Renoir told me, "I found him in his garden, hammer and chisel in hand, before a block of stone. So many modern sculptors merely plagiarise the ancients, but Maillol is such a true descendant of the Masters, that as I watched him disengaging his forms I was reminded of a Greek. I caught myself looking for the olive trees."

Maillol found the olive trees when at the approach of winter he left his studio at Marly-le-Roi to go and seek the sun in his native country at Banyuls-sur-Mer. It is a harsh country where the wind blows at times with savage violence. My printer discovered this when I sent him to the artist, to fetch the plates that the latter had engraved for my edition of Ronsard's *Folastries*.

"I did not find M. Maillol at Banyuls itself," my messenger told me on his return; "I had to go five kilometres beyond it to dig him out at his farm; five kilometres that I had to do bent double, almost on all fours, not to be carried up into the air."

"Ah!" said Maillol absent-mindedly when I repeated this to him, "probably there was a wind that day."

Fortunately the wind does not blow every day at Banyuls. Mr. W. Aspenwall Bradley, who visited the great sculptor, often alludes to the delightful time he spent with him, sitting under the trees of a little café. A girl came out, with a fine, generously moulded figure.

"I have often been rebuked," said Maillol, "for not making my women slender enough. Now you see! I sculpt the women of my country."

For a long while, if one wanted to see the best Maillols, one had to go abroad. There was the *Crouching Woman*, for instance, in the museum at Winterthur; another *Seated Woman*, a splendid marble in the former Kessler collection, now the ornament of M. Oscar Reinhardt's gardens in Zurich; the *Four Seasons* in the Morosoff Museum in Moscow. But now we have the *Hommage à Cézanne* at the Tuileries; the Debussy memorial at Saint-Germain; the *Monument to the Dead* at Céret. And the monument to *Blanqui*.

The story goes that the president of the committee, who was none other than M. Clémenceau, having asked Maillol, "How do you see your monument?", the other answered: "Well! I see a fine woman's bottom."

But alas for the fragility of "historic" sayings! Having reported the sentence to Maillol:

"I didn't say that," retorted the sculptor; "I said, 'Well! I'll do you a statue!'"

All the same, the monument to Blanqui consists in part of the opulent nude figure of a powerful woman, her arms chained behind her back, in which admirers perceive the symbol of "Captive Thought."

Truth to say, it is not from Maillol that one may expect these intellectual interpretations. In fact he hardly keeps up at all with contemporary literature.

"Someone came to see me called . . . Duhamel, Georges Duhamel. He told me he wrote. He looked at the studio. And then he found nothing more to say to me. Nor I to him. So he went away."

"What, Maillol, have you never read anything

of Duhamel's? " asked the friend to whom he was speaking.

Maillol, pointing to a little octavo on the table, said:

" That's what I read."

It was Catullus.

Renoir too thought very little of most of the authors of his time. One day he said to me:

" Would you believe it, Frank Lami is astonished that I haven't read *Madame Bovary*! People expect you to wade through three hundred pages to know how a chemist was made a cuckold! When there are such interesting things to read . . . *The Three Musketeers*, *The Count of Monte Cristo*. . . ."

A statue which had been commissioned by Count Kessler had a very singular adventure. At the time of the Germans' march on Paris, in 1914, Count Kessler, fearing that his countrymen, who were not all æsthetes, might not respect Maillol's studio, sent the artist the following telegram: " Bury statue." The fever into which the declaration of war had thrown everybody was such that this message appeared highly suspicious to vigilant patriots. The obsession of espionage helping, the rumour spread that the little *pavillon* where Count Kessler, a great lover of fine books, had been experimenting with paper-making under Maillol's direction, concealed a rein-forced concrete platform for the guns that were to come and bombard Paris.

The last time I saw Maillol, he was working in his garden at a statue, life-size, representing a pathetic figure of a woman shrouded in veils. On the face, despite its melancholy expression, one detected a quivering of new life.

" It is," the artist explained, " a commission for a monument. The widow of the deceased insisted on sitting herself."

' " She looks as though she were taking some interest in life again, your widow," I said to the sculptor.

" I don't know about that. I merely put down what I see. . . . But the swine who cast the clay for me have given me a hell of a job. The layer of plaster is much too thin, and every minute my tool touches the fibre the armature is made of. It gives me twice the amount of work, but when I think of what it will be like when it is cast in lead . . . what a fine material! "

At that moment the lady arrived, accompanied by a dashing young man. It was her fiancé. She had brought him to admire the monument.

(b) *Rodin.*

I had gone to Rodin to bring him a statuette by Maillol that he had bought of me. I was about to knock at the door of the studio, when I heard a woman's voice imploring:

" Master! Mercy for such a beautiful head . . .! "

Another voice, a masculine one this time, declaimed, with a strong Toulouse accent:

" Rodeïn! le grand Rodeïn! "

Another visitor, in whom I recognised M. Dujardin-Beaumetz, arrived and rang deliberately. Rodin himself came to let us in. He had a great sword in his hand. On the floor lay fragments of statues, severed hands and heads. Among the persons contemplating these with consternation were Loïe Fuller, Mme de Thèbes and the venerable astronomer Camille Flammarion.

" What a crime! " moaned Dujardin-Beaumetz.

The southern voice I had heard began again:

" Rodeïn! le grand Rodeïn! "

This booming voice issued from a little man wearing a thick fringe of beard. I was told he was Bourdelle, the Master's favourite pupil.

Rodin, catching sight of one of the statues, the only one still intact, and which had doubtless called forth the plea for mercy of a minute ago, whirled his sword, and the head fell.

" Such a pretty head! " cried M. Dujardin-Beaumetz.

" It's not a head! " exclaimed Rodin.

We looked at each other in stupefaction. Rodin picked up a foot which he held out to Dujardin-Beaumetz.

" What's this? "

" Well . . . a foot."

The Master cast his Olympian glance alternately at the severed head and foot. All were silent. Even Bourdelle remained dumb.

" I can't find what I want to-day . . . or rather, too many titles occur to me at once. *Hope of the Morning, Starry Night, A Day Will Come, Rêverie* . . . I must allow time for my thoughts to clear. It was in a nightmare that I hit on my best title: *The Kiss*. And again, the other day I was in my cellar when all at once I gave a start: I had thought of *The Earth* to symbolise a woman in travail."

Just then someone came in. It was the hair-dresser. He had a little moleskin bag in his hand, from which he took a wrapper that he made Rodin put on, and which had pinned upon it the rosette of a Commander of the Legion of Honour. The Master seated himself in front of a mirror. The barber opened his instrument case. Respectfully we ranged ourselves in a circle about them.

" To-day, Jules," said Rodin to the wig-maker, " you are going to shave off my beard."

A cry of horror arose from the bystanders.

" The Master without a beard! "

Bourdelle bellowed again:

" Rodeïn! le grand Rodeïn! "

The barber shut up his case.

" The Master must ask someone else to commit a crime such as that."

" Good Jules! " cried Rodin, " I was joking, my friend."

The company heaved a sigh of relief.

" Ah ! my beard! " cried the famous sculptor. " I pull it when inspiration is slow in coming. Besides, like most people, I'm superstitious. They touch wood, I touch my beard."

The door opened. A woman came forward, carrying a little child in her arms. She knelt down. She was a Russian, delegated by a group of political exiles. She told us that she had come from Siberia to bring the Master the homage of his admirers over there. She had had her child on the way:

" Bless him, Master."

Rodin laid his hands on the mother and on the child.

The barber began cutting his illustrious client's hair. When he had finished:

" I must leave you a minute," said Rodin to us, " I am going to see how they are getting on next door."

He went into another room where his pupils were working. Coming back a few minutes later, he said:

" Positively, I have only to go and smoke my pipe before a block of marble that one of my pointers is at work on, and it is as though I myself held the hammer and chisel."

M. Dujardin-Beaumetz had been looking thoughtfully for some time at a little bronze that he was holding in his hand.

" By what signs, Master, may one distinguish a false from a true Rodin? "

" Only I can do so. It's quite simple! A true Rodin is one that has been cast with my consent; the false is done without my knowledge."

Rodin had picked up one of the heads that were

P

lying on the floor, the one that had called forth the disconsolate exclamation I had heard on entering the studio.

" How much more beautiful it is without the body! " he cried. " After all, how could it be otherwise? "

We listened devoutly.

" I am giving away one of my secrets. All those trunks that you see there, so perfect in their forms now that they no longer have heads, arms or legs, belonged to an enlargement. Now, in an enlargement, certain parts keep their proportions, whereas others are no longer to scale. But each fragment remains a very fine thing. Only, there it is! You have to know how to cut them up. That's the whole art."

" Rodeïn! le grand Rodeïn! " began Bourdelle again.

At that moment a footman was shown in, in a rich livery, carrying a plant wrapped up in glassine paper. When the paper was taken off, we saw a little shrub covered with flowers. On one of the branches was pinned a visiting card.

Rodin unfastened it, saying, " Yet another present from the good duchess! "

A little label was tied to the foot of the shrub by a wire. Loïe Fuller read out: " Dwarf acacia, scentless. . . ."

Rodin cried exultingly:

" What a marvellous thing is Science! How fortunate to be born in a century in which one can command nature! "

" Where will progress stop? " threw in Camille Flammarion. " Think of the stars that are giving us up their secrets one by one! This very morning I read that they have invented more than a hundred ways of cooking eggs. When one thinks that the Greeks . . ."

" Yes, we owe them a great many masterpieces,"

said Mme de Thèbes, " but it must be admitted that
they did not excel in gastronomy. Their dinners of
olives, a piece of black bread, goat's milk . . ."

" The Greeks! " exclaimed Rodin. " If we could
only go back to their happy simplicity! "

" Master," said M. Dujardin-Beaumetz, " there
are some little ' snack-bars ' (' Casse-croûtes ') where
one can drink milk fresh from the goat. . . ."

" Really! " murmured Rodin. " Alas! We are
not Greeks. We are civilised. Think of it! If I
were to go, I won't say to the President of the Republic,
but merely to a reception by the Municipal Council,
with my bare feet in sandals—in the costume, in fact,
of a contemporary of Pheidias—it would be no use
my saying: ' I am Rodin.' "

Bourdelle shouted:

" Rodeïn! le grand Rodeïn! "

" I should be chucked out," concluded the
Master.

At this vision of a Rodin expelled from the Hôtel
de Ville, indignant cries broke out on every side.
An expression of melancholy appeared on his noble
visage.

" Not to be the great Rodin any more," he muttered
under his breath. " To be loved for oneself . . . to
be loved, and to be twenty years old! "

" But it is for yourself that we love you, Master! "

The phrase was pronounced by a diminutive little
woman who looked like a former model turned
fashionable lady. Rodin, recovering himself, said:

" That reminds me, Baroness, that I promised you
at least two years ago to use you as a model."

He took a Phrygian cap and put it on her head.

" I want an emblem for my statue of the Republic."

With a lump of clay in his hand he set to work.
Around him there was a buzz of admiration. M.
Dujardin-Beaumetz made himself the interpreter of
the company:

" Illustrious friend, whence do you draw the life
that palpitates in the least detail of your work? "

" From life itself. I make life out of life."

As twelve o'clock struck, we left the studio.

We formed a group around Bourdelle, who was
talking of the lecture he had been giving.

" Your lyricism astonished me! " cried a lady.

" I must admit," said Bourdelle ingenuously, " that
I am carried away by enthusiasm now and then.
But my flights of imagination are always missing
from the shorthand reports—I suppose they have no
signs to transcribe them in."

XXIII GEORGES ROUAULT: DOU-ANIER ROUSSEAU: PICASSO

(a) *Rouault.*

At my first exhibitions in the rue Laffitte I had noticed a young man with a short red beard, wearing a hooded cape fastened by two big buckles of silvered metal. This, I discovered later, was Georges Rouault, the favourite disciple of Gustave Moreau, who used to say, " It is easy to see that he is my pupil, for he wears jewellery."

I did not attempt to make acquaintance with this visitor, who looked about, stopped before this picture and that, then went out without saying a word. This speechlessness will surprise those who have only known the Rouault of to-day. I am speaking of the Rouault of thirty-five years ago, of whom his master used to say: " He only answers ' yes ' and ' no.' But into that ' yes ' and ' no ' he puts so much passion that, if he paints as he speaks, he will go far."

Some time later I came across some water-colours by this young painter. They were so brilliant that I asked him to decorate some pottery for me. The result was a set of vases, plates and dishes that might have come from a factory of the Renaissance.

I said to Rouault one day:

" How do you get those intense yellows, those flaming red-browns, those extraordinary ultramarine blues that make your pictures look like old stained glass? "

" I have been told before," he said, " that my painting reminded people of stained glass. That's probably because of my original trade. As soon as

213

I had my school certificate, my parents apprenticed me to a master glazier. I got ten sous a week. My work consisted in supervising the firing, and sorting the little pieces of glass that fell out of the windows they brought us to repair. This latter task inspired me with an enduring passion for old stained glass. My aunts used to paint china and fans. As a child I messed about with paints. I went off with pencil-ends, old paint-brushes, any tubes of paint left lying about, and tried my hand at painting too."

Georges Rouault was born in 1871, in Paris, during the Commune, in a cellar where his mother had had to be carried during a bombardment. A shell had just burst in the house next door, and as a result of the shock to Mme Rouault the child was born with a very weak heart. In later life Georges Rouault was for ever being told by the doctors to avoid all strenuous exercise and overwork. Laughable recommendations, when one remembers this painter's passion for work! Every branch of art attracted him in turn: ceramics, sculpture, lithography and etching. Not to speak of painting, which to him was a necessary function of life. Rouault had this passion in his blood. His father, a cabinet-maker at Pleyel's, was one of those artisans of the old days who took a pride in their trade. An imperfect piece of furniture, badly-fitting wood that gave or warped, caused him real suffering.

Rouault was very proud of his artisan origin. He told me an amusing story on the subject. On the eve of his marriage, a lady of the family he was about to enter, who was secretly hostile to him, asked him with a simulated interest:

"What was your father, cher monsieur? "

"He was a workman at Pleyel's."

"You mean a clerk."

"No, madame, a workman."

The lady made a disdainful grimace.

"Are you a Christian?" the painter asked her quizzically.

"What a question!"

"If you are, you should honour my father, since you honour Saint Joseph the carpenter, and his apprentice the Child Jesus."

The lady was shocked, and went off, murmuring: "Now I understand why the fellow's painting is so ugly."

Ugly, perhaps, but how compelling! Of this dominant quality of Rouault's work striking proof was furnished me one day by an American couple, on whom it acted like a spell. They lived in Honolulu, and I was envying them for having the splendours of the Pacific always before their eyes.

"Yes," said the lady, "but all that does not amount to a picture by Rouault! We have just found one, absolutely fascinating, but the dealer refuses to sell it. I feel as though we were going home baulked of a treasure."

(b) *The Douanier Rousseau.*

One morning a little man came into my shop with two or three small canvases under his arm: he looked for all the world like a retired clerk.

"I am a painter," he told me.

It was Henri Rousseau, known as the "*Douanier*."

He was not content with painting. He told me he had begun giving music lessons. "My pupils," he said pompously of a few young clerks in his neighbourhood, at Plaisance.

I have often wondered if that simple, not to say slightly bewildered, air, that struck one in père Rousseau, was not a mask behind which he concealed himself, and whether at bottom he was not a sly dog.

Be that as it may, and whether one liked his work or not, one could not help liking the man himself as soon as one knew him, for he was good-nature personified.

It was this good-nature that led one day to his being arrested. One of his music-pupils, taking advantage of his simplicity, asked him to cash a forged cheque for him. When the culprit, who was waiting for Rousseau at the door of the bank, saw him come out between two policemen, he guessed that the fraud had been discovered, and bolted. As the " pupil " was not to be found, the " professor " was brought before the judges. His case appeared desperate, when the advocate thought of showing the magistrates one of the " *Douanier's* " pictures, which he had brought with him.

" Can you still doubt that my client is an ' innocent ' ? " he asked.

The evidence appears to have satisfied the Tribunal, for Rousseau, found guilty in principle, was allowed the benefit of the law of reprieval. On leaving the prisoner's bench, in order to be even with the Tribunal, apparently, in the matter of politeness, he offered to paint the portrait of the President's " lady."

But if he found favour in the eyes of the law, it was otherwise with M. Jourdain, the president of the Salon d'Automne. Someone having said to him one day, *à propos* a picture of Rousseau's, " It is reminiscent of Persian art," M. Jourdain shuddered:

" Persian, in my place! I shall be blamed for not being up to date."

Rousseau's cause, then, was already lost when, thinking a " permanent " situation better than the hazards of painting, he went to M. Jourdain to ask him for a post as keeper in the Salon d'Automne. M. Jourdain saw in this a trick of the " Fauves," whom he fancied always on the look-out to pull his leg.

" You are very badly advised by your friends," he said to the " Master of Plaisance." " I will not give you the job. It would make you ridiculous. I have your interest too much at heart. On varnishing day, for instance, at the time of the presidential visit, I took care to hide the picture you had sent in, behind a curtain. So you see . . ."

What Rousseau saw was that his work ran the risk of being hidden again.

" So of course, M. Vollard, I used to go from time to time to see if my picture was still in its place. And one day when I was sitting on a seat before my *Combat between a Lion and a Jaguar* and had fallen into a doze, instead of my picture I saw a little box beginning to move. . . . Suddenly it opened, and out of it sprang a little devil who was as like M. Jourdain as a brother. Just then a group of painters went past: Derain, Vlaminck, Rouault, Matisse, Marquet. The little devil, brandishing an umbrella, gave them a good whacking on their calves. I woke up . . . A few steps away from me was M. Jourdain in flesh and blood, a pencil in his hand. . . ."

" You say, M. Rousseau, that he had a pencil in his hand? "

" Certainly, M. Vollard, I assure you he had a pencil in his hand."

This showed me how cautious one should be about believing things said even by those who should know best. Did not the late architect Fivas say of his colleague in my hearing, " The extraordinary thing, for an architect, is that Jourdain has never touched a pencil."

It has been said that Rousseau painted his pictures from illustrations in the newspapers. One morning, looking at one of his paintings that certain critics had dubbed an enlarged postcard, and which represented a naked woman dreaming on a red sofa in the midst of a virgin forest, I said to him:

" Tell me, M. Rousseau, how did you get so much air to circulate among those trees, and the moonlight to look so real? "

" By observing nature, M. Vollard."

One afternoon Rousseau arrived at my shop in a *fiacre*. He had in front of him a canvas two metres high. I can see him now, battling with the wind. When his work was under shelter, he stood contemplating it with satisfaction.

" You seem pleased with your work, M. Rousseau," I said to him.

" And you, M. Vollard? "

" That will go to the Louvre! "

His eyes glistened:

" Since you admire my painting, couldn't you give me a certificate to say that I'm getting on? "

" Absurd! A testimonial of that kind would cover us both with ridicule. But why do you want my certificate? "

" I must tell you that I want to get married. . . . At the Customs I was in the outdoor service, whereas my future father-in-law is in one of the offices . . . of course those gentlemen look down on us mere *gabelous*. Besides, to give one's daughter to a man who takes his pictures round to his customers himself . . ."

" Don't let that stand in your way, M. Rousseau! I'll go and fetch them from you, if you like that better."

" Yes, but then, if my bride's family should hear that I'm no longer seen about the streets with my pictures under my arm, they will think I haven't any work. . . . I thought a testimonial from someone with a shop . . . a certificate from a licensed dealer. . . . My situation is becoming difficult. The father of my betrothed is threatening me because he knows that his daughter and I are still meeting in spite of his prohibition."

" Take care, M. Rousseau! If your future wife is under sixteen, her father may prosecute you for abduction of a minor."

" Oh! M. Vollard! She is fifty-four. . . ."

And as this struck me dumb:

" You know, I wish I were called Léon and not Henri. . . ."

" Why Léon? "

" Well, my fiancée is called Léonie. So you see, Léonie . . . Léon . . ."

The " *Douanier* " Rousseau read me one of his poems in which a ghost was concerned:

" Ghosts! Come, M. Rousseau! A sensible man like you! "

" So then you, M. Vollard, don't believe in ghosts? "

" No, I don't believe in them."

" Well, I do. I've seen some. There was actually one that pursued me for quite a long time."

" You don't say so! And what was he like? "

" Just an ordinary man. Nothing special about him. He used to come and defy me when I was on duty at the *octroi*. He knew I couldn't leave my post. So he would put out his tongue or cock snooks at me, and then let off a great fart."

" But what makes you think he was a ghost? "

" It was M. Apollinaire who told me so."

(c) *Pablo Picasso*.

Towards 1901 I received a visit from a young Spaniard, dressed with the most studied elegance. He was brought to me by one of his countrymen whom I knew slightly, a manufacturer from Barcelona called Manache, I fancy, or something like it. One day when I was passing through Barcelona he had made me visit his factory. At the entrance to the workshops a lamp was burning before the statue of a saint. " The workmen pay for the oil," he said to me. " So long as the little lamp is burning, I am safe from a strike."

Manache's companion was the painter Pablo Picasso, who, though only eighteen, had finished about a hundred paintings, which he was bringing me with a view to an exhibition. This exhibition

was not a success, and for a long time after Picasso
got no better reception from the public.

I am not concerned here with his different manners
—his so-called " pink period," " blue period," " negro
period "—that is not my job. But I can say with
truth that I have had in my shop many of his pictures
which are the most sought after to-day, but for which
the artist, at that time, could not obtain the price of
a stretcher. I can also tell a story of the artist's
Cubist period, at a time when not only the man in
the street, but amateurs, art critics and even painters
still refused to admit that nature might consist of an
assemblage of geometrical forms.

Before forcing itself on Paris, Cubism—which was
to exert so profound an influence on decorative art
and on a whole group of young artists—was first to
conquer Germany, greedy as ever of everything new,
and soon after, America and Scandinavia. A New-
Yorker, passionately interested in the controversy on
Cubism and wishing to meet the leader of the new
school, made the journey to Paris. A star led the
Kings to the stable at Bethlehem, but none appeared
to guide the American to the humble studio where
the doctrine was being elaborated. He only knew
that it was in Montmartre. So he set to work to
explore all the nooks and corners of the Butte, hailing
pedestrians, taxi-drivers, newsvendors, concierges on
their doorsteps, workmen in their working clothes,
inquiring of each one: " Cubisme? Cubisme? " the
only word he could say in French. And as no one
answered him, he soon came to the conclusion that
Cubism had died at birth. Without seeking farther,
he gave up hope of penetrating the mysteries of the new
painting and took the first boat back to New York.

What would have been his astonishment had he
been told that he had perhaps passed by the inventor
of Cubism, Picasso himself, coming back from the
dairy, in dungarees, his milk-can in his hand!

XXIV MY PORTRAITS

I have sat for my portrait a number of times.
Renoir, in particular, did several portraits of me,
one of them as a toreador.

I had told him I was going to Spain.

" I have always wanted to paint a *torero*," he said.
" One of my models is about your size, so do try and
bring me back a *torero's* costume that fits you."

But nowhere, either in Seville, Madrid or Toledo,
could I find a costume that fitted me. So I was
obliged to have one made to measure. On my
return to Paris, the Customs officer who was examining
my luggage pounced at once on the swagger costume.

" Those are my working clothes," I said.

" Ah! You are a toreador? All right! Put them
on. We shall soon see! "

I did as I was told. I felt magnificent in the gold-
embroidered jacket and equally gorgeous breeches.
But a crowd was collecting, and I escaped from
their curiosity by jumping into a taxi and driving to
Renoir's.

" Bravo! " cried the painter as soon as he set eyes
on me; " I shall make *you* sit for my picture."

I picked up a rose that was lying on the table.

" You shall be the *toréro à la rose.* . . . No, the rose
would get in the way of your hands. Throw it
down. It will make a jolly note of colour on the
carpet."

I asked Renoir if I ought not to get shaved for the
sake of local colour.

" You don't suppose you would be taken for a real

torero, if you did?" he cried. "All I ask of you is not to go to sleep while you are sitting."

Sitting for Renoir was not at all wearisome. One could move and talk. People came in and out. One day a German couple came to the studio to arrange for the lady's portrait to be painted. Renoir was working at the time from a model whose dress was cut generously low.

"For my wife," said the German, "I *temand* that you shall make it more *indimate*."

"Like that?" asked Renoir, draping a scarf over the lady's bust, to lessen the slight *décolletage* of her dress.

"No. I *dell* you, more *indimate*."

Renoir drew the scarf up to the lady's chin.

"No! no!" reiterated the German. "*Tout-à-fait indime, je fous dis*. . . . So that one can see at least one of her nipples!"

"Don't go to sleep!" Renoir had said. I repeated the warning to myself when I went to sit to Cézanne. In his studio I was required to seat myself on a stool placed on a ramshackle platform supported by four pegs.

Seeing my distrust of the solidity of all this contraption, "I arranged all this myself," said Cézanne with an engaging smile. "Nothing will happen if you keep your balance. And after all, sitting means sitting still."

But hardly was I settled on my pedestal when sleep overtook me. My head sank on to my shoulder. The equilibrium was shattered: platform, chair and myself were all on the floor.

Cézanne rushed forward:

"You wretch! You have upset the pose! You should sit like an apple. Whoever saw an apple fidgeting?"

Motionless as that fruit may be, Cézanne was

sometimes obliged to leave a study of apples unfinished. They had rotted. He came to like paper flowers better. But he ended by giving them up too, for though they did not rot, " they fade, the bitches." In despair, he fell back on the pictures in the illustrated papers that his sisters took in, and the prints in the *Magasin Pittoresque*. What did it matter? Painting, for him, did not consist in copying objects, but in " realising sensations."

But for Cézanne to feel sure that the day's work in the studio was going to be a success, a great many conditions were necessary—the colour of the weather a light grey, and no annoyance such as coming upon the news, in his paper *La Croix*, of a victory of the English over the Boers, or a dog barking, or the noise of a lift near by, which he declared came from a " sledge-hammer factory." About a hundred sittings had to be endured before Cézanne could even announce to me, with satisfaction, " I haven't done so badly with the front of your shirt."

I have sat for other painters besides Renoir and Cézanne. Bonnard did two portraits of me. But with him I did not go to sleep, for I had a little cat on my knees to stroke.

Raphael Schwartz asked if he might do an etching of me. He wanted to publish an album of celebrities. In vain I excused myself by saying I had no right to such a title. The artist's persistence was such that I concluded he must have pitched on me as the publisher of his work.

Although a stranger to Renoir, Schwartz marched one day into his studio with a copper-plate under his arm.

" M. Renoir," said he, " I have come to do your portrait."

" You've chosen a good time. I'm not going out to-day. Sit down over there. Whilst I'm working you can get on with your job."

Some days later Schwartz came back.

" M. Renoir, here is a proof. Will you write a few words on it? "

Without hesitation, the painter wrote: " To M. Raphael Schwartz, thanks to whom I shall go down to posterity."

The etcher also wished to draw Degas, and begged me urgently to introduce him. One day he happened to be in my shop at the same time as an old gentleman who sat leaning with both hands on his walking-stick. After he had gone:

" When are you going to let me meet Degas? " Schwartz asked me again.

He never knew he had just seen him, nor what we should both have " caught " if I had said: " M. Degas, here is M. Schwartz, who wants to do your portrait."

As for the etching he wanted to do of me, I put Schwartz off it at the first sitting, by falling asleep in spite of myself. It was really inexcusable, for pretty Mme. Schwartz had brought me a little clockwork canary to keep me awake. But perhaps it was the bird's song that sent me to sleep.

Picasso did a very notable portrait of me. This painting, of the artist's Cubist period, is now in the Moscow Museum. Of course when they saw this picture, even people who considered themselves connoisseurs indulged in the facile pleasantry of asking what it was meant for. But the son of one of my friends, a boy of four, standing in front of the picture, put a finger on it and said without hesitation: " That's *Voyard*."

Degas, too, said to me: " I shall try and do something of you." But that was towards the end of his life, when he could literally hardly see any longer. Curiously enough, he who had pretended for so long not to be able to see, now that his eyes were failing him, would not admit the fact, although sometimes when he was modelling in wax he would exclaim: " There's no denying it, I shall have to take up a blind man's trade! " One had to be very careful not to appear to notice that his sight was going. A model once remarked, looking at his painting during the rest, " M. Degas, my head isn't properly joined to my neck," and was obliged to go and dress on the landing, where the painter had flung out her clothes in a heap.

On the day he had appointed, I came to put myself at his disposal, but he could do nothing but talk to me of the state of his bladder. It had become an obsession with him. By and by, hearing the bell ring, he went to open the door, with his bowl of cherry-stalk tisane in his hand. A young woman had come to offer herself as a model. Before she had had time to get in a single word, Degas, haunted by his disease, asked her:

" Do you pee properly? I pee very badly, and so does my friend R . . ."

And that was all that came of the appointment to sit to Degas for my portrait.

XXV MALLARMÉ AND ZOLA

I shall always remember my first meeting with Mallarmé. I was walking in the woods at Valvins with one of my friends. We passed a little grey-haired gentleman who, with a stick at the end of which a nail was fixed, was picking up all the bits of greasy paper and putting them into a little basket.

"Why, there's Mallarmé!" exclaimed my friend.

He went up to the poet:

"What *are* you doing?"

"To-morrow," replied Mallarmé, "I have asked a few Parisians to come to tea. I am cleaning up the banquet-hall."

Mallarmé, whose works are supposed to be un-intelligible to the "average Frenchman," was a veritable charmer in conversation. Redon told me that, when Mallarmé received his friends in his modest flat in the rue de Rome, he always talked standing by "his" armchair, in which no one would have dared to sit. Only once did a stranger, introduced by a friend of the house, seeing the chair empty, sit down in it as a matter of course, to the horror of the assembly.

Of the poet's dazzling conversational powers the following is proof. One day, on the top of an omnibus, the editor in chief of the *Figaro*, Francis Magnard, exchanged a few words with the man beside him. As they passed the flower-market near the Madeleine, the latter hit on such original images in which to describe the flowers that Magnard could not refrain from saying:

"Monsieur, I am the editor of the *Figaro*. If you

would care to write down what you have just said, I should like to publish it in my paper."

Some time later, Magnard said to one of his friends:

" I've just had an article on flowers, signed by someone called Mallarmé. He's obviously a madman! "

I went to Zola with an introduction from Mirbeau, in the hope of seeing some of the pictures of Cézanne's youth in his possession.

Immediately on entering the novelist's house, I was faced by an imposing composition of Debat-Ponsan's representing *Truth coming out of a Well*. Two stained-glass windows, the one depicting a venerable anchorite, and the other a character out of the *Assommoir*, completed the decoration of the hall.

The salon alongside, into which I was shown, was a regular museum. Here, a vase on which was painted a Chinaman under a parasol; beside it, the portrait of a child warming a little sparrow on her breast; further on, a picture of naked women; to say nothing of objects in glass cases, miniatures, ivories, etc.

I was looking at an angel with outspread wings which appeared to be hovering, fastened to the ceiling by some invisible cord, when Zola came in. I had hardly had time to greet him when, pointing to the object I had been looking at, he said:

" Mirbeau is very fond of that. In that piece, produced by the tool of some anonymous fifteenth-century artist, there is a chisel stroke that reminds one of Rodin."

And with characteristic good-nature, Zola set himself to do the honours of his treasures:

" That little girl with the bird is a Greuze, painted at the end of the artist's life. That sofa is a period piece. The Chinese vase . . ."

" A Ming," I cried at a venture.

" No, a Jacob Petit. That *Nude* is an Ary Scheffer I picked up in the rue Lepic."

In my anxiety not to let a word of the Master's escape me, I kept my eyes fixed on a horrible little dog that he carried lovingly in his arms, and which kept hurling itself in my direction, showing all its teeth. Zola caressed the hideous animal, saying, " He's very fond of his master, is little Pinpin."

An opportunity of mentioning Cézanne's paintings was furnished me by Zola himself. He picked up a Japanese ivory to show me, and I said tentatively:

" What an influence the Japanese had on the Impressionists! Except for Cézanne, of course. . . ."

" Cézanne! Thinking of him conjures up my whole youth, all our life together in Paris! All our enthusiasms! Ah! Why did not my friend produce the work that I expected of him? It was in vain that I dinned into him, ' You have the genius of a great painter; have the courage to become one.' Alas! he listened to no advice."

Zola walked up and down the room, still holding his dear Pinpin in his arms:

" I have a few of Cézanne's pictures of that period."

And stopping before a Breton wardrobe, he tapped on one of the doors.

" They are in there. So at least, when I say to our old friends, ' No, Paul was not a failure,' I do not risk their pointing ironically to the paintings on the walls."

Zola was obviously distressed. To distract his thoughts I spoke of his books, and asked him which one he preferred. He replied that although a writer always prefers the work on which he is engaged, he had a partiality for *La Débâcle*. " We have got to the two hundredth thousand."

In my book on Cézanne I gave a detailed account of this visit to Zola. My intention had been to reproduce word for word the sayings of the Master, as a conscientious interviewer should. Yet I had a cutting from the *Bonnet Rouge* sent me by the *Courier de la Presse*. It was an article by M. Frantz Jourdain. Shocked by my narrative, he wrote, " If a cur lifts its leg against Notre-Dame, Notre-Dame is not befouled by it."

A few days later I had another surprise. A former *Procureur Général* of La Réunion, an old friend of my family, came to see me and blurted out:

" My dear Vollard, I always thought you such a decent fellow! How can you prostrate yourself like that before Zola! "

XXVI LE SÂR PELADAN AND THE ROSICRUCIANS

When I opened my shop in the rue Laffitte, in 1894, the Impressionist movement had won the day; but by then fresh adventurers were exploring fresh paths. For painting is not stationary, it cannot escape the urge to renewal, the incessant evolution that manifests itself in every form of art. At the same time it may be said with truth that each of these forms reacts upon the others, with sometimes one, sometimes another predominating, providing the impulse in some fresh direction. As a rule, literature heads the movement, furnishing at once the theory and the example from which music and the plastic arts draw their inspiration. But at the period of which I am speaking, music had taken the lead. And what is music? A sort of incantation. It does not define. It does not aim at direct demonstration or description. It captivates precisely by its flowing, vaporous, indeterminate qualities. It feeds at the sources of mystery, on myths, on legends; and with what it borrows from these it creates moods, an atmosphere propitious to passion or reverie. Under its influence, and by way of reaction against the brutalities of realism on the one hand, and cold Parnassian perfection on the other, the writers, and the poets especially, were attempting to capture the almost immaterial charm that resides in the vagueness of the subject. They were endeavouring to induce the same moods, the same enthusiasm, the same transports of sensibility into which they were thrown in moments of musical exaltation. They would no longer describe, they would evoke. They would not state precisely, but suggest. The poet would consider it his mission merely to open up vistas. The poem was to prolong itself in the free and emotional meditation of the reader. The fascination exercised by Wagner's work thus gave rise to the esoterism of Mallarmé, and the " music before all things " of Verlaine. It was the symbolic epoch.

In the plastic arts, and particularly in painting, the same influence was at work, an influence undergone directly by some, but propagated for the most part through the media of literature and criticism. It is not for me to quarrel with this sort of tutelage of painting. I would merely recall that it was to produce the school of the Rosicrucians, which, compared with other manifestations of symbolism, appeared to derive its inspiration more expressly from religion.

These new æsthetics were presented by a number of painters in exhibitions of a somewhat boisterous character. I attended these first exhibitions; and I must admit that I could not get up any enthusiasm for those paintings of filiform, bloodless women, nor for those green, blue or yellow Ophelias who looked as though they had just had a bath at the dyer's.

The influence that literature can legitimately exert on painting has been determined by Degas in a word. When he was asked to admire a picture:

" Wouldn't you say, M. Degas, that the influence of Debussy can be felt in that painting? "

" Oh, come," said Degas; " blue paint comes out of a tube, not an ink-pot."

All this brings me to my first acquaintance with Josephin Peladan.

It was not merely his works that had caught my fancy; I was also very much impressed by the title of *Sâr*, that is to say *Mage*, with which he had adorned his surname. In my earliest childhood Tante Noémie had told me so many lovely stories about the Three

Wise Kings! So I wrote to the author of *Le Vice Suprême*. I told him I was one of his most obscure admirers and that I solicited the favour of being received by him. He replied that he would be very glad to see me; and greatly delighted, I rang at his door.

At the sound of the bell, a voice inside cried, " Light the candles! " The door opened. I found myself facing an individual with a jet-black beard, in a sort of dressing-gown of red turkey twill.

The Sâr—for it was he—showed me into a room in which were a number of young men all garbed in the same red robes. The Master and his disciples received me with the utmost affability.

I then saw the meaning of the phrase I had heard through the door. Five candles were burning before a picture representing a flower, from the calyx of which a woman's head emerged. One of the young men was turning over the pages of some art reviews, and tearing out violently every picture of any subject that the Rosicrucians prohibited in painting, such as still-lifes. I accepted a cigarette offered me by one of these gentlemen. The Sâr condescended to do me the honour of giving me a light; and finding no matches, plunged his hands into the waste-paper basket, where his disciple was throwing the condemned reproductions. He seized one, which he twisted up and lighted at one of the candles wasting before the altar.

After a time, too long I fancy for the tastes of my hosts, whose mystic communion was disturbed by my presence, I retired. From the hall I heard, " Put out the candles! " Such was my first encounter with the Sâr.

Later, happening to be at Nîmes, I went to listen to a lecture by Peladan. He still had his fine black beard; but in a simple morning coat he appeared less of the Sâr. I made this observation to a lady beside

me. She retorted with much vivacity that if he had
worn a red robe, people might have thought that
M. Josephin—as she called him familiarly—had
become a vendor of specifics for corns or of love-
philtres, and he might have suffered the same mis-
adventure as another man in a red robe and a pointed
cap who used to read people's hands. . . . "It was
last week," the lady began, " in the square in front of
the church . . ." But at that instant the general
attention was attracted—I should say captured—by
these words of the Sâr: " People of Nîmes, I have
only to pronounce a certain formula for the earth to
open and swallow you up."

The audience looked at each other as though it
were a joke, but I fancy they were really in a bit of a
funk. The Sâr, being good-natured, did not pronounce the fatal words. As I came out of the hall, I
said to someone:

" Supposing they had said to him ' Rats! Pronounce your famous formula then!' Do you think
a disaster would have occurred? "

" You can't tell! Josephin's a decent fellow, but if
you defy him . . ."

I made a note of the procedure of intimidation, and
determined to try it upon occasion.

A few days later in a pastrycook's window I noticed
some very appetising little cakes. I went in and asked
the proprietress if her tartlets were really " to-day's."
She declared that if I had come a few minutes earlier
I should have seen them being taken from the oven.
I tested one, but the first mouthful proved the cake
to be irrefutably stale.

" Madame," I said to the shopkeeper, " do you
know the story of Ananias and Sapphira? "

She stared at me.

" Do they belong to these parts? "

" No. They were people of the time of Jesus
Christ. One day they went to the Apostle Peter and

said, 'We have sold all our possessions and brought you the whole proceeds for the poor.'

" 'You have kept some of it for yourselves, you liars!' retorted the chief of the Apostles. 'To punish you for your lie . . .' He made a gesture. The earth split and swallowed up the two deceivers. And suppose your floor, madame, were to open in the same way, to punish you for having told me this little cake was fresh this morning? "

The woman listened to me with her mouth open. But at the mention of the floor she cried:

" Well! just you touch my floor! "

The husband, huge and covered with flour, came out of his bakehouse.

" What's the fellow after? " he asked with scant affability, pointing to me.

" Never mind him. He's trying to pull my leg," replied the *patissière*.

I thought it more prudent to decamp, for the maker of tartlets had two great rolls of dough in his hands which I fancied he might be thinking of flinging at me. Later, in a Charlie Chaplin film, I saw a scene of the kind and thought it great fun, but that time I was a spectator.

XXVII STATESMEN AND JOURNALISTS

That night the bellowing of the sirens announced that German aeroplanes were making for Paris. Like everyone else I went down into a cellar, and to pass the time began chatting with my neighbours. One of them told me he was one of the editors of the *Gaulois*.

"What do you think of the paper?" he asked me.

"It's very good, of course."

"And Arthur Meyer, the editor?"

"He has a very fine mind."

A few days later, M. Arthur Meyer wrote to me, saying his collaborator had told him of my flattering opinion of his newspaper and of himself. He thanked me, and begged me to go and see him. "We may be useful to each other at some time," he added.

In effect I persuaded Bonnard to do him a sketch for his copy of my book, *Ubu-Roi*.

Every book in M. Meyer's library was enriched by the original work of some artist. His choice always showed a sure taste. For instance, for *La Maison Tellier* he had thought of Degas, and he showed me a letter from the painter promising him a drawing. Not long after, I saw a sketch on Degas' desk.

"It's for a book in Arthur Meyer's library," he told me.

"What? You who dislike the Jews . . ."

"Ah, but he's on the right side."

Renoir was very angry when M. Meyer wrote asking him to do a drawing for a book he was sending him. But after letting fly for a bit, he said:

"What are you doing, Gabrielle?"

235

" Sir, I'm packing up the book to send it back."

" No . . . leave it there."

And he painted a water-colour on the fly-leaf.

Degas never finished his drawing, but that was through over-conscientiousness. He was in the habit of improving his work by corrections on tracing-paper outside the original lines, and the sketch he intended for M. Arthur Meyer ended by attaining a metre in height, so the bibliophile had to forgo the promised illustration. But he would not be beaten. By way of illustration to *La Maison Tellier*, he bought a mono-type by Degas of two women on a sofa, which suited de Maupassant's story far better than the drawing of a dancer that the artist had thrown aside. At the sale of Meyer's library, a good price was obtained for this book, to which the letter from Degas promising the drawing had been added.

I went one day to see M. Arthur Meyer at the *Gaulois* office, and found him with a book in his hand. As I was leaving, I asked him the title of it, thinking I could not do better than read a book that appealed to so enlightened a mind.

" It is *The Odyssey of a Torpedoed Transport*," he said, referring to the title on the cover.

" And who is the author? " I asked him.

Again he consulted the cover:

" The work is anonymous." [1]

" And the subject of the book? "

" I have not the slightest idea! " he replied, shutting it up. " The fact is, you see, I think too much. I take up a book to stop myself thinking; but as I can't help thinking all the same, I end by not knowing what I'm reading."

" How strange," I replied. " Xavier de Maistre said the same thing."

" Xavier de Maistre said that too, did he? "

[1] The author has since dropped his anonymity: He is M. Maurice Larrouy.

And M. Arthur Meyer bridled and stroked his whiskers.

I was waiting for one of my friends in his flat in the rue Franklin. I saw a pigeon tapping hard with its beak on the pane of a window near me. I opened the window. The pigeon hopped into the room, followed by another pigeon which had a straw in its bill. The bird went and perched itself on a dwarf palm that stood on the piano; then, cautiously, it placed the straw between two of the branches. Meanwhile its companion strutted about with its tail spread. All at once they both flew away. They came back again, and this time each pigeon carried a strand of wool which was laid alongside the straw.

My friend's son, a boy of seven, came in.

" Do those pigeons belong to you? " I inquired.

" They belong to a neighbour."

" But what are they doing in that palm? "

" They're making their nest."

" Why don't they build it in that dove-cot in the garden? "

The child did not answer.

Then I saw some cats prowling along the garden wall; and they were not the only creatures that threatened the pigeons. For now a manservant brought the ring-doves their food; he had hardly turned his back before two enormous rats ran out and made a clean sweep of the lot. I thought of telling the owner of the garden, but he was no less a personage than M. Clémenceau, and I should not have dared to approach him.

I noticed an old fellow perpetually bending down over the flower-beds; but I hardly liked to report the misdeeds of the rats to him either, he seemed so indifferent to everything but his rose trees. And behold, in the evening, as I was going away, I found myself face to face with the old gardener: this time he was in a morning coat and a bowler hat, and I saw he was M. Clémenceau.

Later, during a conversation at which I was present and which concerned the political activity of the former President of the Council:

" He saved France," said one.

" Granted," retorted another, " but think of his post-war policy . . . the oil-fields of Mosul abandoned to the English ! "

" Well, what does that matter? " cried the child of the house. " The grocer's boy was saying to the maid this morning : ' *Ma petite*, we can supply you with as much paraffin as your employers want ! ' "

During the War, when I was staying with Renoir at Cagnes, he gave me a letter to read from his son who was serving in the Air Force, saying :

" Look at that, Vollard ! Read what Jean says. He complains that they are being given aeroplanes they can do nothing with. Do go and see Clémentel, and tell him about it ! "

As soon as I got back to Paris, I telephoned to M. Clémentel to ask him for an appointment on behalf of Renoir.

" Look in at the Ministry," he replied. " You can tell me what Renoir is doing now, it will do me good. I shall expect you the day after to-morrow, Sunday. Come at half-past seven in the morning, so that we can have the place to ourselves."

At the appointed hour, I found the Minister with his cup of tea, making notes on some papers he had on his desk.

" Just give me a minute," he said.

At that moment a secretary came in, bringing a letter that was to be sent off at once.

The missive read and signed, M. Clémentel said to me :

" I am yours."

But again the door opened, and an usher presented himself, a visiting-card in his hand.

" Ah! yes," said the Minister, " it is an Air Commander who insists on seeing me, although it is a matter for the Ministry of War. As this visit may delay us, will you come and fetch me at twelve? We will go and lunch at my house in Versailles; there, at least, we shall not be disturbed."

At twelve o'clock, M. Clémentel was chatting with two gentlemen in the courtyard of the Ministry; a little way off, the Air Commander was waiting. The Minister dismissed the civilians, then he said to the officer:

" I'll take you with me to Versailles, where we can have a good chat."

Just as the car was starting, a secretary came running up. He was carrying a file of papers which he gave to the Minister.

" That's right," said the latter; " I had forgotten that I have that to go through."

He immersed himself in the dossier, which kept him busy till we got to Versailles.

As we entered the house, a cook rushed into the hall, shouting:

" I've made the sauce for the langouste . . . I can promise you it's good! "

So saying, he took off his " chef's " insignia and appeared in usual attire. M. Clémentel introduced us. Our *maître-queux* was the painter Dumoulin, whom I had not recognised in his get-up.

After lunch, just as the Air Commander thought M. Clémentel was at last going to spare him a few minutes, some visitors arrived, who also tried to secure the Minister for themselves. At the same moment, Mme Clémentel said to her guests:

" The children want to show us their cinema."

Then on the screen of a toy *Pathé*, *Red Riding Hood*, *Puss in Boots*, *Sleeping Beauty* passed in procession; and this lasted till tea was announced.

Soon after, the Minister begged permission to go to his study. It was time for the visitors to return to Paris.

As we were leaving, the Minister, turning to the Air Commander, said:

"You see how it is, Commander: I have not had a minute to myself. You had better write me what you wanted to say: I will pass the note on myself to the Ministry of War."

We walked to the station.

"That's the second time I have played cook," said Dumoulin, "and I wasn't able to get the Minister to myself for two minutes. Every Sunday it's the same thing, and as for getting hold of Clémentel during the week . . ."

M. Clémentel said to me, one day when I ran across him after the session had broken up:

"Bernheim wants me to exhibit at his gallery. I am going to Auvergne in a few days. There's a place for a painter! What ripping holidays I shall have!"

For to M. Clémentel, painting is a relaxation.

Some weeks later, happening to be at Vichy, I had a note from him asking me to lunch. It meant a journey of about fifty kilometres in a magnificent region, the appearance of which reminded me of the Midi.

On the terrace of the Minister's house, which overlooked some vineyards, I caught sight of an armchair surmounted by an immense straw hat.

"That's M. Bourdelle," said the housemaid who was showing me the way.

I was about to go up to him.

"He is asleep, sir."

At that moment M. Clémentel arrived, and carried me off to his studio. On the walls were freshly painted canvases in numbers that showed the painter's energy to be at least as tireless as the Minister's.

My host was called away, and I went back to the terrace. The great sculptor was still asleep. I was hesitating to awaken him, when a chestnut detached itself from a neighbouring tree and fell on his hand. He stretched himself.

"Hullo! That you, Vollard? . . ."

Bourdelle threw out his arms.

"Isn't this landscape fine! In the presence of these mountains I close my eyes, to construct things in my mind before modelling the clay. The hour I have just spent in communion with nature has taught me more than a week in the studio."

This is how I came to know the socialist Marcel Sembat. Renoir had said to me: "They are persecuting the schoolmistress in my village because she refuses to sleep with the *maire*. Sembat has often offered me his help if ever I should need anything. Will you go and tell him from me that I beg him earnestly to intervene, so that the poor girl may not be tormented any more."

I went to Sembat's house. They told me he was at his office. There I was shown into a rather sordid little ground-floor room, smoky from a log fire that would not burn up. I explained the object of my visit to Sembat. He said at once:

"Tell M. Renoir to be easy. I will have this disgusting fellow sent to the right-about."

Not long after, M. Sembat went to Renoir and said, as though it were a matter of course:

"I can't do anything for your schoolmistress! The *maire* belongs to the 'party'."

Another time when I had to see Sembat about something, I went to his house. He received me in the dining-room, where he was expecting one of his colleagues of the Right to lunch, a comrade of Stanislas. A maid appeared, and put a carafe of wine on the table.

R

" What are you thinking of? " said Sembat. " Get out a bottle of *Nuits*. . . . You know quite well that the *ordinaire* is for when M. Cachin comes."

In the rue Caulaincourt, opposite Renoir's house, there was about an acre of ground belonging to the city of Paris, on which stood a number of wooden shanties.

" You will see," Renoir said to me. " They will pull down those hovels to build six-storey houses! "

A fire broke out, which destroyed most of the huts. A Municipal Councillor of the quarter took the opportunity of suggesting to his colleagues that the place should be turned into a square, in the interest of public health. The notion was taken up for consideration. Upon which, great consternation among the publicans of the quarter. Invited to appear before a sort of tribunal presided over by a chemist supported by three pub-keepers, the Councillor, in mortal terror, was told:

" For the last fifteen years we have been expecting to have houses built on this piece of ground that would bring in a profit. You go and fool us by asking for a square. If your proposal passes through the Council, you'll know what to expect at the next elections! "

Needless to say, the Councillor withdrew his proposal without delay.

I mentioned this affair to Sembat, who was the deputy for the arrondissement. I thought to embarrass him.

" It's the fault of the régime! " replied the author of *Faites un Roi*. " In the old days it was the marquis who had the upper hand. Now it is the publican."

XXVIII THE *PRIX DES PEINTRES*

Men of letters consider themselves judges of painting. Why should not painters turn judges of literature?

This reflection led me to offer a prize, to be awarded to a writer by a jury of artists: *Le Prix des Peintres*.

When the founder of a prize selects his jury himself, he may be suspected of weighting the scales. To avoid laying myself open to any such accusation, I appealed to painters representing the most opposite tendencies, from Albert Besnard to Vlaminck, including Van Dongen and Paul Chabas. Thus the Institute and the *Fauves* would be gathered about the same table, at the luncheon after which the Laureate would be nominated.

I met with the greatest readiness on the part of the artists, to serve on the jury. They can certainly have had no idea of the avalanche of books that was to overwhelm them. Sem was a member of the jury. I went to his studio to see him on some other matter, and as I came in he pointed silently to the books overflowing in every direction.

" And there's another whole week before the allotting of the prize," he said sadly.

" Still," I remarked, " I imagine all these volumes came to you by day? "

He assented with some astonishment.

" You are luckier than So-and-so," I went on. " It was midnight when somebody knocked at *his* door—a candidate for the prize bringing him his complete works, a pile of seventeen volumes. He explained that he had been wandering about for three hours, looking for the house. When at last he found it, he did not know which was the right floor, and not daring to wake the concierge for fear of being turned out, he had knocked at all the doors, right and left, on all the landings, before arriving at his destination."

On the day of the ballot, when the painters were assembled for lunch:

" At last! " said one of them. " How nice to think we shan't get any more books! "

At that moment a postman called, and made me sign a paper for the receipt of a big package. Sent from Algiers by air, the wrapper contained a volume of typewritten poems, and a letter from the authoress asserting that typewritten poems had as much right to be considered as printed ones, and that she was sure we should be delighted with hers.

I must admit I was not without a certain anxiety as to the choice that so unusual a jury would make. To everyone's surprise, these artists of such diverse tendencies showed the most discriminating, and at the same time the boldest taste: their almost unanimous choice fell upon Paul Valéry, who had not as yet been elected to the Académie Française.

After the *Prix des Peintres* I thought of having another awarded, again to a writer, but this time by booksellers' assistants. I have always admired their activity, their intelligence, the art with which they handle their customers and size them up.

One day when I was at Flammarion's, two ladies came in.

" That will be for a *Don Juannes*," said one of the salesmen to me.

He went up to the ladies, one of whom said immediately, " Give me Marcel Prévost's *Don Juannes*."

I was astounded.

" But how could you guess it was the *Don Juannes* they wanted ? "

" Oh, well, by the ladies' hats, their way of walking, everything in fact."

Besides their psychological qualifications, I had been struck, when listening to booksellers' assistants, by the interest they took in many of the books they sold, and I felt sure that if they were asked to award a prize, they would make an excellent choice. But the booksellers' Trade Union, to which I applied in order to set my plan going, pointed out politely that my idea was absurd. " A bookseller's assistant, being an employé, must not be concerned with anything but the interests of his chief; if he advances a personal opinion, he is not a good bookseller's assistant." In short, I was advised not to go on with my Booksellers' Assistants' Prize. I was prepared to disregard this advice, but I saw that, owing to the great number of booksellers' assistants, I could not arrange the competition unless their professional organisation took it up. And it turned out that the booksellers' assistants had no Trade Union.

So my plan went by the board.

" You talk of a Trade Union," said a friend to whom I was recounting my failure. " Well, there's the concierges' Trade Union. Why shouldn't you institute a prize to be awarded by concierges? "

I mooted the idea to the concierge of a house I frequented, whom I always saw with a newspaper in his hand.

" You couldn't do better," he said to me. " There's an enormous amount of reading done in our profession. Just think of all the papers that come to us first, with at least two novels each in them! By the end of the year that constitutes a fine asset for the brain of a concierge.

" But," my interlocutor continued, " you'll want a jolly big hall for the luncheon! "

" What luncheon? " I asked.

" Why, the luncheon at which we award the prize. There will be the Paris concierges, the delegates from the provinces . . ."

Seeing me recoil, he reassured me:

" Of course they won't all come. . . ."

By that time I had reached the door, and the *Prix des Concierges* went the same way as the *Prix des Commis-Libraires*.

But a further plan did mature: the prize to be given to the small artisan who, with the least material, should invent the most ingenious object, be it only the most amusing toy.

XXIX AMBROISE VOLLARD, PUB-LISHER

I had always had a taste for engravings. I was
hardly settled in the rue Laffitte, about 1895,
when I began to dream of publishing engravings, but
they must be engravings by painter-gravers. " Painter-
graver " is a term which has been wrongly applied to
professional engravers who are not in any sense
painters. My idea was to obtain engravings from
artists who were not engravers by profession, and
the result was a great artistic success. All the painters
I approached produced, at their first attempt, engravings that are eagerly sought after at the present
day.

I can still see Lautrec, a bandy-legged little man,
saying to me with that astonishingly ingenuous look
of his :

" I will do you a *femme de ' maison '.*"

In the end he decided upon the *Governess-cart*, which
to-day is considered one of his masterpieces.

Cézanne, Bonnard, Vuillard, Maurice Denis,
Toulouse-Lautrec and Sisley all did colour-prints;
Whistler, Renoir, Edouard Münch and Puvis de
Chavannes executed theirs in black; Redon worked
in both media. All of these, with others, I published
under the title *Les Peintres-Graveurs* in two albums, of
which only a hundred copies were printed. Neither
of these albums sold very well, and a third series
remained unfinished.

But if the collectors were indifferent, the painters
themselves were becoming more and more interested

247

in this alternative mode of self-expression. Some of them even did me an album apiece. From Bonnard, for instance, I had a series of coloured lithographs of Paris—" Here's my wife and daughter in this *Retour du Bois* ! " cried Helleu, looking at them, so recognisable were the figures in the crowd. Other lithographs included a series of *Interiors* by Vuillard and of *Landscapes* by K. X. Roussel. Maurice Denis did a series entitled *Amour*, and Redon an *Apocalypse* in black.

In spite of the low prices (100 francs for the first album, 150 for the second) the *amateurs* continued to fight shy, and twenty years later the edition was not sold out. But the times have greatly changed. Not so long ago, a print of Lautrec's *Governess-cart* sold for fifteen thousand francs at the Hôtel Drouot.

Cézanne did me a self-portrait, a lithograph in black. Renoir also, with the kindness he always showed me, composed several lithographs, among them his *Chapeau épinglé*, which he decided to carry out in black and colour. But he dislocated his right arm. " Suppose I tried with my other arm? " he said to himself. And he went on with his plate as though nothing had happened. Then he undertook other lithographs in black and colour: *Les petites filles jouant à la balle*, *L'enfant au biscuit*—an astounding composition—and *Mère et enfant* in black. I was forgetting his admirable portraits of Rodin, Cézanne and Wagner. The last of these plates I obtained in this way. I went to Renoir's house, followed by a porter carrying a lithographic stone, and found him just leaving to go to his studio. When he caught sight of the stone, he flung up his arms:

" There! And I'm up to the eyes in work just now! "

We went along together, but could not get far, as there was a cordon of police barring the street leading to the studio. We had neither of us remembered that it was the First of May, when the " Festival of Labour " is celebrated by disorder in the streets. The police warned us that traffic would not be free before two o'clock.

" Let's go back to my house," said Renoir; " I'll do your litho straight away."

After this he executed a series of little lithographs in black. Among them is my portrait, and that of the painter Valtat. But the album is chiefly composed of female nudes. One day when Renoir was asked how he preferred painting women:

" Naked," he replied without hesitation.

Some of Fantin-Latour's finest prints were done for me. He took a kindly interest in my efforts to awaken a taste for prints among the public, although my " bold " tendencies frightened him. When I told him I thought of taking a still-life by Cézanne to the Louvre, to compare it with a Chardin, he stiffened:

" Don't play about with the Louvre, Vollard! "

A visit I paid to an exhibition of decorative art was a revelation to me. I had no idea till then how beautiful pottery could be, and from that moment I longed to " publish " vases, plates and dishes. At that time there was a Master-ceramist called Methey. At my request he put his kilns at the disposal of the younger artists—Bonnard, Maurice Denis, Derain, Puy, Matisse, Roussel, Rouault, Valtat, Vlaminck— and they decorated a number of fine pieces for me. I was again unable to get the public to appreciate them, but they had a great influence upon contemporary decorative art.

Pottery was not the only thing that tempted me. I persuaded Maillol to let me have one of his wooden statuettes cast in bronze, with such happy results that he repeated the experiment more than once.

One day I saw Bonnard kneading a piece of bread.

In his fingers it gradually assumed the shape of a little dog.

"I say, Bonnard, that looks like sculpture to me?"

"I beg your pardon?"

"Suppose you were to do me some statuettes?"

Bonnard was not averse, and after a few attempts he undertook an important centrepiece for a table.

From the basement of my shop one afternoon came sounds as though a coppersmith were at work there.

"Have you got workmen downstairs?" I was asked.

It was Bonnard, hammering his bronze.

I hardly hoped to have the same luck with Renoir. When I first suggested he should do a statue:

"Come, Vollard, you know I hardly have a hand left! . . . I might perhaps manage to do a little head. . . . All the same, I should rather have liked to model a big figure."

Was a hand needed for a big statue? Had I not seen Rodin surrounded by pupils enlarging the Master's *figurines* while he stroked his beard? I said as much to Renoir.

"That reminds me," he said, "of an engraving in a *Lives of the Artists of Antiquity*, showing stone-masons busy in a workshop, while on a couch reclined a man crowned with roses. He was the sculptor."

In the end, Renoir set to work and brought off his little *Vénus à la pomme*. But he wanted to see it in stone, and as enlarging is apt to throw certain parts of the work out of scale, Renoir, with his habitual care, decided to do fresh drawings for the bigger statue. While the enlargement was in progress, I many a time found him standing under the silvery olive trees of his garden, a long wand in his hand, directing the work of the pointer.

"You see, Vollard, it's as though my own hand were at the end of the stick. To do good work one should not be too near. How can one see what one is doing, with the clay right under one's nose? "

When the statue was finished:

" It's not bad," said Renoir; " all the same, there's something wrong with it. . . ."

About a year later he said to me with a waggish air:

" I've at last discovered what was the matter with my Venus. I shall have to raise her breasts a little."

When the alteration had been made:

" Now I've got it! " he cried.

I tried Degas too. A number of wax figures in his studio bore witness to his activity as a sculptor. When I suggested having one of them cast:

" Have it cast! " he cried. " Bronze is all right for those who work for eternity. My pleasure consists in beginning over and over again. Like this. . . . Look! " He took an almost finished *Danseuse* from his modelling stand and rolled her into a ball of clay.

Strolling along the quays, I dipped one day into the books in a second-hand dealer's box. On the title-page of a fine octavo I read: *Ambroise Firmin-Didot, éditeur.*

" *Ambroise Vollard, éditeur* . . . that wouldn't look bad either," I thought.

Little by little the idea of becoming a publisher, a great publisher of books, took root in my mind. I could not see a fine sheet of paper without thinking: " How well type would look on it! " Soon my only remaining hesitation was whether to publish prose or verse.

I decided on verse, after a visit to the Imprimerie Nationale, which was still housed in the magnificent *hôtel* of the rue Vieille-du-Temple. I was with a friend who wanted to see the famous " Salle des Singes." While he was studying every detail of that

celebrated decoration, I had opened a book published by the Institution, and was admiring a page
printed in Garamond, that magnificent type engraved
by order of Francis I, the italics of which seemed
to me expressly designed to print the work of a
poet.

But what poet should I choose? Chance helped
me to a decision.

One day, on the top of an omnibus, I was sitting
near a poorly-dressed man. A scarf barely concealed
the absence of a collar. He was holding a large
picture in both hands—his own portrait, I fancied.
This painting got in the way of the conductor as he
went to and fro to collect his fares.

"Look here, you," he broke out at last, "why
not bring your wardrobe next time?"

"I haven't one," said the other, simply.

"That's Verlaine," whispered somebody beside
me.

It was Verlaine. He got down at one of the
omnibus stops, and I saw him going towards a
picture-dealer's shop. Hearing the name of Verlaine, a passenger turned round:

"Who's Verlaine?"

"A poet, the greatest next to Stéphane Mallarmé."

This reply was made by a passenger carrying an
impressive portfolio. A young man sitting near him
addressed him as "My dear Master!" I had thus a
warrant that Mallarmé and Verlaine were the two
greatest contemporary poets. The next day, outside
Flammarion's, I opened a book by Mallarmé and
read his admirable *Don du Poème*. I confess that for
the moment I remained insensible to the charm of
that subtle music. Next I began turning the pages
of Verlaine's *Parallèlement*, which corresponded better
to my notions of poetry. It seemed to me exactly
what I wanted.

But whom should I get to illustrate a book at once

so tender and so voluptuous? I decided to ask Bonnard for some lithographs.

For the printing, I thought at once of the Imprimerie Nationale. They told me there that I must first obtain the authorisation of the Minister of Justice. I did not know that certain parts of *Parallèlement* had drawn down the thunderbolts of the law, and therefore took it quite as a matter of course that I obtained the required permission. What did astonish me was the remark of the business manager of the Imprimerie: " That's a queer idea, to put a book on Geometry into verse! "

One of the foremen thought differently—a man with the head of an old faun, who would certainly have pleased Verlaine, and whom I found reading aloud to two young work-girls, winking slyly at them the while:

L'une était brune, l'autre blonde,
Toutes deux s'aimaient d'amour tendre. . . .

When the printing of *Parallèlement* was finished, a copy was sent as usual to the Keeper of the Seals. The next day I received a visit from a high official of the Ministry of Justice.

" The Ministry begs to inform you," he said, " that you must return all the copies of *Parallèlement* to the Imprimerie Nationale. It is considered inadmissible that a book banned on moral grounds should be republished in a cover ornamented with the effigy of the Republic, and that the title-page should bear the inscription: *By special permission*, etc."

I had distributed a certain number of copies of the book. For those that remained Bonnard designed a cover more in keeping with the spirit of the work.

The incident, reported in the press, had its echo in the Chamber. But parliamentary controversy did not help to sell a single copy more.

This work, and *Daphnis et Chloë*, which I published two years later, also illustrated by Bonnard, were in fact a complete failure at the time, one reproach against them being that they were illustrated by lithography, the only method of illustration admired by the bibliophiles of that day being wood-engraving.

" Well, if they want woodcuts," thought I, " why shouldn't I give them woodcuts? " And I published the *Imitation of Christ* with a fine series of cuts by Maurice Denis, and later *Sagesse*, illustrated in colours by the same artist. But I was told: " Painters are not illustrators. The liberties they permit themselves are incompatible with the ' finish ' which is the whole merit of an illustrated book."

I once heard a bibliophile voicing his admiration of an engraving in which, on the setting of a ring on a man's finger, the body of a woman could be discerned:

" And you could actually see she was pregnant! "

I had given the bibliophiles the wood-engravings they were so keen on; it now remained for me to give them " finish." I thought of Armand Seguin, whom I knew capable of " working up " a design without losing his qualities as a painter, and I commissioned him to illustrate *Gaspard de la Nuit*, qualified by its author, Louis Bertrand, as " Fantasies in the manner of Rembrandt and Callot."

When the book came from the press of the Imprimerie Nationale, where they had made a veritable typographical gem of it, a bookseller went to offer it to one of his customers—a true blue in the way of bibliophiles, M. Béraldi himself. The latter, to begin with, could not find praise enough for the book. But all at once:

" Who is the publisher? "

" Vollard."

" The man who published *Parallèlement* and *Daphnis*

et Chloë? Ah, no! That would be letting the Devil into my library. . . ."

At each rebuff from the book collectors I said to myself: "All the same, I shall have the last word." And I replied to their hostility by publishing yet another book.

For the illustrations to *Les Fleurs du Mal* I went to Emile Bernard. This book, on which he lavished woodcuts, was also printed by the Imprimerie Nationale in its splendid Garamond. The printing was begun at the end of July 1914. When the War broke out, a newspaper friendly to literature congratulated the Imprimerie Nationale on not having stopped the hand press that was being used for my Baudelaire. Thereupon, according to another paper, certain parliamentarians wrote to the Minister of Justice for a copy of the book, which, as they imagined, was being printed at the expense of the State. Not long after, the *Figaro* revealed that all these requests, with the exception of three, had Baudelaire spelt *Beau*. The *Figaro* was perhaps exaggerating.

After *Les Fleurs du Mal*, Emile Bernard illustrated *Villon* for me, and Ronsard's *Amours*. For the *Villon* he found a type that went so well with his work that one could have sworn he had designed it himself. He was less fortunate with the *Amours*, and decided to write out the pages of the text in a style that harmonised with his drawing, after which they were engraved.

" It is not a real book," the collectors now declared.

Rodin, then at the height of his fame, had undertaken to do some lithographs for the *Jardin des Supplices*, by Octave Mirbeau. Of course I did not expect to be the publisher. Too many powerful competitors were sure to contend for the masterpiece.

So my joy was only equalled by my surprise when Mirbeau came to suggest my publishing the book. No other publisher would have anything to do with it.

I turned once again to the Imprimerie Nationale, but this time without success.

"Oh, no!" exclaimed the Keeper of the Seals, when the request for permission reached him, "I don't want to get into hot water, as Monis did over *Parallèlement*."

I then thought of having the book printed by Didot, and took him, at the same time, Mallarmé's poem *Jamais un coup de dé n'abolit le hasard*. When I came back by appointment, the director himself received me:

"Monsieur," he said, without further preface, "we shall not print the *Jardin des Supplices*. We consider ourselves, in this old firm, as having a cure of souls, as much with regard to our workmen, who are honest fathers of families, as to our apprentices, who will become such one day."

So in the end the book was printed by Renouard.

Didot's refusal was equally categorical concerning the *Coup de dé*. "It's a madman wrote that," the works manager said to me. This verdict did not make me abandon the publication of Mallarmé's work; but with my habit of always putting everything off, the years pass. Still, I have kept the lithographs Odilon Redon did for this book, and I hope some day to publish it, as well as another poem of Mallarmé's, *Hérodias*. The author himself was for a long while dissatisfied with this: "It is a diptych. I want to make a triptych of it."

At last he felt he had brought it to the desired pitch of perfection. Here is the letter he wrote me from Valvins, the 12th May, 1898: "I am glad to know I am being published, *mon cher*, by a picture-dealer. Don't let Vuillard leave Paris without having given you a favourable reply " (he was to illustrate it). " Tell him, to encourage him, that I am pleased with the lengthened poem. For once this is true."

At this juncture the poet died. When I claimed the continuation of *Hérodias* from his son-in-law, Dr. Bonniot, " It is still unfinished," he objected. " My father-in-law's reputation would suffer by it."

I had not overcome the strange scruples of Dr. Bonniot when he, too, died. But his heirs will surely allow the poem to appear, in conformity with the poet's wish?

Madame de Commanville, Flaubert's niece, had scruples of another kind. I wanted to publish the *Temptation of St. Anthony*, with illustrations by Redon. But the heiress of the great novelist had not forgotten that the Devil, in order to seduce Anthony, caused naked women to appear to him, and in the contract that I wrote at her dictation, she stipulated that I was to submit the artist's compositions to her. Redon's illustrations comprise more than twenty original lithographs and about fifteen compositions designed as woodcuts. I had mislaid the latter, but to my great joy I have just found them again, and the book can at last be published.

Another book that I had the good fortune to publish was *La Belle Enfant* by Eugène Montfort.

From the number of chapters in *La Belle Enfant* may be seen the quantity of headings, full-page plates and tailpieces its illustrations necessitated. This did not worry Dufy, who engraved a hundred plates. His conscientiousness was extraordinary. After several journeys to Marseilles—a Marseilles that is beginning to disappear, which adds still more to the interest of these illustrations—just as he was about to engrave one of the last plates, representing

s

Aline's "salon," the artist felt doubtful. It seemed to him that his drawing did not express the atmosphere sufficiently. He had tried to find it in Paris, in *maisons closes* of the same order, but had not succeeded. He decided to go to Marseilles again. . . .

One most important part of Degas' work is little known: his *Scènes de "Maisons Closes."* As Renoir said to me, "Any treatment of such subjects is likely to be pornographic, and there is always a desperate sadness about them. It took a Degas to give to the *Fête de la Patronne* an air of joyfulness, and at the same time the greatness of an Egyptian bas-relief."

All these little *plats du jour*, as Degas called them, were executed by him in printer's ink, on a copperplate. The plate not having been bitten, he could only pull one good proof. As a rule Degas executed these monotypes after dinner, at Cadard the printer's. He sometimes touched them up with pastel.

When the sale of the painter's studio was being arranged, his brother René, out of respect for the artist's reputation, destroyed about seventy of these little masterpieces, which would have served brilliantly to prove how much Toulouse-Lautrec owed to his old master. The *Scènes de Maisons* were not included in this hecatomb. I had the good fortune to persuade their owners at that time to release them from the portfolios in which they kept them jealously hidden. In this way I was able to illustrate de Maupassant's *Maison Tellier* and Lucian's *Mimes of the Courtesans*, which Pierre Loüys has so happily reconstituted for us. Reading these *Mimes of the Courtesans*, one is astonished to see to what degree these "little ladies" are of all time. Pierre Loüys himself, in his preface to his translation, says of the dialogues of Lucian that one might at times think one was listening to the *midinettes* of to-day.

In order to reproduce these compositions of Degas', I had to find an artist capable of fathoming the sensitiveness of his drawing, the subtlety of his tone. I turned to the painter-graver Maurice Potin, who accomplished wonders. He spared neither time nor trouble. To reproduce a certain monotype, even in black, as many as three copperplates had to be engraved!

One would have said Degas' compositions had been made specially to illustrate *La Maison Tellier*. But would it be the same with the *Mimes of the Courtesans*? Conforming to the custom of the *maisons*, Degas' women were dressed only in stockings. Stockings! Did the ladies of antiquity wear them? Should I not be guilty of an anachronism? I confided my difficulty to a lecturer in Greek literature, who took me to an old archæologist, in whom I fancied I recognised M. Salomon Reinach. I told him my perplexity. The savant reflected a few moments, then:

" Degas must be right. As it often happens, the artist has intuitions which reveal what remains a mystery to the learned. I am inclined to think the Greek courtesans wore stockings, for after all, without stockings, where would they have put their wages? "

It would be hard to give an idea of the emotions I went through while the reproduction of Degas' monotypes was being carried out.

Only a few belonged to me personally. Most of the others, in particular the famous *Fête de la Patronne*, were the property of an art publisher, M. Exsteens, to whom I can never be too grateful. M. Exsteens had agreed to lend me his Degas, on condition that I brought them back to him if he wanted to show them. So it was in a state of perpetual *qui vive* that I started on this enterprise. At the end of three years, when everything was on the stocks, M. Exsteens sent me word that the representative of an American museum wanted to see his Degas. I took them back, therefore, with what anxiety may be imagined, since I could not get anything finished if they were taken away from me. But the gods were propitious. More collector than dealer, M. Exsteens could not bring himself to sell his treasures, and he let me keep them the three more years that were needed to carry the thing through.

But what were these six years compared with the time taken by K. X. Roussel over his preparatory studies for the illustration of Maurice de Guérin's *La Bacchante* and *Le Centaure*? It was about 1910 that I asked him to interpret these two little master-pieces. Since then he had often said to me, " I'm working at them, you know."

I must confess I had ceased to count on him, when one day he showed me a whole pile of drawings.

" There! Now they've only got to be carried out."

And once at work on his lithographic stones he never left them.

Although the chief characteristic of Roussel's work is his intoxicating frenzy of colour, he felt that *La Bacchante* and *Le Centaure* called indisputably for plates executed in black.

One of my most cherished ambitions had been to publish a *La Fontaine*, worthily illustrated. As a child I had detested La Fontaine. My Aunt Noémie, who used to make me copy out the fables as impositions, was responsible for this distaste. But as I began to grow up, many a verse of the poet's came back to me, and I gradually discovered their charm.

When the time came, it was the Russian painter Marc Chagall that I thought of for the illustration of the book. I was sharply criticised for it. People could not understand the choice of a Russian painter to interpret the most French of all our poets. But it was precisely on account of the Oriental sources of

the fabulist that I had pitched on an artist whose
origins and culture had rendered him familiar with
the magic East. My hopes were not deceived:
Chagall did a hundred dazzling *gouaches*. But when
it came to putting them on copper, so many technical
difficulties arose that the artist decided to substitute
etchings in black.

I had asked Chagall before this to illustrate Gogol's
Dead Souls, a work for which he also did a hundred
full-page etchings, besides a number of headings,
tailpieces and decorations of all kinds. Chagall contrived to suggest, with remarkable truth, the rather
Louis-Philippe appearance characteristic of Russia in
Gogol's time.

A lady complained, in my hearing, of the high
prices of fine books.

" But, Madame, when you're buying jewels? "

She answered sharply:

" One can't wear a book as one does a jewel."

Maillol, who is illustrating Ronsard's *Folastries* for
me, has taken upon him to give the lie to this feminine
assertion. " I see the *Folastries*," he says, " as a tiny
book, something like those miniature books that can
be slipped into the pocket."

Rouault, on the other hand, is engaged on two
volumes that no collector's shelves can accommodate.
They will have to be kept on lecterns. I met Rouault
one morning laden with files, rasps, burnishers and
emery-paper.

" What's all that for? "

" For your damned plates! "

" Etchings? Aquatints? "

" I don't know what they will be called. They
give me a copperplate . . . I just dig into it."

But of all the works I have published, the one
that most puzzled the bibliophiles when it was

announced was Balzac's *Chef d'Œuvre Inconnu*, with original etchings and woodcuts by Picasso, in which cubist realisations rub shoulders with drawings that remind one of Ingres. But each new work of Picasso's shocks the public, till the day when astonishment gives way to admiration.

Other books are in preparation: Hesiod's *Theogony*, with etchings by Braque; Suarès's *Cirque* and *Passion*, illustrated by Rouault; *Cirque de Étoile filante*, by Rouault, with illustrations by himself; lastly, Virgil's *Georgics*, with etchings by Segonzac, whose first attempts already show with what moving aptness of expression the artist is inspired by the Virgilian aspect of the country round St. Tropez.

XXX AMBROISE VOLLARD, AUTHOR

Not satisfied with being a publisher, I tried my hand at writing as well. The first book I wrote was *Paul Cézanne*, which appeared in 1914 in an expensive edition to begin with. I had fixed the subscription price at 65 francs. My few subscribers backed out at the last moment under pretext of the War. I then put up the price to 100 francs. The subscribers who had " faded out " came back at once; others followed, and the book had what might be termed a success. It was later translated into German, English and Japanese.

In the joy of seeing myself in print, I hung about the machines all day; not that I had any fears for my text. I had been told the corrector, Lelong, was an " ace " who would let nothing slip. One day this " ace " of correctors said to me, " This painter of yours doesn't seem to know his own mind. Here he says, ' Woman, divine creature, whether she be mother, wife or sister . . .' and directly after, ' Women are bitches and schemers.' " Now this latter formula was authentic Cézanne, but not the preceding one. It turned out that the work of a convinced feminist was being set up at the same time, and a line of his text had slipped in amongst mine.

Another day Lelong hailed me with:

" This time, M. Vollard, the mistake is yours. You've put *Cabaner* for *Cabanel*."

And turning to his assistants:

" What are you waiting for? You can get on with it."

I had come in the nick of time, for it was not Cabanel the painter I was referring to, but Cabaner, a modest musician from the provinces whose repartees had procured him a certain notoriety. To someone who asked him:

" Could you suggest silence in music? "

" Certainly," he replied without hesitation. " But I should need the assistance of three military bands."

And on his arrival from the provinces:

" I had no idea I was so well known in Paris," he said to his new acquaintances. " I found everyone taking off his hat to me."

Cabaner had not noticed that he was following a funeral.

Cézanne was inclined to credit Cabaner with the flair of a connoisseur. One day the painter started out carrying his big painting of *The Bathers*, which is to-day one of the gems of the Barnes collection.

" There's no money in the house," he said to Renoir, whom he met on the stairs. " I am going to try and find an *amateur*."

Soon after, meeting Renoir again, he said:

" I am very pleased. I ran across someone on the way who liked my painting of *The Bathers*."

This *amateur* turned out to be Cabaner. He had fallen into an ecstasy over the picture and the painter had made him a present of it.

In my book on Cézanne I tried to write simply, colloquially, so to speak, eschewing the slightest hint of art criticism. The material was rich enough without. First the boy's irresistible vocation thwarted by an anxious father; and his mother's retort to all who doubted it: " After all, he's called Paul like Veronese and Rubens." Then his arrival in Paris, his diligent study of the Masters at the Louvre, his eagerness to work, his failure to get into the École des Beaux Arts with a painting of which a member of the jury said: " Cézanne has the temperament of a colourist: unfortunately he paints to excess."

Then there was the friendship with Zola, and the latter's solicitude on Cézanne's account: " Work hard at your drawing. Don't degenerate into a commercial painter." Cézanne's perpetually renewed enthusiasms and perpetual recommencements, and the publication of *L'Œuvre*, in which Zola represented his friend in the character of an artist who commits suicide because he is incapable of expressing himself. To which Cézanne retorted, " Damn it all, when a picture isn't a success, one chucks it in the fire and begins another."

There were also Cézanne's vain attempts to get into Bouguereau's Salon; the consolation afforded him by an enlightened *amateur*, M. Choquet; the exhibition of his works that I got up in my little shop in the rue Laffitte; my visit to Cézanne at Aix, the sittings for my portrait and many other episodes of the painter's harassed existence. But the outstanding lesson of Cézanne's life to which I tried to do justice was his modesty and his unremitting toil in the service of his art. He was a Don Quixote of painting. In his hours of depression he went to the Louvre in quest of renewed energy and came out refreshed, saying, " I think I shall do some good work to-morrow."

In my book on Renoir I gave a great deal of space to painting, though merely, I must add, as a reporter of Renoir's sayings on the subject. But here also the person and life of the artist deserved the fullest treatment I could give them. His career had something of the fairy-tale about it: a little decorator of plates rising to the incomparable brilliancy of the art of the *Loge*, the *Moulin de la Galette*, the *Danseuse*, the *Canotiers*, and the marvellous *Nudes* of his latest period. What an example to younger painters was this man who at the height of his fame still had doubts of himself, and at a time when others were demanding that the Louvre should be " burnt down," could put himself to school again under the Masters.

I had read in a history of the painters that Pliny the elder complained of the " youngsters " who wanted to introduce new colours into painting. I mentioned this to Renoir:

" New colours! " cried he.

" But," I said to him, " isn't Impressionism something like that? "

" Bother Impressionism! " cried Renoir impatiently. " To think it was I who insisted on keeping that title for our Group, after the public had seized on it to make fun of a painting by Monet called *Impression*. I simply meant it to signify to the man in the street ' You will find the sort of painting here that you don't like. If you come in, it's your funeral. You won't get your ten sous entrance money back.' "

" But didn't the Impressionists discover how to make black by a mixture of blue and red? "

" You call that a discovery? In painting, you know, there is not a single process that can be made into a formula. For instance, I once attempted to fix the quantity of oil that I add to the paint on my palette. I couldn't do it. Each time I have to add my oil at a guess."

This is sufficient proof that the painter of *La Loge* was not a fanatic of " progress." " I tried to change my yellow," he told me again, " and I messed about with it for ten years! " Renoir loved to talk of those days when, instead of dreaming of a new palette, a painter would direct all his efforts to researches in his craft while founding himself on tradition. Happy days, when his works were witness to the balance and serenity of the artist.

The aristocratic side of Renoir's nature revealed itself in the nobility of his art, his tastes, his opinions, even his outbursts. He had a passion for everything that bears the mark of the French genius: order and balance in art, clarity of ideas, simplicity of style. He did not hesitate to say he preferred Alexandre Dumas to Victor Hugo, such a grudge did he bear the poet for having disaccustomed the French from expressing themselves simply.

Renoir was not fastidious in the matter of models. Someone said to him one day, " We are trying to get you the portrait of the Duchess of X. to do." " Oh, don't bother," he said hastily. " I am content with the first draggle-tail that comes along, provided she has good firm buttocks and breasts."

And to those who knew that these were the only qualities he demanded of his servants, it may have seemed at first sight surprising that Renoir's house was so well kept, that his children were so well cared for, his meals always punctually served. But one had only to see Madame Renoir supervising everything, even to the washing of the paint-brushes; and in those pretty glazed earthenware pots that she picked up on the stalls, arranging flowers with that sure taste that made Renoir declare, " When my wife has made a posy I have only to paint it."

No one loved the Old Masters so much as Renoir. Under his guidance I made, so to speak, an excursion, the most original and instructive of excursions, through the museums. At Cagnes, at Essoyes, where I was often his guest, Renoir would amuse himself smoking a cigarette after his *café au lait*, before the model came to sit, looking through little catalogues of the museums that I myself had craftily left lying about on the table, at the other end of which I was supposed to be writing my letters. I was able in this way to note down the painter's remarks on the pictures that reminded him of the time when he could come and go at his will. Now he was condemned to spend his life in an armchair, his legs useless, his hands twisted with rheumatism. His fingers were almost dead and had to have now a paint-brush attached to them, now the wand which the painter, turned sculptor in the last years of his life, used for dictating to the pointer the volumes of his Venus.

Re-reading my notes one day, it occurred to me that I might publish them. When my manuscript was finished, I submitted it to Renoir.

" Well! " he said when he gave it me back, " you can boast of having ' had ' me. I saw you scribbling on bits of paper while I was talking. So it was for the public, was it? But whom do you suppose it will interest? Fortunately you haven't made me talk too much rubbish."

The interest of Renoir's personality was in itself a guarantee of the book's success. The reviewers thanked me for having brought the reader into such intimate relations with the painter. I was pleased, but I remembered the saying of Albert Wolf, of whom an author begged an article:

" A eulogistic article," he replied, " will be 25 louis. A thrashing, 50 louis."

I had not long to wait for my thrashing. A Socialist Deputy, somewhat of a dilettante, and who since then has figured as a statesman, M. Paul Boncour, compared me in *l'Europe Nouvelle* to the " worms that thrive on corpses."

Happening to meet someone of the parliamentarian's circle, I asked him:

" What was the matter with your friend? "

" That's a good one! You make Renoir say that he likes a curé better than a Socialist, because a curé wears a uniform and can be recognised from a distance, whereas if a gentleman wears a coat like everybody else's you can't tell that he's a Socialist who will bore you to death. Boncour couldn't attack Renoir, so naturally he fell upon you."

In my book on Degas I tried to fix certain traits of

the man's personality, a personality compounded of a seeming cold cruelty and a controlled sensibility.

So soon as one mentioned Degas' name, one was sure to hear his latest "malicious" saying quoted. Most often this dart was aimed at one of his colleagues and transfixed him like a butterfly on a cork. Painters were not the only people threatened. Whoever came within reach of Degas ran the risk of being caught. He gave the impression of a hunter stalking his prey. One must, however, do him this justice, that if he showed himself intractable where art and good principles were at stake, he never indulged in personal gossip: for Degas the "wall" of private life was no vain expression.

It has been said of M. Ingres that he was "a Chinese painter astray among the ruins of Athens in the middle of the nineteenth century." It might be said of Degas that as far as social life went, he was astray in a time that was not his own. He belonged to another period, a period in which politeness still existed, and a sense of hierarchy and the cult of one's own country. When he praised these virtues he was accounted a madman.

The chief characteristic of Degas as a man was the ease with which he went from one extreme to the other. He was sometimes so uncompromising that he would turn his favourite model violently out of the room with " You're a Protestant! You all go hand in hand with the Jews for Dreyfus." But let one of these "Jews" be in trouble, if Degas could alleviate his misfortune he would not fail to do so.

One day I met an Israelite on his staircase, M. M. . . .

" I am going to see Degas," he said to me.

" Do you want to be devoured, then? "

" It was Degas himself who wrote to me about my poor wife's death. He wants to give me a few sketches he did of her in the old days."

There were the same quick changes of temper in Degas' relations with all his contemporaries. Witness his fury, now with the painters who worked out of doors: "Hang it all, did Ingres set his easel up on the high-road?" Now with women who used scent, who invaded omnibuses and *métros* with their arms full of flowers. Witness again his exasperation when he found flowers upon a dining-room table or when dinner was served later than half-past seven. And this same Degas, so shy, so apparently unsociable, did not hesitate to brave the crowds in the big shops to buy toys for children; would plead for the little girl who was being deprived of dessert because she had made mistakes in her spelling, and let his servant lead him by the nose:

"Zoë, my brother is coming to lunch to-morrow."

"No, not to-morrow. To-morrow I've got my jam to make."

Rather than go to an exhibition by some other painter he would often exclaim:

"I can't see now-a-days. . . . My eyes! My poor eyes!" And immediately after this refusal he would take out his watch and say without the slightest hesitation, "It's a quarter past two."

No more was needed for the legend of unsociability to grow around the painter.

But when nightfall drove him from the studio and he no longer had to defend himself against those who were always ready to disturb him at his work, he could be delightfully genial.

He met Mirbeau in my shop one evening and stopped to chat with him. When Degas had gone, the writer, greatly touched, said:

"You saw how pleased Degas appeared to be to see me again."

In reality Degas would have accorded the same welcome to anybody else. On seeing me again a little later he asked me:

" Who was the gentleman I met at your place the other evening? "

" Why—it was Mirbeau."

" Mirbeau? He's a man who writes, isn't he? "

When he was obliged to leave the house he had inhabited for thirty years, and which a new owner was going to pull down, I said to him:

" M. Degas, you would only have had to open your portfolios to have the three hundred thousand francs they were asking for that house."

" Can an artist chuck away three hundred thousand francs like that? " he said.

After moving, he lost even his taste for destroying his wax figures in order to remodel them, and, really attacked now by the infirmity he had simulated for so long in order to get rid of intruders, he spent his days wandering about. In the course of his perambulations he always came back, nostalgically, to his former home. With his bowler hat, turned greenish, on his head, wrapped in a faded ulster, his eyes failing him more and more, he was obliged, when he wanted to cross the street, to ask a policeman for his arm. I once overheard an ironmonger, on his doorstep, saying to his wife:

" Do look! Is that really M. Degas? You would take him for an old pauper. . . ."

XXXI THE WAR

(a) *The Fourth of August*, 1914

In July 1914 I was expecting a pastel of Degas' back from Berlin, where I had sent it on approval, when I received the following telegram: "Emperor authorises purchase Degas National Gallery."

The Emperor William had hitherto shown nothing but antipathy to modern French painting. It was actually with great difficulty that the National Gallery had obtained permission to accept the Degas, Renoirs and Monets offered it by Berlin patrons of art. This sudden interest evinced by the Emperor in a French picture led me to suppose that despite the gravity of events, the "War Lord" was not preparing to attack us, and I agreed that my picture should remain in Berlin till the bargain was concluded. I discovered later that the Emperor's admiration for Degas was a piece of bluff on the part of my correspondent. A customer had taken a fancy to the pastel at the last moment, and he feared I might insist on its immediate return. My belief in peace being thus confirmed, what was my astonishment a few days later, when on passing a post-office I saw these words on a little hand-written poster: "A general mobilisation has been ordered."

A crowd has gathered. A workman cried " S—! "

But his anxiety was not justified by events. On the contrary, the working classes soon found themselves in a privileged position. While the lower middle class, the intellectuals and the peasants maintained at the Front went on getting their heads

smashed, the proletarians of both sexes filled the
munition factories, where the combatants' five sous
were replaced by wages that became ever more and
more alluring. I heard their gratification expressed
by a fellow in corduroy trousers who was buying a
fine fowl. " At last the chickens are going down
someone else's gullet ! " he cried.

When Paris was threatened and began to empty of
its inhabitants, I felt some anxiety about a friend of
mine who must, I thought, be in difficulties, with a wife
and eleven children. He was too old to be called up,
and as they had a house in the country I should not
have been surprised to find their Paris one empty.
But my friend was there in his shirt-sleeves, sawing
wood in the little garden behind the house.

" You see," he said to me, " I'm developing my
muscles, so as to be able to join up."

On leaving this hero I met a little boy crying on the
pavement. I asked the reason of his tears.

" When our grocer was supposed to have gone off to
the War," the brat explained, " Grandpa said the
man must be a Boche, and we'd go with a few good
Frenchmen and revictual ourselves from his shop,
and we'd eat little fishes in tins and green peas in
bottles; but the grocer's wife smelt a rat and sent for
the police. . . ."

" You go to school, I suppose? " I asked the child.

" Yes," he said. " This morning teacher made us
say the rabbit."

" Well, and what is the rabbit? "

" The rabbit is a vertebrate, a herbivore and a
mammal."

" What is a vertebrate? "

" I don't know."

" And the teacher is pleased with you? " I went on.

" Yes. I got the prize for history and for civic
instruction."

T

" Well then, tell me who it is that governs France."

" I know that! . . . It's the King."

" The King! What King? "

The child did not hesitate:

" Charlemagne! "

On my way home I saw a taxi which, owing to a clumsy manœuvre of the chauffeur's, had dashed up on to the pavement. And all at once I recognised the driver as a masseur, who not long before had been treating me for a sprain. One morning he had said to me:

" You mustn't count on my coming to you any more, M. Vollard. I'm not due to be called up just yet, but I'm going to forestall the call. You see, if I don't hurry up, all the best places at the Front will be taken by the others, and I shall be stuck somewhere at the rear."

I had not seen him since.

" What the devil are you doing here? " I asked him. " I thought you were at the Front."

" That's right, M. Vollard; I was even going to get someone to shove me up there right away, but I didn't know then what war was like! Three days ago I was taking the concierge's little dog out to do its business, when all at once something began farting away over our heads. Toto started howling as though they were tearing out his guts, and the fact was a bit of shrapnel had sliced his tail off level with his backside. He bolted like a shot into the house. I took to my heels behind him, and bumped down the cellar steps on my bottom. Toto had already taken the stump of his tail to show his mistress, and was looking at us as though taking us to witness what had been done to him. My wife was in tears. ' Now Jules,' she said, ' there's not a moment to be lost. Run along and enlist this minute, because if you go before you're due, you can choose your own arm.' So, you see, I've chosen the motor. I'm learning to drive."

To put a bit of heart into this honest fellow, I told him I had just seen a father of eleven children who, although free of all military obligations, was in the act of developing his muscles so as to go and fight. But the ex-masseur shook his head:

"That's because your friend hasn't seen an aeroplane chucking muck at people's head, nor all the blood that ran from Toto's behind. . . . Excuse me, I must get on with learning my job," he continued; "I'm passing my chauffeur's exam. in three days from now."

I left him, and went, like many other Parisians, to see the defence works prescribed by the military authorities. They had been actively advanced. At the Porte de Montrouge, for instance, where I went first, the railings had been provided, as a sort of shield, with a revetment of tin, on which an urchin was amusing himself by drumming. His mother gazed lovingly at her offspring: "Now we needn't worry about the cannon-balls." And it was in perfect quietude that I bought one of the cardboard *semelles* of Montreuil peaches of which there was a glut in Paris since it had become difficult to send things over to England. That was one of the first effects of the War: Montreuil peaches at four sous! Relishing my fruit, I went on exploring the fortifications that the Governor of Paris had reinforced. I noted that the roads leading into the capital had been barred with trunks of trees and big branches, the ends of which had been sharply chamfered. With the fault-finding tendency natural to all Frenchmen, I was inclined to think it would have been preferable if the points had been turned towards the enemy rather than towards Paris; but after I had bumped into one of them I guessed there was a stratagem in this. We should let the enemy enter unsuspecting, and then drive him back in disorder upon this spear-tipped apparatus. In order that the closing of Paris should not entirely prevent the inhabitants from going about their business in the suburbs, a pathway had been preserved on either side of the barricades—another subterfuge to attract the enemy.   As a warning against the danger of spies there were little posters everywhere—on the kiosks, in public conveyances, even inside the urinals, which read: " *Taisez-vous, méfiez-vous, des oreilles ennemies vous écoutent!* "   So it was almost in a whisper that I heard a soldierly-looking old man, with an 1870 medal on his jersey, telling people of an excellent means of annihilating the effects of cannon-balls, shells and other infernal machines, which he had used in the preceding war.   The secret consisted in placing a pail of water in the middle of every room, this liquid having, the veteran explained, the property at once of attracting shells and preventing them from bursting.   " And in '70," he added, " we hadn't got water *ad lib.* as we have to-day."   It may perhaps be thought that this revelation has no object, now that with the League of Nations all danger of war is averted. But I am merely reporting what I heard.   I congratulated myself more at every step on this stroll of mine among the working population, from whom so many useful hints may be picked up.   Everywhere the measures taken by the authorities were unanimously approved.   Where tree-trunks were wanting, soldiers were digging trenches under the direction of an adjutant of engineers.

" We shall get them!   We shall get them! " the crowd asserted enthusiastically.

In the event, the trenches turned out to be considerably more efficacious than the tree-trunks and branches.   But at night at any rate these must have the advantage; for in the darkness, what would happen? The first rank of the assailants would stumble against the obstacle, now invisible, the second rank would fall on top of the first, the third on the second, and so on . . . till, one after another, everybody would be on the ground! Or so I heard a citizen expounding, whose reeling gait attested the number of *petits verres* he had civically absorbed since the morning.

" Because by day, you know, if you see a road barricaded you stop in spite of yourself."

I little thought I was about to verify in my person this patriotic boozer's belief in the intimidating effect of a barred road.

Having shut my shop from the first day of the War, I left Paris for the hamlet of Le Home, a dependency of Varaville, where I had a little house.

The most direct way, coming from Paris, is to get out at Cabourg. From there to Le Home is about a kilometre. I was setting out on foot when I saw a handcart drawn across the road, bearing the inscription: " No thoroughfare." This brought me up short, and after the first moment of surprise I discovered a second placard: " Show your passes at the Controller's office on the left." I am in the habit of obeying imperative instructions with docility. For instance, one day when I was going up a flight of stairs, I read on the wall: " Hold your umbrella outside the banisters." Without reflecting that this notice only held good in wet weather, I instinctively held my umbrella out over the well of the staircase . . . and broke a gas mantle. Now again at Cabourg I did what the placard relating to passes told me to do. I turned to the left, where, under a sort of pent-roof, three individuals were playing cards. They had caps trimmed with gold braid such as hotel porters wear. All this braid—you know the respect it has always inspired me with—intimidated me greatly, although I had immediately identified two of the players. They had worked all the previous season in the garden next to mine, and when I passed them, never failed to wish me " *bonjour, monsieur*," cordially and respectfully. The president of the office—at least I assigned this title to the one with the most gold braid—began to question me. He asked me my surname and Christian names, those of my father and mother, if I was married, and how many children I had, although I had declared myself a bachelor.

I began to lose patience.

" But you know me, hang it all! Surely it was you who used to work in M. Duchâtel's garden? "

" Yes, I know you as the M. Vollard of peace-time. But it's war-time now. . . . Your pass, please."

I handed him my paper. Without even looking at it, the man let fall an " Ah! you have one, have you! " in the vexed tone of someone saying to himself: " Now we shan't be able to bully him." His neighbour leant over to him and murmured a few words in his ear, upon which my interlocutor announced:

" This is a pass for Cabourg, but not for Varaville."

" There's hardly five hundred yards between them! "

" Five hundred yards or a yard, I don't care a damn. You'll have to send another application to Paris."

" Why not read my pass right through? You'll see it says Cabourg *and* Varaville."

" Ah! You thought of that, did you? "

I wondered at the time if I had not had to do with impostors—if these could possibly have been *bonâ fide* officials. My doubts vanished later, when I came in contact with duly authenticated officials—the Special Commissary, for instance, who claimed our passports with such arrogance at a frontier railway-station.

In the same train as myself was a lady belonging to the Red Cross, who was going to Switzerland.

" Your papers are in order," the Commissary said to her, " but I see you are married. So you leave your husband in Paris while you go gallivanting abroad? "

" But you might have seen, too, that it is by order of my doctor."

" What about other people, then, who are ill and

can't afford to travel? Besides, I saw you talking to a Belgian officer a minute ago."

" I was asking him when we were due at Bâle."

" And it was in the train that you made the acquaintance of this officer? "

" Why are you asking me all this? My papers are in order: you've just said so yourself."

" In order or not in order, I have the right to detain passengers for further information if the situation doesn't seem clear to me."

And as the lady stood there trembling with indignation:

" I have even the right to have them stripped, and their skin rubbed with lemon-juice. That's how one of my colleagues discovered a correspondence written on a lady's back in invisible ink."

This man, without any possible doubt, was a *bonâ fide* agent of the Administration. But I feel sure he must have suffered *in petto* at having to show himself so ungallant. For, as I learnt afterwards, it was by way of remedying our lack of fuel that our officials vied with one another in putting the public out of conceit with travelling.

So now-a-days, when in any public office an official makes game of people, myself included, I take off my hat to him, mentally, with a great sweep. For I know that he is only sending people to the devil because it is important, in view of the next war, to break them into it beforehand.

(b) *At the Ministry of Investigations*

During the course of the War I had occasion to see a friend of mine who was a private of the Auxiliary forces on duty at the Ministry of Investigations. I found my way into his office just as he was telephoning: " Give me the War Office. . . . Colonel So-and-so. . . . That the War Office? . . . Ministry of Investigations speaking. . . ." And in a louder voice:

" The Minister is very surprised that you haven't yet
sent us Private So-and-so, whose technical knowledge
is so badly wanted here. . . . Right. . . . We count
on you, then, absolutely. . . ."

My friend hung up the receiver; then turning to
me:

" That's the third time I've rung up that ass."

" Do you mean to say you can treat a Colonel like
that? " I asked in astonishment.

" Good Lord, yes! " my friend replied. " You've
only to speak on behalf of a Minister. . . . Except
under fire, there's no one so terrified as a soldier facing
a superior, especially if the superior is a civilian.
Look here, I'll show you. . . ." And turning to
another private, he said:

" I say, Verdier, ring up that fellow again yourself."

The other did not hesitate:

" War Office? Investigations speaking. Give me
Colonel X. . . ."

And the conversation proceeded as before, except
that this time the Colonel's interlocutor invoked his
personal responsibility, which he " wished to safeguard," he said, thereby insinuating that the Colonel's
responsibility might also be implicated.

" By Jove! " I said, " it must mean quite a lot of
work, telephoning every minute to a Ministry here,
and a Colonel there. . . ."

" Between ourselves, it's on my own account that
I've just been telephoning. The technician we're
asking for is my grocer. When I said to his wife;
' Come now, Madame Louise, what about that jam? '
she shook her head: ' It'll be a wonder if you get any
this year. My husband is a Guard of Railways and
Bridges in the Oise; I hoped they were going to send
him back to me, as the surgeon-major has declared him
unfit for armed service. But his captain, who is none
too friendly to him, says one doesn't need to be in the

pink to get oneself killed. . . . So, you see, it doesn't look as though your jam . . .' "

" But surely," I interrupted, " for you to get your man back, your Chief must first have requisitioned him? "

" Of course. So . . . when I gave him the mail to sign, I said to the Chief: ' We simply can't get the War Office to send us so-and-so—you know, the specialist we need so badly for the Commissariat. . . .' And the Chief, who doesn't care a damn about any of it, said: ' Insist, *mon cher*, insist! If anything were to go wrong it's you who would be held responsible.' "

" All the same, if I were in your place, I should be afraid the Chief might find out, one day . . ."

" No fear! He's so worried about the affairs of his firm as it is that he doesn't know which way to turn."

" But he doesn't manage them from here, I imagine? "

" It would be much better if he did. The Service would gain by it, seeing the time he wastes going to and fro between his business and the Ministry."

Just then a little typist came into the office. My friend held out his cigarette-case. " Gasper? " She took one, and inhaled it voluptuously. " This is real tobacco, anyway. It's not like our rouge—since the War started one can get nothing but rubbish. It used to come from the *Boches*, apparently." When she had gone:

" Not a bad little girl," I said to my friend.

" No. She's a typist I managed to get allotted to me. One day I marked down a room with a table and a green tablecloth in it. No one was using it. I had four chairs put into it; that made an office. And then I went to the Chief and said: ' Haven't we got our typist yet? ' You see, it would have begun to look as though I had nothing to do! An office consolidates your post; it may help me later to go over into the permanent services.   That happened to a pal of mine who was no higher up than I in civil life, and who gradually worked his way into the Mixed Tribunals.   And that's a juicy enough job, isn't it? Still, for the moment, the position isn't too bad.   By the by, Verdier, if you like, I'll try and shove you up so that you can be incorporated with us."

" Oh, no," said the other, " I don't want to change. Of course when I was at Rennes, it wasn't all beer and skittles.   That was chiefly because they knew that in civil life I was an examining magistrate.   You can imagine the sort of thing. . . . And then the Commandant took it into his head to make me his secretary ; so of course the adjutant fell foul of me at once.   I had started on a big legal work which necessitated research at the Library of the Faculty.   If I copped it for four days even, that meant four days lost to my work.   So I used to be damned careful.   But one day, as I was passing the adjutant, he called out to me :

" ' Hi!   You there!   Man! '

" ' Sir? '

" ' Your overcoat.'

" ' Sir? '

" ' You can do four days.   That will teach you to put your buttons on straight.'

" I had sewn one of them on crooked.

" But I didn't do my four days, for just at that moment the lieutenant happened to go by.   Seeing the adjutant splitting his sides with the sergeant-major :

" ' We're in very good spirits to-day, adjutant? '

" ' Yes, I've just given the examining magistrate four days.'

" ' Oh, but, I say!   Do you mean Verdier? '

" ' Of course I mean Verdier.   There aren't two examining magistrates in the regiment, thank God! '

" ' Isn't he secretary to the Commandant or something? '

" ' That doesn't matter.   He'll be in quod outside the Service.'

" ' All the same, he may make it awkward for us. One never knows with those chaps. . . . At any rate I don't mean to have any trouble. . . . Cancel your four days.'

" The Commandant certainly thought rather a lot of me.   The good man, having once got some information from me, had gradually got into the habit of asking me about everything under the sun.

" ' Now this time, Verdier,' he said to me one day, ' I fancy I'm going to stump you. If you can't answer, I shall excuse you, for it's a medical question. Do you know what salpingitis is?   I have a request for leave here from a man who wants to go home because he's got acute salpingitis! '

" Seeing my expression of astonishment:

" ' There's no mistake about the name of the disease, he's written it clearly, " salpingitis." '

" ' Pardon me, Commandant, it can't anyhow be the man himself who has salpingitis, it's his wife. . . .'

" Putting on his glasses, and re-reading the request for leave:

" ' You're right, by God!   But how could you guess what was written on a request you hadn't read? '

" ' There was no guessing about it, Commandant; salpingitis is a female complaint.'

" ' Are you sure?   Ah, here comes the M. O.; now we shall see. . . . Tell me, Doctor, I've got a man here who wants a week's leave because he's got salpingitis.'

" ' I beg your pardon, Colonel? ' said the M. O.

" When I had to leave Rennes for Paris, I was afraid I might no longer have time for my own work, but in the end things turned out so well that I'm secretary to a Commission that hasn't yet assembled. And anyhow I hardly ever come to the Ministry now."

" How's that? "

" It's like this.   One day when I was absent, some-

body came to see me at the office. The lieutenant,
who was reading about a woman who had a *liaison*,
replied mechanically: ' Verdier? He's at the *Liaison*.'
And he repeats this automatically now, every time he
hears my name. So there it is, you see, I'm at my
Liaison."

At this moment my attention was attracted by the
antics of one of the young soldiers, who was pirouetting
on one foot, and repeating jubilantly: " They didn't
get *my* leg, anyway ! "

" Who are *they*? " I asked with curiosity.

" The sawbones with four stripes who wanted to cut
it off. . . ."

Seeing my look of astonishment:

" I'll tell you the story. I was wounded at Les
Eparges. In hospital they found I had moist gangrene
in one leg. It didn't worry me too much, because I
knew there was a scientific chap from the Institut
Pasteur on our staff, Doctor Winberg, who had discovered a serum that cured it in two shakes. But
apparently this doctor only held the rank of a lieutenant. So the ' Four-stripes,' who couldn't allow a
' Two-stripes ' to cure people without them, refused to
let him apply his remedy, and went on cutting off
arms and legs worse than ever. A pal of mine did
succeed in saving *his* leg, by sending an S.O.S. to his
uncle, a deputy, who interfered, and got the ' Four-
stripes ' sent to the rightabout. But my pal had gone
back to the Front, I didn't know where. So my leg
was seriously threatened, when at last the Service got
frightened at the number of pensions that would have
to be served out to the mutilated, and decided to
bestow on Doctor Winberg the four stripes that would
give him the right officially to use his serum. So I
was able to keep my leg."

It was after hearing this story that I wrote my
Ubu à l'Hôpital, in which a wounded man begs mercy
for his leg, that a " Five-stripes " is about to cut off

while sending to the devil the " Two-stripes " who had had the effrontery to cure without operating. The Censorship opposed the publication of my pamphlet for cogent reasons; and I came back, of my own accord, to a saner appreciation of the military method. For it is easy to see how contrary to all hierarchy, and even to common sense, it would be if a " Four-stripes " were not twice as clever as a " Two-stripes." Obviously, any cure obtained by an inferior, after a man of superior rank has failed, can only be considered null and void. I wrote my *Ubu à la Guerre* to this effect, and this time the Censorship bestowed its full approval.

On leaving the Ministry of Investigations I felt both embarrassed and saddened. What about all the other young men they were finding no use for, while their friends were being gloriously killed, or shot by way of example? I had got thus far in my reflections, when on the Boulevard Saint Germain I met L. M . . ., Commissary of the First Class. He seemed very much preoccupied, and I remarked on it.

" The fact is," he said, " a post of Commissary-General is vacant, and I'm afraid that once again someone will cut the ground from under my feet. . . . In spite of all my qualifications. . . . But then, qualifications have to be brought into the limelight. . . . I've got an Admiral on my side, but between ourselves he's rather a broken reed. He doesn't know how to insist. . . . I must try and get hold of General Carence."

The name made me at first suspect a joke.[1]

" What, haven't you heard of Carence? A splendid man, who has Painlevé's ear. . . ."

To change the subject, I told my interlocutor the reflections my visit to the Ministry of Investigations had aroused in me.

[1] *Carence,* insolvency.

" First of all," he said, " it isn't given to everybody
to be killed. So you see what an encumbrance all your
auxiliaries would represent. Really, you know, it's
quite right not to send them to clutter up the
Front."

" But," I suggested timidly, " when the Front is
decimated, they would help to make up the numbers
a bit."

" It's easy to see you haven't been to the War, or
you would know that gaps at the Front are automatically filled by troops from the rear."

I thought of the method invented by *Père Ubu*,
who, in order to keep his Front immutably intact, was
careful never to throw any but troops of the rearguard
into line against the enemy.

I mentioned these tactics to my interlocutor.

" There may be something in that," he said; and
then with a frown: " Although, to tell the truth, I
don't quite get you."

" But," I cried suddenly, " don't all these auxiliaries
clutter up the Ministries too? Besides all the trouble
they give the Commandant, not to speak of the
Colonel, whom they keep badgering over the
telephone! "

The Commissary interrupted me:

" A soldier, no matter what his rank, is always on
his guard with a Civil authority. Let me give you an
instance. On the occasion of a ministerial visit to
the Front, Lieutenant André Tardieu was recognised
by the Minister of War, then M. Millerand. The two
parliamentarians chatted together for a few minutes
in the most familiar manner. The General-in-Chief
was horrified. ' Did you see,' he said to his Chief of
Staff, ' the free-and-easy way in which that lieutenant
was talking to the Minister? ' "

Coming back to my idea of making some use of
all these auxiliaries who were kicking their heels in the
Ministries, or at any rate occupied in useless tasks:

" If it would be bad for the service to send them to the Front, why not send them back to civil life? There, at least . . ."

But again the Commissary interrupted me:

" That would be very dangerous too. In the Ministries they are at least officials of a sort. If they adopt official habits, the chief of which is never to worry, they are at least obliged to respect certain rules; and if they accomplish useless tasks, at least they are occupied. . . . Whereas, suppose you send these people back to civil life, where nothing is demanded of them—left to themselves, plunged into idleness, they would soon fall a prey to funk; and then do you suppose they would go on ' holding out '? Remember Joffre's saying: ' If the civilians don't hold out, we are done for! ' "

In the course of this conversation we had arrived at the War Office, where I had to see one of the Chiefs of Staff. As it was not quite time for him to be at his office, I watched the behaviour of the people coming and going in the hall where the forms were filed in, stating the object of one's visit. A sergeant took the slip that was handed him, and passed it on to the person it was intended for. I noticed the deferential manner of the visitors towards this sergeant; they seemed to be saying to themselves, as they politely handed him their request, " We must be nice to him, for it depends on this swine whether the other fellow is told we are waiting."

Meeting the Comte de Comminges, I could not help pointing this out to him.

" There," I said, " look at that Colonel giving his card to the recruit who is assisting the sergeant; he looks positively as though he were begging a favour of him."

" Well," said the Comte de Comminges, " perhaps he's in a hurry."

I went in my turn to hand my slip to the sergeant.

Coming back to my place, I saw the Comte de Comminges was smiling:

"Ah! M. Vollard," he cried, "if you could have seen yourself holding out your slip to that little soldier! You looked even more deferential than the Colonel just now."

XXXII PAINTING AND THE WAR

It is said that on the evening of mobilisation M. Frantz Jourdain gave vent to a shout of relief:

" This means that Cubism is done for! "

But then a frown gathered on the brow of the President of the Salon d'Automne:

" So long as the reaction doesn't sweep the collectors back as far as Bonnat! "

The fear was groundless. Bonnat's painting did not gain a single customer by the War. Pictures by the " Master "—portraits with hands—for which the painter had been paid as much as thirty thousand francs, sold with difficulty at 600. Cubism, on the other hand, and modern art in general, did not suffer at all from the course of events—quite the contrary. For it was soon discovered that in time of war anything would do to speculate in, and that pictures might be as fruitful of profit as Camembert cheese, wine or scrap iron. The prestige enjoyed by Art made the investment doubly tempting, since it might enable one to pose as a connoisseur.

One morning there was a knock at my door. A man came in carrying a prospectus of the books I had published, and inquired if I still had any " tall " copies. Some of them were sold out, and he seemed very disappointed. When I offered him copies on vellum, he made a grimace. " My friends only go in for ' *Chine* ' and ' *Japon*,' you know."

I asked him if his passion for books was a long-standing one.

" Passion? Passion? " he repeated, and went on:
" How many *de luxe* books ought one to possess to be
classed as a great bibliophile? And what, exactly, is a
collector? "

I gave him a definition of the word.

" So then, as I have a great many expensive books, I
am a bibliophile-collector? "

I confirmed this, and he seemed very pleased.
Gaining confidence, he told me his history.

" I was a potato-peeler in a big restaurant, when I
met a pal from the days when we were both street-
hawkers. He told me he had become an army con-
tractor, and suggested my joining his firm. I left
the potatoes with pleasure, and soon became his right
hand as a buyer."

" But you knew something about what you were
buying? "

" Hang it! You know well enough that at that
time the great thing was to get lower prices. I had a
dodge. I pretended to be uncertain when they showed
me the stuff. I said ' Hum! Hum! ' and then I was
sure to get my reduction. It was a good trade, and I
made my pile. And money is meant to be circulated.
I know lads who spend their money on buying pearl
necklaces for tarts, but I'm all for something that
lasts . . . stuff that they say is likely to go up in
value . . . pictures, books."

This attitude explains the success of Degas' sale,
right in the middle of the War. Counting pictures,
drawings and sketches, there were two thousand
items, which four sales sufficed to disperse. On one
occasion the bursting of shells shook the glass roof of
the Georges Petit auction-room, but business was not
interrupted. In fact, a painting which had been
sold and turned to the wall was still being " bid up "
when a passer-by rushed into the room and shouted,
" All clear! "

The liquidation of Degas' studio produced nearly

twelve million francs—and they were not francs at
four sous!

During the War, the Service of Propaganda asked
me to go abroad and give some lectures on painting.
I decided to speak on the two painters I knew best:
Cézanne and Renoir.

I went first to Switzerland.   Crossing the frontier, I
remembered what had happened to M. Paul Adam,
the writer, when he got into a train in a Swiss station,
with his two big dogs:

" I am M. Paul Adam," he said to the guard, who
wanted to turn the animals out of the carriage.

" And I am here to enforce the rules."

It was delightful to be in a country where so much
order reigned, and I resolved to enjoy my happiness
without delay.   In the restaurant car a passenger
lighted his pipe, in spite of the notice: " *Défense de
fumer.*"   I protested vigorously.   But a head-waiter
intervened:

" We are in French Switzerland here; we are free."

A little humiliated to see that the colour of my
country " came off " on the borderland, I was eager
to reach the region that I, like everybody else, had
hitherto called German Switzerland, a mistake that
occasioned this somewhat tart retort from a native:

" There is no German Switzerland, Monsieur.   We
say Germanic Switzerland."

My ignorance on this point was all the less excusable
as I had long been in touch with that part of Switzerland, where there are so many fervent admirers of
French painting.

On getting out of the train, I was surprised not to be
assailed, as in France, by an ear-piercing shriek.

" Is there something wrong with your engine, that
you're not whistling? " I asked the engine-driver.

" No, but I don't want to be had up for infringing
the rules," he replied.

Winterthur is a charming town, standing like an outpost in the direction of Germany. And what picturesque surroundings! I must admit, however, that I was greatly disappointed with the Falls of the Rhine. I thought the spectacle decidedly poor. I had so often heard the famous Falls celebrated in enthusiastic literary tirades, that I expected a gigantic cascade falling straight from the clouds, and was faced with a miserable sheet of water trickling down from artificial rocks recently consolidated with reinforced concrete.

I had an invitation from M. and Mme Hannloser, who are among the most zealous propagandists of French art in Switzerland. What a collection they have! Renoirs, Matisses, Roussels, all our moderns, in fact!

But it was not only the pictures I enjoyed at the Hannlosers. There was real refreshment in that atmosphere of intimacy that I could wish more usual in my own country. Here, the daughter of the house handed the dishes, while her young brother poured out the wines. And both so quiet, so attentive! How different from our faithful but imperious domestics whose temper is not always restrained even in the presence of guests.

The notables of the little town of Winterthur constitute a veritable artistic *élite*. I need only mention the Hannlosers, the Reinharts, the Sulzers, the Butlers. One of these notables said one day at the club: "Why have we no picture-gallery? Why should we lag behind Zurich?" It was decided there and then to open a subscription, and in a few days they had collected fifteen hundred thousand Swiss francs. This enabled them to build a gallery, that might almost be termed a temple, dedicated to the genius of French art, by reason of the Cézannes, Renoirs and Degas which are its chief ornaments, together with Roussel's admirable frescoes by which the vestibule is, so to speak, illuminated. It is worth mentioning that they have here solved the problem of lighting and heating, usually considered unworthy of the attention of a curator.

I was to give a lecture at the Gallery at half-past eight. Used to Parisian habits, I thought that if I arrived punctually, I should still have time to look at the pictures. When I was twenty yards away from the building, the half-hour struck, and immediately a keeper, who was behind the door, pushed it to and hurriedly turned the key. I had great difficulty in persuading him to let me in, and I should certainly not have succeeded if I had not been the lecturer. So a few days later, in Geneva, when I had again to give a lecture at half-past eight, I was up to time. But my punctuality was wasted, for the hall was still three-quarters empty. The audience, more accustomed to Parisian ways, hardly turned up before nine o'clock.

It may be said of the Swiss, that they know how to listen, and that they think about what they have heard. Thus the day after one of my talks, a member of my audience suddenly burst out laughing and said to me: " I've just tumbled to what you were telling us about Cézanne's models."

The wines in Switzerland are excellent. Besides the much-admired local growths, all the most famous French wines are to be had. What a splendid means of propaganda our wines are! With our books and our pictures, they have always been our most accredited ambassadors abroad.

At Zurich I imagined I had discovered a gift for attracting birds. Walking along the quays of the town, I saw a crow in the branches of a plane tree. The bird seemed to be looking at me as though he knew me. I stirred the leaves with my walking-stick, saying, " Pretty Crow! " and the bird fluttered from branch to branch and began pecking the end of my walking-stick. I was delighted. On my return, I told the hotel-keeper of my adventure. "Ah! That must be the water-bailiff's crow. He bothers everybody that goes by like that."

I had another curious adventure in Zurich.

From my open window I could see, at the end of the garden, a tiny pond reflecting the branches of the surrounding trees, which at break of day were crowded with birds. I used even to get out of bed at that time to watch them skimming the water in pursuit, as I supposed, of insects they took on the wing.

One morning the pond was no longer to be seen.

I rang for the waiter:

"Tell me, there *is* a pond at the bottom of the garden, isn't there?"

"A pond, monsieur? There's never been a pond here! I can tell you that for certain. I rake the garden over myself."

"All right!" I said. "My mistake. . . ."

Coming out of my room, not without some anxiety as to my mental state, I met a friend staying in the hotel.

"You know," I said to him, "that pretty little pond I showed you from my room . . ."

"Yes. Well?"

"Disappeared . . . evaporated. And the waiter seemed to take me for a madman when I asked him what had become of it."

"Let's go up to your room."

When we got there, and had opened the window, my friend exclaimed:

"Now then! What nonsense are you talking? The little pond is still there."

So it was! I was dumbfounded.

"Are you still looking for your pool?" said the waiter, bringing me my letters.

"I'm not looking for it. It's come back. See for yourself."

He burst out laughing.

" Ah! That's what you take for a pond, is it?
That's the table with a mirror on top, on which the
English family takes tea. It wasn't carried down
this morning because they had breakfast in their
room. . . ."

Soon after this I went to Spain. The two famous
Athenæums of Madrid and Barcelona had asked me to
speak on Renoir and Cézanne.

As soon as one has crossed the frontier, the impression made on one by Spain is an impression of
desolation. The same thing had struck Renoir.
" And yet," he said to me, " the Spaniards have not
got a Republic, the régime that succeeds in banishing
trees from the forest, birds from the air, hares from
the plain, fish from the water. . . . On the other hand
the Spaniards have goats, and they ravage everything."

They said to me in Paris, " You are going to Spain?
It is the dirtiest country in Europe." Now Spain is
perhaps the only country where one has no qualms
about drinking out of doors from a glass that is used by
everybody. I shall always remember drinking barley
syrup from a glass which was afterwards placed
under a running tap. I also remember that when, in
a *pâtisserie*, I pointed to one of the cakes inside a glass
case, the waitress pushed my arm down hurriedly:
" Oh, monsieur, if anyone had seen you pointing at
that cake they might have thought you had touched
it." So saying, the young lady picked up the cake
with a long pair of metal tongs, and handing it to me
on a plate, turned her head slightly aside, so as not to
breathe on it. This made me think of the slaves of
Carthage who waited at table with nose and mouth
swathed in bandages.

On arriving at Barcelona, I thought it proper to go
and pay a visit to the Consul-General of France. I
was accompanied by the President of the " Association
of young painters " and by a member of the *Athenæum*.

I handed the Consul a letter from the *Service of Propaganda*, recommending me to him.

" Another lecture ! " exclaimed the Consul-General. " If I give permission for it . . ."

" But," interrupted one of the Spaniards who were with me, " we have not come to ask your permission to give a lecture, M. le Consul-Général ; we have come to invite you to be present. . . ."

After my *causerie*, during which I had spoken chiefly of Renoir at home, some of the audience decided to send an address to the painter, expressing " how happy they had been to feel themselves admitted for a few moments to the intimacy of the Master." They made a point of sending their telegram by courtesy of the Consul-General, since he was the Frenchman who seemed to them best qualified to serve as intermediary between the painter and themselves. It was not till three months later, through a note in the *Petit Niçois*, that Renoir heard of this deferential undertaking. The telegram had never reached him ! Inquiries were made at the Consulate, and it turned out that it had never been sent off.

At Madrid, where I went next, I was gallantly received by the Ambassador, to whom I took my letter of introduction. Most courteously he expressed his regret that his occupations prevented him from being present at a lecture on an artist for whom he had so great an admiration. In which, as a matter of fact, he was mistaken. I was not long, in effect, in realising that he was confusing Renoir the painter with Renouard the designer; but rather than muddle him still further, I did not undeceive him. My lecture, as a matter of fact, did not suffer by the diplomat's absence, and Renoir's prestige sufficed amply to make my Madrid audience favourable to me.

After the War I had occasion to go into Alsace. I arrived with my head full of Erckmann-Chatrian's stories, which had peopled the dreams of my youth with pretty girls with long fair plaits, and storks' nests on the roofs of the houses! I may say that the fair plaits and the storks' nests disappointed me: most Alsatian girls wear their hair cut Paris fashion, and as for the storks . . . I was told that for the moment they were in Egypt.

From Alsace I went to Wiesbaden, where I was thinking of opening a Gallery of Modern Art. I found a town of scrupulous cleanliness with a most friendly population, and how many details to remind me of Old France!

I seemed there to be recovering my entire childhood, with that definite stamp that La Réunion had preserved from the days of the first colonisers from the mother-country: on the walls, a Louis Philippe wallpaper, with its round posies and its little wreaths of ferns, bon-bon boxes decorated with Watteau and Lancret scenes, that are hardly to be found now-a-days except in a few old Parisian *confiseries*, such as Seugnot's or the " Marquise de Sévigné." Another time, walking in a park, I saw an old man with a fine white beard, giving his arm to a lady in a dress with panniers. Two children walked soberly in front of them: a little girl with a doll, a little boy carrying a hoop. And Wiesbaden at the time of the great religious festivals! What beautiful processions I saw passing, with their banners, along roads shaded by cherry trees laden with fruit! And what scrupulous honesty among these Rhinelanders! I went up to a young man who was standing under one of the cherry trees, and taking him for the owner of the tree, held out a five-franc note, asking him to let us pick a few cherries. He refused my money. " The cherry tree isn't mine," he said.

At that time, on account of the devaluation of the mark, the hotel porters would offer you houses of five stories for twenty-five thousand francs of French money. I was present at one of these sales. A lady had come to order the omnibus for her luggage.

" How pleasant it is at Wiesbaden! " said she. " I should love to own a house here! "

" What part of the town does madame prefer? " inquired the porter.

" Oh! you know I'm leaving in two hours' time."

" That's plenty long enough."

The man pointed to a poster depicting a number of small villas.

" There is a batch of houses to choose from."

While the lady was looking at them, hesitating, the porter seized the telephone, said a few words in German, and announced:

" I have told the hotel lawyer . . ."

A few minutes later the man of law arrived and had soon got the better of all the client's objections. While she was at lunch, the notary began drawing up the deed of sale. He informed the purchaser that the law obliged him to read the deed over to her, although she did not understand German. In the middle of the reading he stopped suddenly and rushed across to the balcony. The lady had gone out there and was leaning over. He said to her piteously:

" We shall have to begin the reading all over again. The law forbids leaving the room in which it is taking place. Being on the balcony is the same as being out of doors."

The marvellous cleanness of Wiesbaden made me think of Holland, where, as I was made to believe when I was a child, animals were forbidden to go into the street without a little basket under their tail.

Of all the countries I visited during my wanderings outside France, England made the strongest impression on me. As a foreigner, you are struck first by the formalism that chills you at your first contact with the soil. It is as though our neighbours across the Channel, in order to affirm their particularism, make it a point of honour not to answer anyone whose pronunciation is not faultless, even though they understand perfectly.

I admit there are words belonging to the English dictionary which have not the same meaning as in France.

When the French-speaking porter at my London hotel was off duty for the night, I was only saved from a difficult situation by the kindly intervention of a Dutch visitor, as well versed in the language of Shakespeare as in that of Voltaire, who informed me that across the Channel " waters " are " toilets." He also told me that " No Smoking " on the windows of railway-carriages is not intended to exclude wearers of dinner-jackets, but merely means " *défense de fumer.*"

The dinner-jacket, on the contrary, is rooted in the English national habits. I had heard of the official in the Indian Civil Service who, having climbed a tree to escape from a lion, would not touch the food he had in his pocket because he had left his dinner-jacket among his kit.

I had therefore been careful to take this indispensable garment with me, and I put it on for a dinner-party to which I had been invited. On going into the drawing-room I felt myself followed by a persistent stare that I could not account for, but back in my room I found my evening trousers, recognisable by their stripe of broad silk braid, lying on a chair. In dressing, I had absent-mindedly retained the trousers of my morning suit. Hence the astonishment of my hosts, who were perhaps under the impression that my blue trousers and black jacket represented the latest Paris fashion.

Speaking seriously, I cannot sufficiently express my

liking for this England, which gives one so powerful an impression of greatness and order. I have seen London in spring, its parks clothed in a green that seems peculiarly their own. I have seen it in the thickest fogs; and never did London seem to me more beautiful. One goes along feeling one's way, and suddenly one comes upon ghostly buildings reminiscent of the Arabian Nights. The day when this fairy-like London was revealed to me, I had for guide my friend Paul Maze, the well-known French painter, who has adopted England as a second fatherland. I spent a whole afternoon admiring the monuments of London under this impressive cloak of mystery lent them by the fog.

Though the man in the street, owing to a sort of exaggerated nationalism, refuses to answer you if you do not question him in faultless English, yet, on the other hand, the representative of authority who is in closest contact with the crowd, the magnificent English policeman, is always on the look-out to help the passer-by. One day, coming out of my hotel, I was looking about for a pillar-box. A policeman, seeing me hesitate with a letter in my hand, ran up to me and pointed out the Post Office with his white-gloved hand.

But what surprised me most agreeably was the sympathy, the warm hospitality that one meets with from the Englishman as soon as one has been introduced to him. Paul Maze having taken me to see one of his English friends, the manservant said to us: " Mr. . . . is not in, but tea is ready for any of his friends who may turn up." We had tea while waiting for the master of the house. Then, as he had still not come, we went back to Paul Maze's. There we found his friend having tea while waiting for us.

That year there was a mummy in the British Museum which was reputed to bring bad luck to visitors. I have always been a little afraid of the occult, of every-thing suggestive of malevolent powers, ghosts and phantoms. I therefore put off my visit till some future time. But the other museums! . . . What I was most delighted to observe was the more and more obvious importance given to French art in English collections, both public and private. Less than fifty years ago, in our own country, the Impressionists were still pleading with official painters: " Let us set up our little table alongside of yours, O sumptuous banqueters! " It is remarkable, therefore, that in a country so devoted to tradition as England, these same Impressionists should have obtained citizens' rights alongside of Gainsborough, Lawrence, Turner, and all the most famous English painters. One cannot, in fact, be completely acquainted with the work of Renoir, Degas and many others until one has visited the London museums and the galleries of the English collectors, to one of whom, Samuel Courtauld, the museums themselves owe some of the finest Impressionist paintings.

American readers may think it strange that I have not yet been to the United States, a country it is indispensable to visit if one wishes to see the best French pictures. I myself am all the more surprised, as America has always had the greatest fascination for me. As a child I once came across a picture of a bright red carriage drawn by four white horses, in which sat an imposing personage in a grey top-hat, distributing a number of toys to the children who crowded round him. The picture was entitled " *Un Oncle d' Amérique.*"

" Have all children got uncles in America? " I asked my mother.

" Yes, if they are very good."

I shall have to hurry if I am still to find mine. But in any case I hope some day to go over and take another look at those of my pictures—some of the finest—which, after being exhibited at Knoedler's, have remained in the United States. And then I promise myself the pleasure of renewing acquaintance with my many American friends.

XXXIII MY HOMES: FONTAINE-BLEAU — LE TREMBLAY-SUR-MAULDRE

I had always longed for a place in the country, with trees of my own, and the district of Fontaine-bleau in particular appealed to me very much.

The Forest of Fontainebleau is a wonderful place, affording endless variety in its area of forty thousand acres of chalky soil—pine-tree-covered plain, slopes feathery with bracken, glades that might have stirred Corot to serene emotion, and plateaux where narrow paths wind among a maze of stones fantastically grouping themselves in ever-changing combinations of form and size.

But as though with all this she had done enough for the Forest, Nature has refused it the benefit of natural springs. The few existing wells have been obtained by digging to great depths in the soil.

For this reason I had abandoned the project of buying a piece of land that tempted me very much, when one day, having wandered back to that neighbourhood, I heard what I took to be the sound of a brook. I called to my companion, who was lagging behind to botanise:

"Listen! Don't you hear a murmur like running water?"

"Water? There isn't a drop in the whole Forest of Fontainebleau!"

"Let's go and see, all the same."

After a few minutes' search, we came upon a brook which lost itself again a little further on in the sand.

"There must have been a seismic shock recently,"

said my companion, " which has made a spring break out."

I returned later on, alone, to explore. Following up the brook, I came to an imposing aqueduct, from which water was pouring out on every hand. I knew that openings are left in aqueducts to allow for an overflow, but I could not help admiring the genius that had given to these gushing waters all the fantastic effects of ruined fountains. There were little cascades, and a thousand fantasies of a facetious and invisible Mannekenpiss, bursting out in a jet now as thick as an arm, now as slender as the spirt of a syringe; further on was a shower as from the rose of a giant watering-can. I was quite carried away by this unexpected sight, and as the land watered by the aqueduct was for sale, I acquired bit by bit a respectable number of acres. Then one day on coming to the aqueduct I found a team of workmen there.

" What is up? " I asked them.

" We've come to repair the aqueduct. It must be at least thirty years since the damage began, but as no one complained, of course the Government was not in a hurry."

This meant not only the destruction of my fairyland, but the cutting off of my water-supply. I was obliged to have recourse to a water-diviner, who, armed with his hazel twig, discovered a spring, by good luck, not twenty yards from the house I was building.

What had captivated me as much as the gushing waters of the aqueduct was the number of enormous rocks covered with moss and lichen. One of the grandest of these overtopped my house by its bulk. A girl-student, who was working for her doctor's degree in Natural Science, came with some friends to spend the day with me. Pointing to a pine tree that had spread its roots all along the rock:

"M. Vollard," she said to me, "aren't you afraid that some day the pine supporting that rock may give way and your house may be crushed?"

I reassured her, smiling at her youthful thoughtlessness.

Not long after I got a letter saying: "Next week the workmen will be planting the little flag on the roof-tree of your house."

All eagerness to behold my finished house, I arrived. I gazed. I admired: "What a fine block of masonry!" I cried, "but where is the flag?"

"Oh, my God!" exclaimed my chauffeur, coming up behind me, "the house has fallen down!"

There was nothing left of it but a heap of stones. The foundations had been laid on a gigantic, possibly prehistoric, rabbit-warren. It had, of course, to be rebuilt, and the architect, having learnt his lesson, took care this time to safeguard me against the underground conspiracies of the rabbits. All the same, the affair put me out of conceit, for a time, with landed proprietorship.

Le Tremblay-sur-Mauldre is a little village fifteen kilometres from Versailles, out of reach of the railway, in a region beloved of many artists. At St. Germain-en-Laye, Maurice Denis owns an ancient Abbey. Maillol lives at Marly-le-Roi. K. X. Roussel, the painter of nymphs and fauns, at Étang-la-Ville. Here too is the valley of Chevreuse with its acacias, whose blossom forms a sweet-scented carpet on the roads in spring. Further on lies the Vaux-de-Cernay, with a whole colony of painters. There are fruit trees everywhere, and I know no sight so beautiful when spring is come. We hear a great deal of the Feast of Cherry-blossom in Japan, but there Nature, even at blossoming time, proclaims her mutilation at the hands of man. Here the trees grow freely, on a scale in keeping with the surrounding hills. The land-

x

scape is enchanting at all times of the year, even under snow, perhaps especially under snow. My most vivid impression is of that mass of whiteness against the blue of the surrounding hills, one winter's day when I was walking in the neighbourhood of the château of Pontchartrain. It was quite near the little village of Tremblay-sur-Mauldre.

One day in the following summer I remembered that the writer Blaise Cendrars lived there. A little pink house, next to the local joiner's, he had told me. I found it easily. Cendrars was at his typewriter in the midst of a field of poppies—poppies of every colour.

I expressed my delight.

" Everything grows marvellously here," he told me.

" By the by, Vollard, there's a little house to be sold, in a big garden with the most ripping views. Do come and look at it! "

The doorway had delightful pilasters surmounted by bunches of flowers carved in the stone, the stone itself weathered to a delicious hue. The house, with its rustic character, and its old well, belonged to a period when everything, even the peasants' cottages, had a charming *cachet*. I noticed a barn that could easily be turned into a studio. A painter who was working for me had often bewailed the fact that he had no peaceful little place, far from the noise of the town, where he could paint in comfort. I let myself be tempted, and bought the property. But hardly had I signed the deed of sale when my tribulations began. First the well ran dry. They explained that as the soil was sandy, I must have a well with a special apparatus. This took time and cost money. All the time the work of fitting up the barn and the well was going on, the painter to whom I had promised the studio never ceased to pester me:

" Here we are in the middle of April. Will the studio be ready by July? When will the well be

covered in? That gaping hole gives me nightmares
—I can see my children falling headlong into it."

At last, towards the 14th July, I was able to say to
him: "It's ready. Come and see it."

The artist expressed his entire approbation of the
well, the hermetic sealing of which deprived him of
all anxiety. He was satisfied with the studio too.
Scratching the wall with his nail:

"Look," he said to me, "the plaster comes off in
powder, a sign that it is quite dry. I shall be very
comfortable here."

He never came back to Le Tremblay.

I experienced a like disappointment with a cat that
I had at the rue Laffitte. It was in the habit of
climbing up a curtain fixed to a shelf on which it
liked to doze. When it awoke, it humped its back
—*tirait sa paresse*, as they say in my country—and its
back then touched the ceiling. "Poor creature!" I
said to myself one day, "I'll have that shelf lowered,
it's too near the ceiling." When this had been done,
I watched him climb up his curtain, settle down and
go to sleep. But when, after his doze, he humped
up his back and no longer felt the ceiling in the way,
he jumped down in a hurry and never climbed the
curtain again.

XXXIV PAINTING AFTER THE WAR

After the War, the enthusiasm for painting did not die down. Everybody went on buying and selling pictures. Galleries sprang up like mushrooms. Over the length of whole streets, every shop-window was the show-case of a picture dealer. To say nothing of private traders. One day my attention was drawn to a little lady going by with canvases under her arm. It appeared she had complained that her husband's pay did not allow her to have two servants, and someone had said to her: " There's nothing like buying and selling pictures nowadays, if you want to make money." A friend of the family, who had confidence in the lady's business capacity, advanced her a few thousand francs, which she spent on having everything knocked down to her, at the Kahn sale, that " did not go too high." In this way she acquired some Cubist paintings, which at that time had gone down a great deal in value, but went up again soon after. She got her two servants straight away, then her car, and then her " At Home " day.

But if the picture dealers prospered, they were very soon faced with the growing demands of the painters, all anxious to share their prosperity.

One day I met one of my colleagues, who said to me:

" I've just been with So-and-so " (mentioning one of his " colts "). " Only a year ago I had to give him a Talbot, and now he wants to touch me for a Packard."

I had occasion to visit this same colleague a few months later.

"Is M. A. . . . in his office? " I asked the lady secretary.

"You've come at an unlucky moment, M. Vollard! The boss is in such a state! . . . X. . . . has just been here."

The name was that of the Packard man.

"Just fancy! He came in like a whirlwind, and without saying a word, rushed up to a *Nude* of his own—a painting for which we had refused seventy-five notes, *oui, Monsieur!* Before he could be stopped, the picture was . . . Look, that's all that's left of it, those scraps in the corner over there. ' That picture is no longer worthy of my reputation! ' he shouted to us as he went away. And he carried away a piece of the woman's belly, to make sure the canvas shouldn't be repaired. All that after the Packard he's cost us! A painter, too, that the firm has actually made, you might say. Not three years ago he was swearing to the boss: ' You can count on my eternal gratitude.' "

I myself was caught by the general fever. One day I thought I had stumbled on a good thing. In a dealer's window I saw a picture of a cathedral, signed Utrillo, a name unknown to me. " Aha! " I said to myself, " there's a painter to take up."

I went in and asked the price.

Fifty thousand francs.

I was too late. Only a few years earlier, I was told, Utrillo's work was to be found hung out in the open, at the junk-dealers' on the Boulevard Clichy, or in eating-houses, where the artist had left them with the proprietor for the price of a meal.

It was much the same with another artist, Modigliani, an exhibition of whose work, in the rue Laffitte itself, had attracted my attention by its strangeness. Out of curiosity I had bargained for one of his paintings, although I rebelled somewhat against his figures,

which had necks so long that they looked as though
they had been dragged out.

"Three hundred francs, that's dear for such
stuff!" I thought at the time.

A few years later, walking along the rue de la
Boétie, I noticed a *Nude* by this artist, which recalled
the rather mannered grace of certain Japanese prints.
But what a voluptuous texture he had given to the
skin! I said to myself: "Only four years ago the
biggest Modiglianis were priced at three hundred
francs. They're not likely to want more than three
thousand for this."

"How much?" I asked.

"Three hundred and fifty thousand. But there's
an option on it already. And we have every reason
to believe that the traveller who has taken it is acting
on behalf of Mussolini!"

The post-war period saw the rise to popularity of
the cafés on the Boulevard Montparnasse. On the
terraces, and within-doors, people pointed out to one
another the new groups of painters and their models.
The latter, convinced that they had film faces, all
dreamed of appearing on the screen. There was no
resemblance to the old Montparnasse. Nothing of
the Good-natured Artist, smoking his pipe before a
sparkling *bock* and announcing jubilantly: "Things
are moving, I've got one of my pictures on show in
the rue Laffitte." An anecdote that I had from
Guillemet is characteristic of that period. One day
when he had gone to see Corot, the latter said:
"What! You tell me an *amateur* has given you
thirty louis to buy two pictures for him, and that if I
were not Corot you would have come to me? But,
my boy, thirty louis is a good sum. We'll choose
two paintings for this Mæcenas straight away."

The new Montparnasse was a Babel, where the
painters for the most part talked in dollars, piastres,

pesetas, kroner, pounds sterling. What a contrast with their elders, who painted simply for the joy of painting!

But it is not easy to work with pleasure when everything conspires to disturb your peace. It was not only the snobs and profiteers who had " gone in for painting," the more enlightened collectors were no less ardent in their pursuit of the artists. Only one means of escape from such a conspiracy remained: running away. Running far away. Fleeing to places where there was no railway. Alas! villages, even the most remote, are not safe from the motor, and the painter had hardly settled into the retreat where he thought himself to be undiscoverable, when he was tracked down.

" We happened to be coming your way . . ."

And besides these confirmed admirers, there were insolent individuals to be dealt with, who, as soon as the " Master's " removal was rumoured, rushed in pursuit of him. In vain did the artist, to secure a peaceful seclusion, put up notices at his gate, such as " Wolf-traps " or " Beware of the dog," they always found means of forcing his door. " Monsieur," the maid would come and say, " there are three very respectable-looking gentlemen at the gate. They are giving Black sugar, and he is licking their hands." A fresh lot of intruders were attempting to corrupt the dog so as to get in.

Who would suspect the chauffeur, come to ask for help in a breakdown? The help obtained, a lady would get out of the sumptuous limousine and insist on thanking the painter for his kindness. Of course it was quite by chance she had discovered it was to the " Master " Renoir that she owed the possibility of continuing her journey. Yet as she knew that Renoir had once said nothing was so difficult, and at the same time so exciting, to paint, as white on white, everything in the lady's get-up would be white, from the hat to the shoes. And Renoir, greatly struck, would exclaim: " I have no luck: for once that I see a good portrait to paint, of course the model must escape me." Then, by mere chance again, it would turn out that the lady was staying quite close by. She would offer to come back—" only too happy to be of use in her turn to the ' Master '." Before she had got back into the car, a day would have been fixed for the sitting. And after the portrait she would want a bunch of flowers, a landscape " that would remind her, when she was back in Paris, of the silvery olive trees she loved so much."

Two gentlemen left the train one day at Cagnes.

" Now we must get at Renoir," said one.

" I'd give a thousand francs to anyone who would introduce us," declared the other.

" Is that serious? " asked a fellow who had overheard them. " I can easily introduce you to Renoir, I know him quite well."

So he did, but merely from having seen him go by.

Having duly pocketed the thousand francs, he took the others to the painter's house, and persuaded the maid to fetch him. When Renoir asked what was wanted of him:

" M. Renoir," said the fellow imperturbably, " allow me to introduce M. So-and-so and M. So-and-so," and decamped.

Renoir could not even get rid of importunates by telling the maid to say he was out, since in a village one is always to be found. It is easier to escape from visitors in Paris. One day at an artist's house I suddenly saw his little boy run into the hall and pick up his father's coat, hat and stick. I was puzzled. "Didn't you hear? " said the painter. " There was a ring at the door. It may be a visitor for my wife, but it may also be someone for me."

What a contrast with pre-war days, when people

of fashion were far from caring to be taken for connoisseurs of painting!

When the *Gioconda* was stolen from the Louvre, I came upon a lady of my acquaintance one day, standing before a kiosk.

" Who was Mona Lisa? " she asked me, showing me, in an illustrated paper, the portrait of a man, entitled, " The husband of Mona Lisa."

" She was the *Gioconda*, of course! "

" The *Gioconda*? "

" Why, yes. You know, Leonardo da Vinci's masterpiece! "

" Leonardo da Vinci? "

" Have you never been to the Louvre? "

" To the *Magasins*, often. To the Museum, *ma foi*, no! It would mean crossing the rue de Rivoli. I have never had time."

Yet this was the person of whom Forain, at one of my dinner-parties in the " Cellar," had said to me: " If you want to give me a treat, put me beside Mme Z. . . . I love hearing her talk. She has ideas."

She had taste as well. I came across her another time in a friend's drawing-room, seated beside a member of the Académie des Beaux-Arts, whose formal mien recalled that of an English lord, and with whom she was carrying on a very animated conversation. When he had gone, I said:

" You seem to find that gentleman profoundly interesting? "

" We were talking painting. He wanted me to explain why I like those *Women bathing* so much. You know—in the hall."

This was a water-colour by Cézanne. I did not think it a good time to ask the lady for her reasons, but I promised myself that when I saw the academician again, I would lead the conversation to the water-colour in question. When we did meet, however, before I could open my mouth, he exclaimed:

" What a painter's eye that pretty woman has that I was sitting beside the other day, at the X.'s! With my craze for always talking shop, I asked her if she cared for painting.

" 'When I was taking my cloak off in the hall,' she replied, ' I saw a picture of some women bathing. Now I call that really pretty.'

" 'What! That thing that looks like a cheese with big white maggots coming out of it!' I cried, like the bloody fool that I am . . .''

(I thought it my duty to protest against this description of himself.)

" Shut up. . . . You think worse of my painting even than that," said he.

" The lady," he went on, " retorted: ' I get the same pleasure from it as I should from a beautiful piece of china.' Well, that opened my eyes to Cézanne. So that now, when I sit at my easel, in front of my little pink bottoms and waxen breasts, all those horrors that got me into the Institute, they make me feel sick."

" It's a different art," I ventured.

" It's muck. But I'm trying to turn over a new leaf. At the moment I'm studying Picasso and Matisse, before making a serious attempt at Cézanne."

A Cézanne, a Matisse, a Picasso are not merely a joy to the eye, they may procure one advantages of another sort. I knew a big Jewish banker who wanted at all costs to get into the Faubourg Saint-Germain set, of which one of the most representative personalities, in his eyes, was Baron Denys Cochin. He opened his batteries by buying an estate alongside the Baron's, but in spite of his advances, he could never get anything out of him, socially speaking, beyond a visiting-card. Whereas if he had possessed a few Cézannes, M. Denys Cochin might very well have been the first to make advances.

And besides fine acquaintance, one may even derive lasting profit from the fact of having a collection and allowing it to be seen. I knew a collector whose modest means only permitted him to buy sketches. One day I found him engaged in showing some paintings to an individual with a patronising air, whom he was trying to persuade to admire them.

"Oh, of course," I heard the visitor say, "I don't know anything about it, but you will never convince me that any of this stuff is serious painting."

At that moment the maid came in:

"They have sent to tell Monsieur that the Prince of X . . ., who was to have come at ten o'clock, cannot get here till half-past. The Prince hopes it will not put Monsieur out."

The visitor stood agape:

"What! The brother of the King of . . . is coming here?"

"Oh, yes! Whenever he goes through Paris he comes to see my little gallery."

"Look here, my friend, I'm a plain-dealing man. I know you're in love with my daughter. I have never encouraged you to propose. Well! put it there! Only let me stay here when the Prince comes. I should so love to be able to say I had had a *tête-à-tête* with the brother of a king! Of course I don't expect you to introduce me straight away. But you might say, for instance, referring to that picture over there: 'My dear father-in-law, would you mind helping me to take down that picture? I want the Prince to look at it more closely.'"

So there was an *amateur* whose collection helped him to a brilliant marriage.

A certain financier, too, owed his salvation to the portrait a famous artist painted of him.

I was in John Lewis Brown's studio when someone came in, and seizing both the artist's hands, cried:

" Do you know you have positively saved me from ruin ? "

" I ? " exclaimed the artist.

" Do you remember my asking you one day to get Bonnat to do a sketch of me for ten thousand francs? How did that strike you at the time? "

" I said to myself: 'How rich he must be to fork out ten thousand francs like that!' "

" What would you have said, my good Lewis, if you had known the fix I was in? I was literally at the end of my tether. I expected to go smash from one minute to the other, when the idea came to me of bluffing with that portrait by Bonnat. . . . *Coup de théâtre*: when they read in the *Figaro* and the *Gaulois* that the eminent painter of the Presidents and other big-wigs of the Republic was at work on a portrait of the 'great banker,' you can imagine it gave all the people who were preparing to hang me something to chew! I immediately found all the money I needed to set myself afloat again."

" Well," said Brown, when the other had gone, " now you see the true uses of painting."

" Yes, I see. Why don't all the manipulators of capital buy pictures, and the company promoters, and the States that are in debt—everybody, in fact, who wants to restore public confidence? "

Seeing the *amateurs* " stocking " pictures as though they were shares that promised to go up, the dealers themselves, convinced that prices would continue to rise, formed a reserve stock, and when a chance customer, attracted by some picture in the window, asked: " How much is that *Snow Scene* by Monet? " he was told: " Not for sale."

" That Derain, then? "

" Not for sale either! "

Dumbfounded, he might still persist:

" And that big Matisse? "

" Everything in the window belongs to the boss's private collection."

I did not go so far as to refuse to sell, but it might well be said that the way I conducted business at that time was not calculated to make the customer buy.

" How much are those three sketches by Cézanne? "

" Do you want one, two, or three of them? "

" Only one."

" Thirty thousand francs, at your choice."

" And if I take two? "

" That will be eighty thousand francs."

" I don't understand. So then, all three would be . . .? "

" All three, a hundred and fifty thousand francs."

My customer was flabbergasted.

" It's perfectly simple," I said. " If I sell you only one of my Cézannes, I have two left. If I sell you two, I have only one left. If I sell you all three, I have none left. Do you see? "

My man was more and more perplexed. Suddenly he tapped his forehead:

" You've given me a jolly good lesson! "

And he ran off in a hurry. He thought he had discovered that, in any kind of business, the more people buy of you, the more you should put your prices up. Unfortunately for him, his trade was in shoes.

Amateurs and dealers, hanging on jealously to their treasures, had reckoned without the Slump.

What a far cry now to the time when buyers came as suppliants! There was the American who persisted: " Come, M. Vollard, be a sport! It's for the United States! Let me have that Renoir." Deaf to that pathetic appeal, confident in the continuance of the rise, I did not sell him the picture. I still have the Renoir, but I have not seen the American again.

In spite of everything, we all try to persuade ourselves that the bad time will be over some day, and that money, sooner or later, will begin to circulate again. We go on confidently expecting the customer. The bell rings. The door opens. Suppose it were HE! It *is* an *amateur,* but . . . he has merely brought something to sell!

EPILOGUE

The rue Laffitte is no longer the Street of Pictures. One dealer, unable to find a shop there, was reduced to going as far as the rue de la Boétie. Contrary to all expectations, his business prospered there. One by one his colleagues followed. They were equally successful. So the rue de la Boétie has become to-day what the rue Laffitte used to be: the picture-market.

I myself was forced to emigrate. The building in the rue Laffitte in which I had my shop was to be taken over by a Bank, and at the same time No. 28, rue de Gramont, the house in which I had lived for more than twenty years, was to be pulled down. I therefore came to an important decision, which was to unite my picture-gallery, my publishing house and my personal quarters under one roof; and I set about finding appropriate premises.

The task was complicated by the fact that, from a sort of superstition, I wanted to find a house bearing the same number as my former dwelling, twenty-eight. In La Réunion, in the days of my childhood, it would have seemed quite simple to carry off the number of the house one was leaving, particularly if it happened to be engraved on a finer plate than that of the new one. But in France, and especially in Paris, the numbering of the houses is controlled by the order of the numbers, and the Administration would hardly have tolerated a sequence resembling a lottery list.

But it happened that the first house I was offered was a *hôtel* in the rue de Martignac bearing that very

319

number, 28.[1] I was not in the least astonished. It was my luck that had ordained it thus.

I have been settled in the rue de Martignac these twelve years, and every day, for twelve years, I have been meaning to organise exhibitions in my house. To-day I have got a step further—I am preparing to do so. I am even thinking of inaugurating them shortly by an exhibition of Degas' works, to be followed by one of Georges Rouault's. And I have many other plans in my head.

As regards Degas, it is the works of the artist's last years that I am concerned with—works as yet little known to the public, and of which Renoir said: " If Degas had died at fifty, he would have been remembered as an excellent painter, no more; it is after his fiftieth year that his work broadens out and that he really becomes Degas."

---

[1] Formerly the *hôtel* of the Princesse de Ligne.

INDEX

Plates

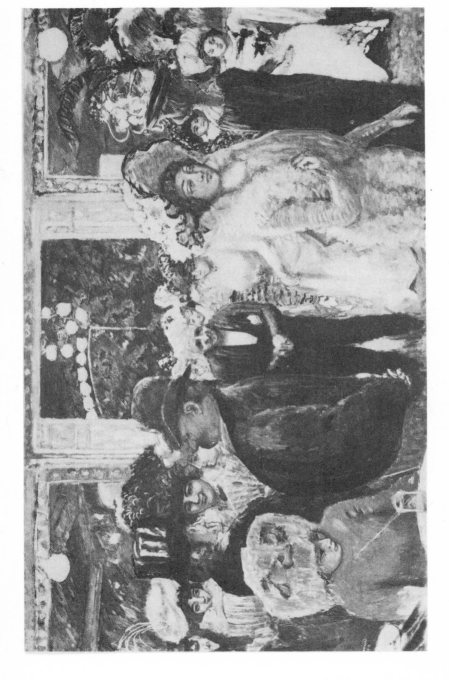

"SORTIE DU MOULIN ROUGE, MONTMARTRE"
Painting by Bonnard

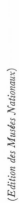

(Edition des Musées Nationaux)

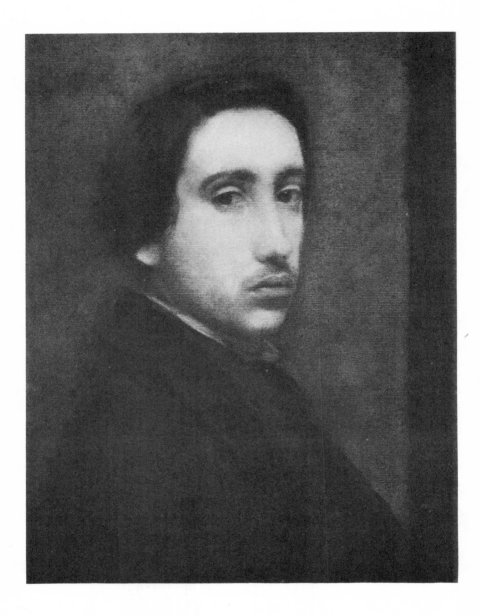

SELF-PORTRAIT
Painting by Degas

(*Edition Durand-Ruel*)

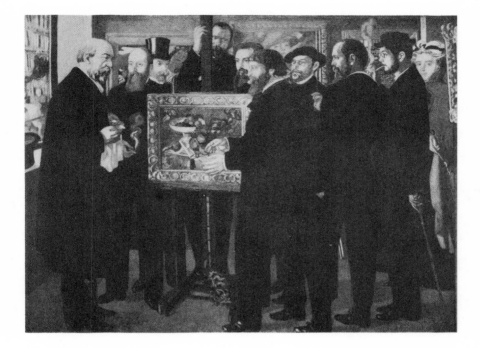

L'HOMMAGE A CÉZANNE
Painting by Maurice Denis
Left to right : Odilon Redon, Vuillard, K. X. Roussel, Ambroise Vollard, Maurice Denis,
Sérusier, Mellerio, Ranson, Bonnard et Madame Maurice Denis

(*Les Archives Photographiques d'Art et d'Histoire*)

This picture was painted in 1900 and exhibited the following year at La Nationale, where it was purchased by André Gide. The still-life by Cézanne, which is represented on the easel in the centre, belonged first to Gauguin and then to Dr. Viau, at whose house Maurice Denis saw and copied it. The actual gathering painted by Denis was staged in Vollard's shop in the rue Laffitte

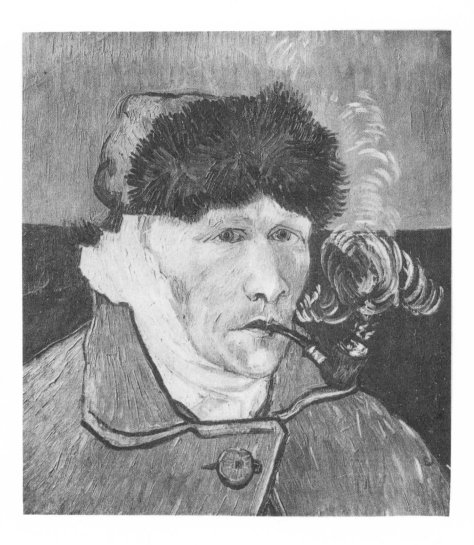

SELF-PORTRAIT
("THE MAN WITH THE SEVERED EAR")
Painting by Van Gogh

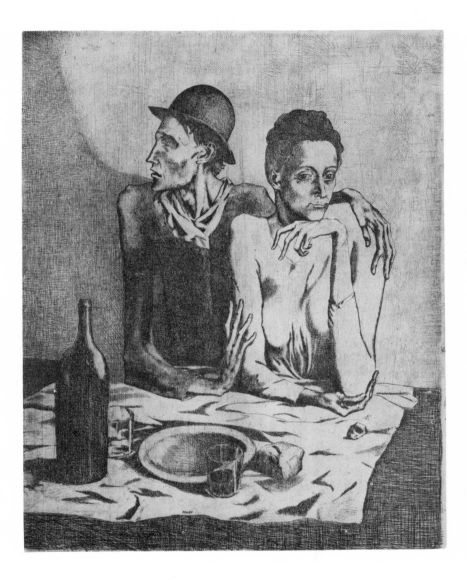

"SALTIMBANQUES"
Etching by Picasso

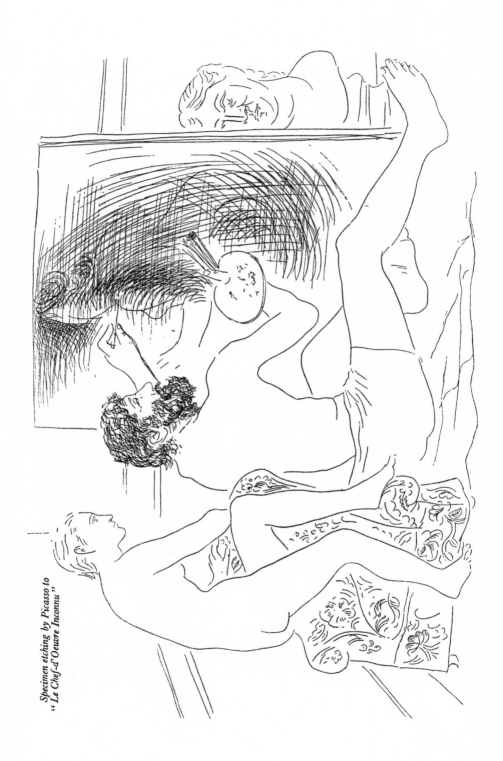

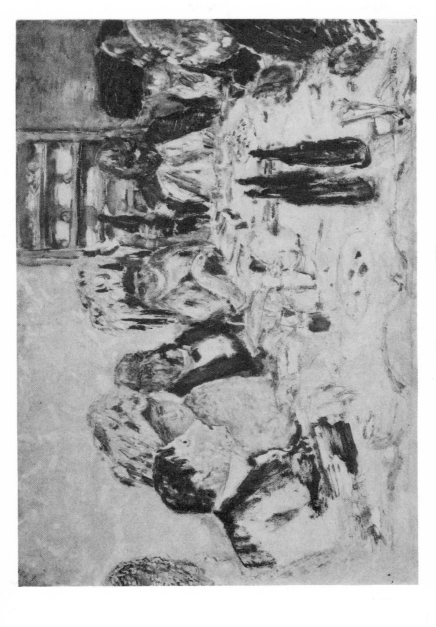

DINNER IN LA CAVE
Painting by Bonnard

Left to right: Forain, Redon, Vollard at the far end of the table pouring wine

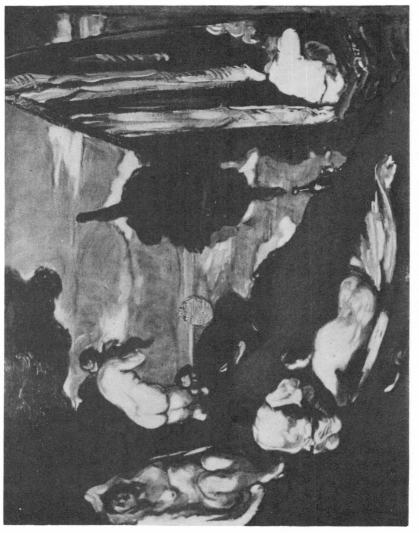

"REPOS A LA CAMPAGNE"
Painting by Cézanne
The central bearded figure is a portrait of the artist

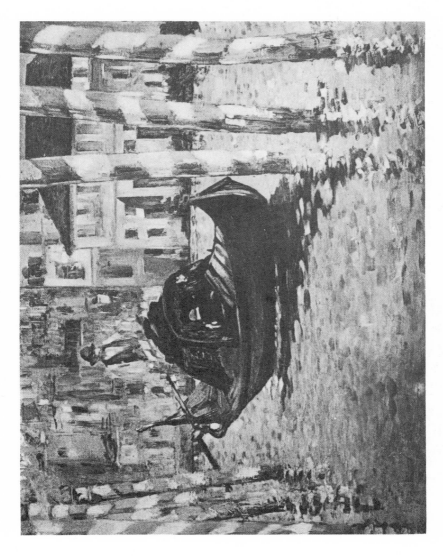

THE GRAND CANAL, VENICE
Painting by Manet (1875)

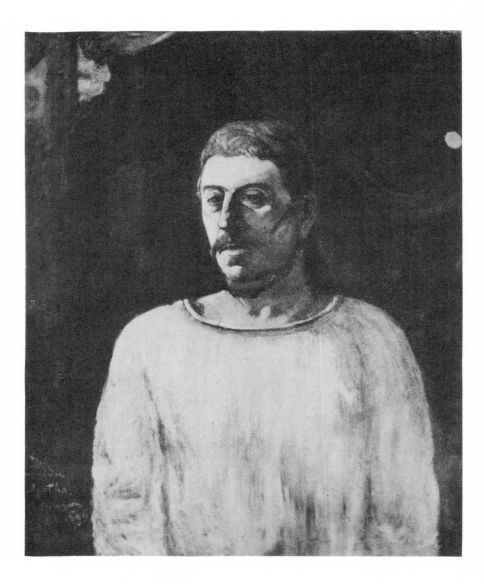

SELF-PORTRAIT
Painting by Gauguin

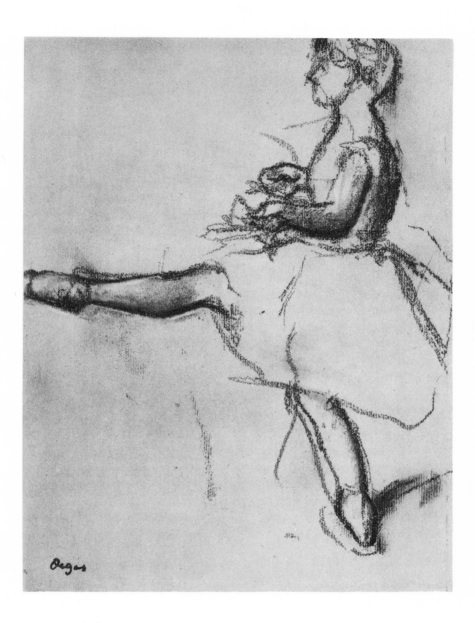

À PROPOS DE LA DANSE BY PAUL VALÉRY
Illustrated by Degas, and to be published by Vollard
Specimen illustration

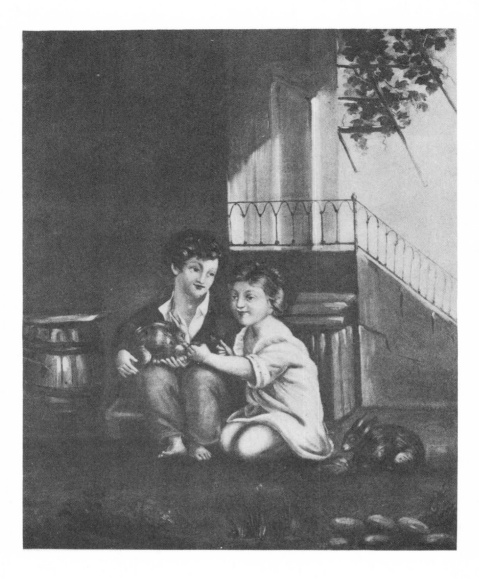

PICTURE PAINTED BY CÉZANNE AT THE AGE OF 18

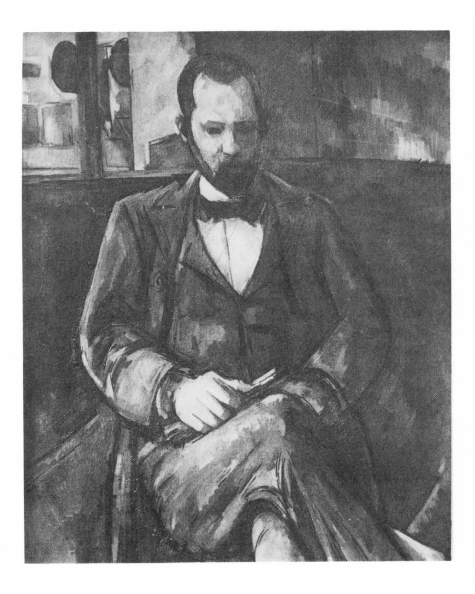

PORTRAIT OF VOLLARD IN 1900
Painting by Cézanne

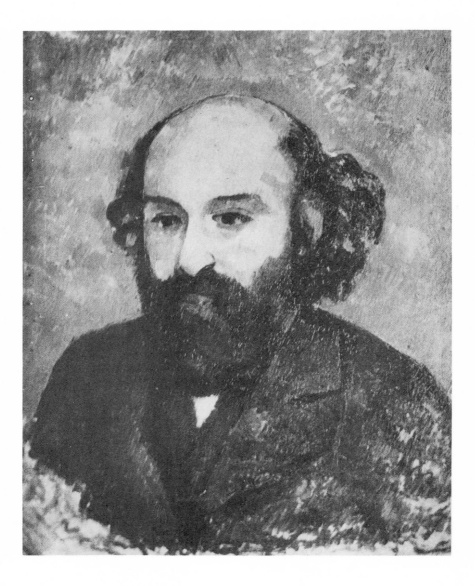

SELF-PORTRAIT
Painting by Cézanne

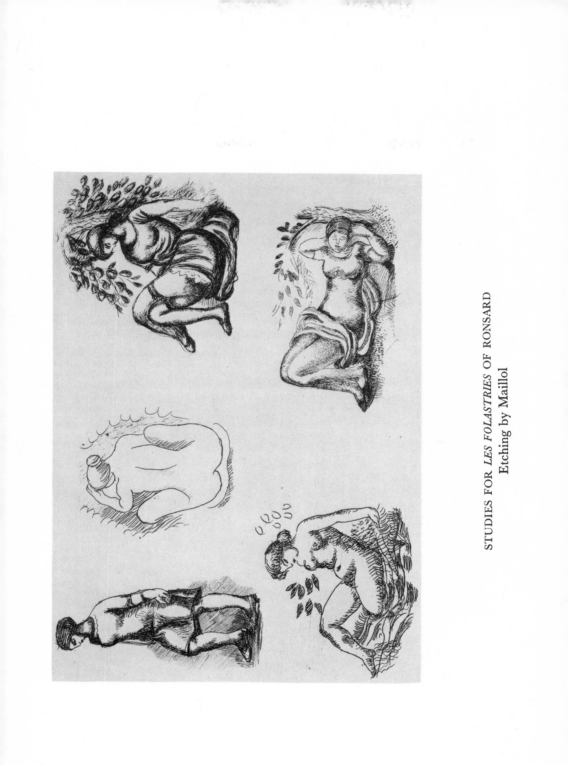

STUDIES FOR *LES FOLASTRIES* OF RONSARD
Etching by Maillol

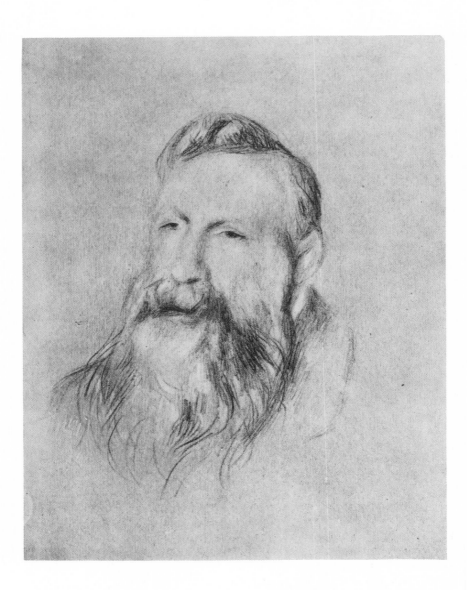

PORTRAIT OF RODIN
Lithograph by Renoir

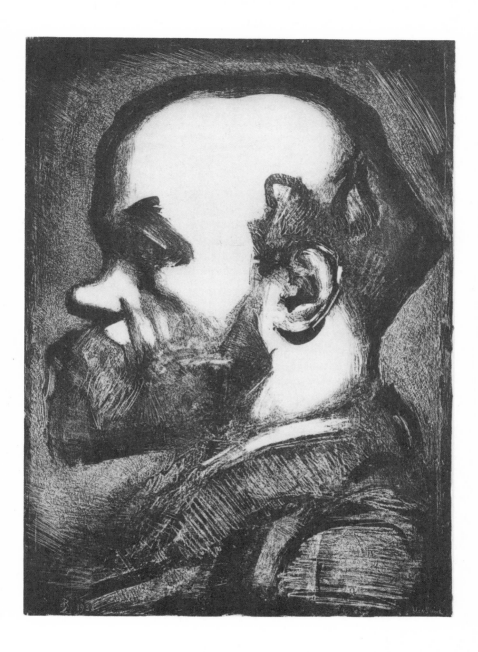

PORTRAIT OF VERLAINE
Lithograph by Rouault (1933)

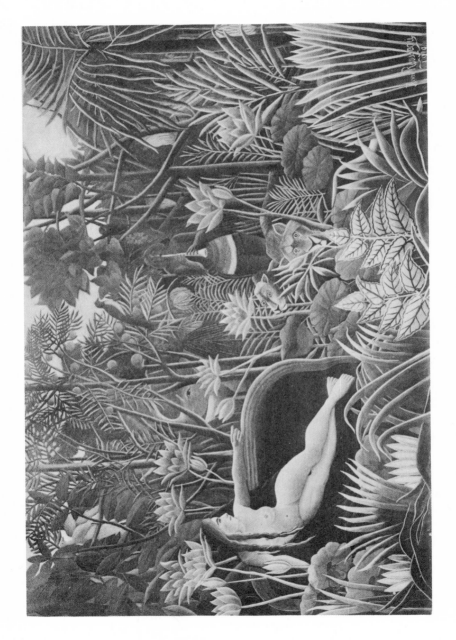

THE DREAM
Painting by the Douanier Rousseau

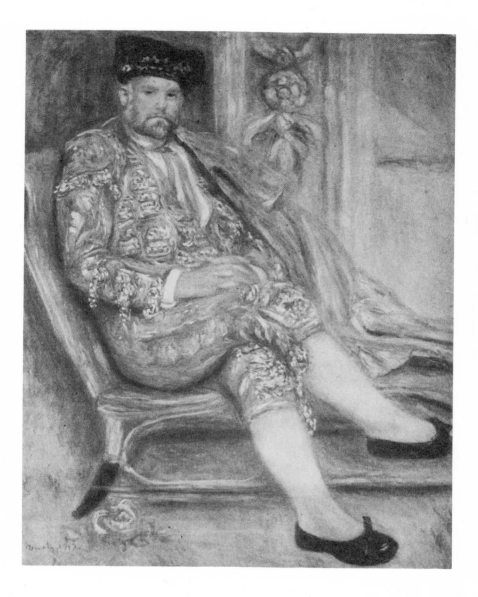

VOLLARD AS A TOREADOR
Painting by Renoir (1917)

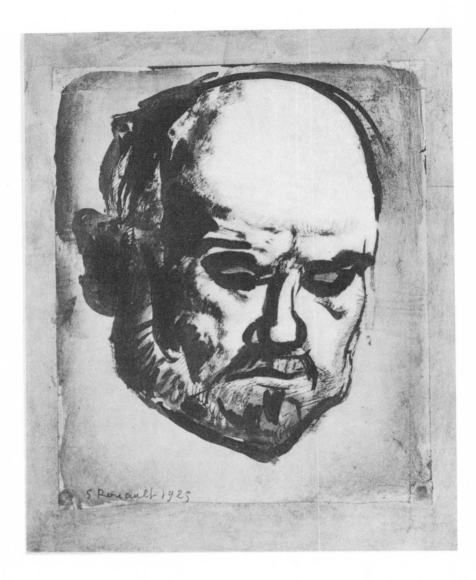

MASK OF VOLLARD
Wash-drawing by Rouault (1925)

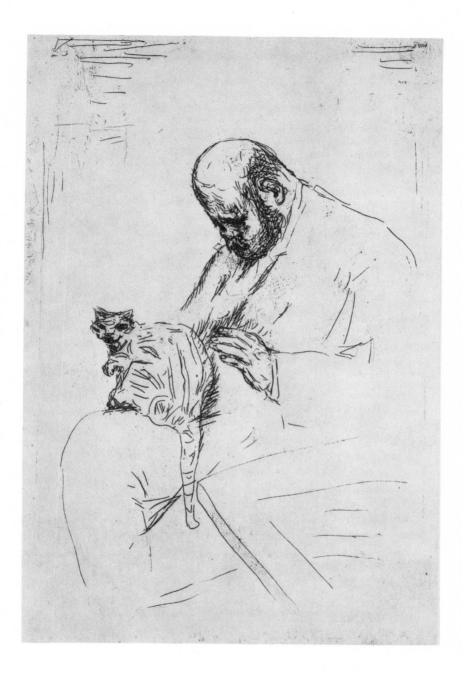

VOLLARD WITH A CAT
Etching by Bonnard

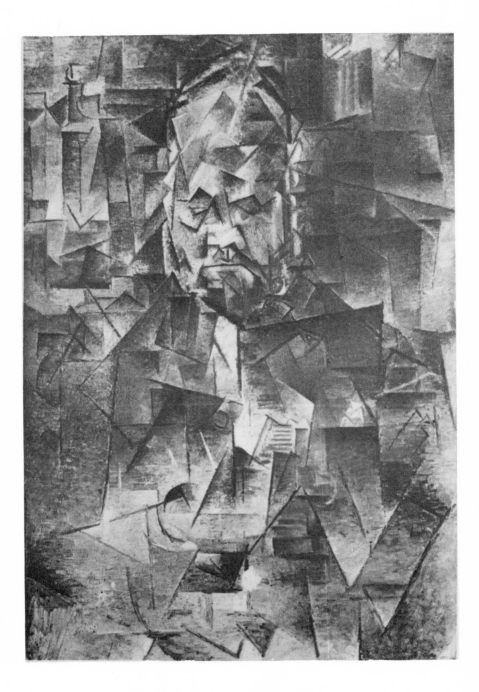

PORTRAIT OF VOLLARD
Painting by Picasso

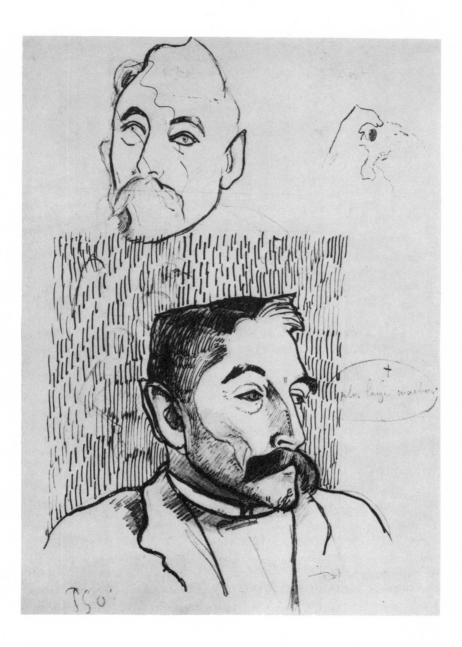

PORTRAIT OF MALLARMÉ
Pen-drawing by Gauguin

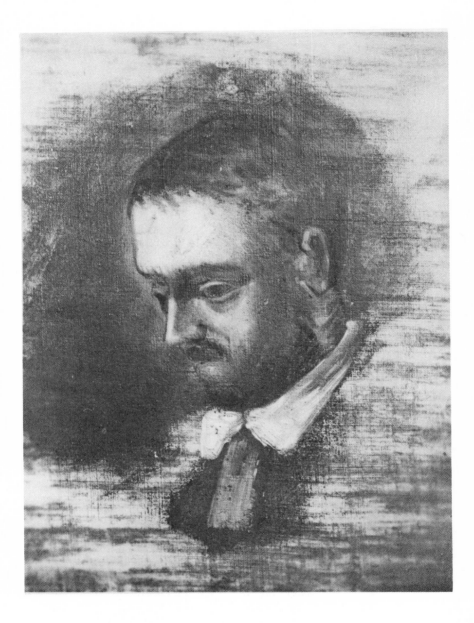

PORTRAIT OF ZOLA AT THE AGE OF 20
Painting by Cézanne

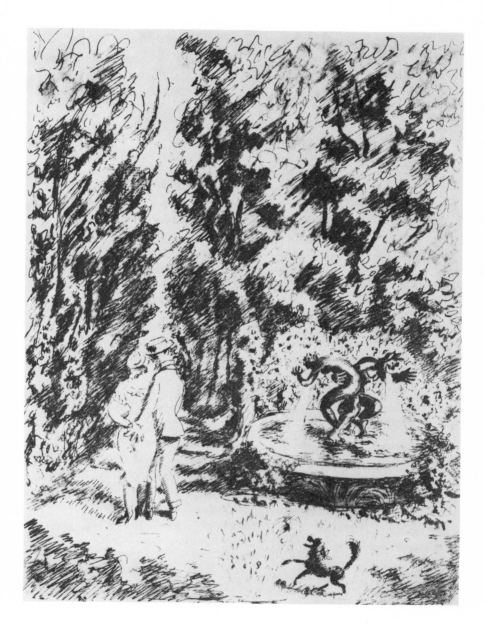

LE POT DE FLEURS DE LA MÈRE UBU BY VOLLARD
Illustrated with Lithographs by Puy.   Published by Vollard
Specimen illustration

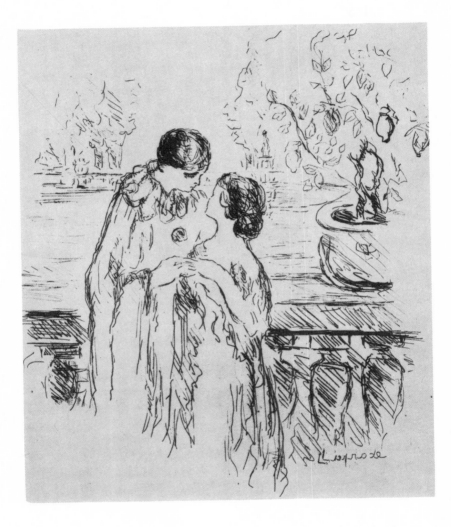

FÊTES GALANTES BY VERLAINE
Illustrated by Laprade.   Published by Vollard
Specimen illustration

CHAPITRE XXXIV.

QUE CELUI QUI AIME DIEU LE GOÛTE PAR-DESSUS TOUT
ET EN TOUT.

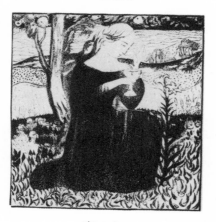

L'ÂME FIDÈLE.

1. Vous êtes mon Dieu et mon tout! que voudrais-je davantage et que pourrais-je souhaiter de plus heureux?

L'IMITATION DE JÉSUS-CHRIST
Illustrated by Maurice Denis.   Published by Vollard
Specimen page

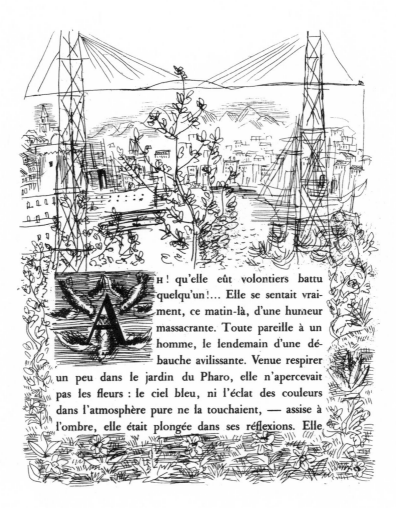

A H! qu'elle eût volontiers battu quelqu'un!... Elle se sentait vraiment, ce matin-là, d'une humeur massacrante. Toute pareille à un homme, le lendemain d'une débauche avilissante. Venue respirer un peu dans le jardin du Pharo, elle n'apercevait pas les fleurs : le ciel bleu, ni l'éclat des couleurs dans l'atmosphère pure ne la touchaient, — assise à l'ombre, elle était plongée dans ses réflexions. Elle

LA BELLE ENFANT BY EUGÈNE MONTFORT
Illustrated with Etchings by Dufy.   Published by Vollard
Specimen page

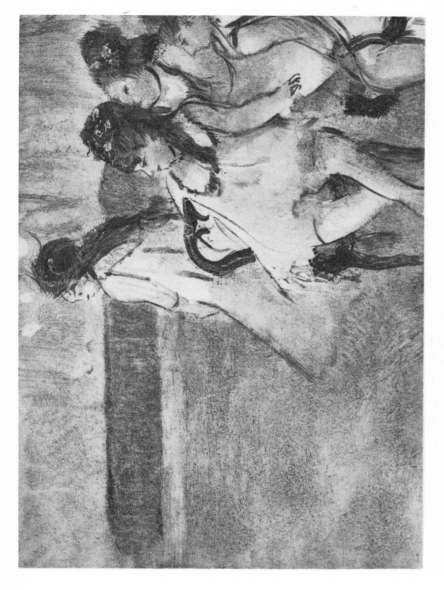

THREE DANCING GIRLS
Illustration by Degas to *Mimes* by Pierre Louys
Published by Vollard

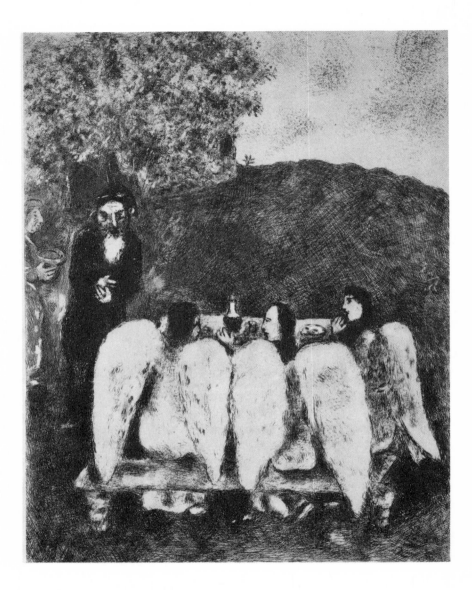

ABRAHAM AND THE THREE ANGELS
Etching by Chagall for *Le Livre des Prophètes*
Published by Vollard

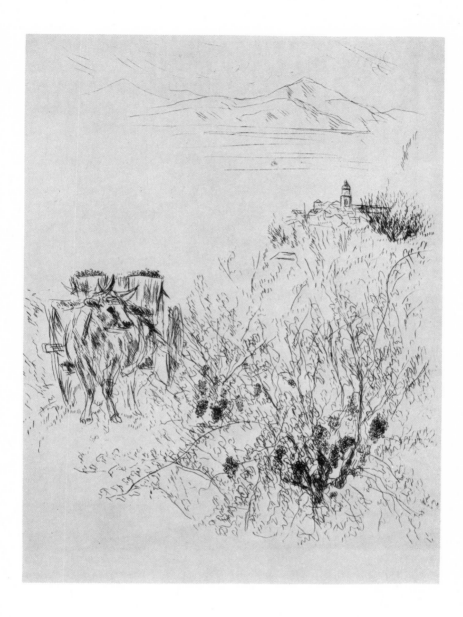

LES GEORGIQUES
Illustrated with etchings by Dunoyer de Segonzac
Published by Vollard.   Specimen illustration

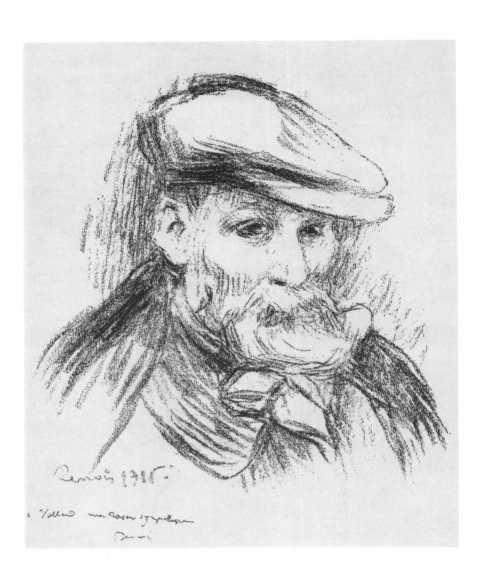

SELF-PORTRAIT
Drawing by Renoir, inscribed to Vollard
"à Vollard, mon raseur sympathique, Renoir."